Defending Democracy in an
Age of Sharp Power

T0385718

Defending Democracy in an Age of Sharp Power

Edited by WILLIAM J. DOBSON, TAREK MASOUD, *and*
CHRISTOPHER WALKER

Johns Hopkins University Press
Baltimore

© 2023 Johns Hopkins University Press
and the National Endowment for Democracy
All rights reserved. Published 2023
Printed in the United States of America on acid-free paper
9 8 7 6 5 4 3 2 1

Johns Hopkins University Press
2715 North Charles Street
Baltimore, Maryland 21218
www.press.jhu.edu

Library of Congress Cataloging-in-Publication Data is available.
A catalog record for this book is available from the British Library.

ISBN 978-1-4214-4804-6 (paperback)
ISBN 978-1-4214-4805-3 (ebook)

*Special discounts are available for bulk purchases of this book. For more information,
please contact Special Sales at specialsales@jh.edu.*

CONTENTS

ACKNOWLEDGMENTS

OUR FIRST DEBT is to the contributors to this volume. They represent some of the finest thinkers on the evolving dangers and threats posed by authoritarians' use of sharp power and how democracies should respond. Some of these chapters developed from the "Sharp Power and Democratic Resilience" series organized by the National Endowment of Democracy's International Forum for Democratic Studies. Others were first commissioned and appeared in the *Journal of Democracy*. Collectively, they represent a comprehensive, forward-looking, and insightful body of analysis, and we are incredibly grateful to each of our authors for sharing their time and expertise for this endeavor.

A number of staff members from the International Forum for Democratic Studies contributed in important ways to the development of the material in this volume, including Ariane Gottlieb, John Engelken, and Kevin Sheives. Former staff members Shanthi Kalathil, Jessica Ludwig, and Rachelle Faust also made valuable contributions to this effort.

We are also indebted to our partners at Johns Hopkins University Press. Editorial Director Greg Britton enthusiastically encouraged and championed this book from the start, and the Books Division's managing editor, Juliana McCarthy, worked closely to ensure a smooth production process. Kristina Lykke was a great ally in spearheading the book's promotion and marketing. We have long worked with Bill Breichner and his colleagues Carol Hamblen, Maria Kummerfeldt, and Mary Alice Fallon Yeskey of the Journals Division, and we value their help and good counsel at every turn.

We wish to acknowledge the Smith Richardson Foundation, which has provided critical financial support for this volume.

Our deepest thanks go to the *Journal of Democracy*'s editorial staff. We are fortunate to work alongside an exceptionally talented team who make indispensable and all-important contributions to each issue of the *Journal,* and their commitment to the fine details and preparation of this volume was no less. Executive Editor Phil Costopoulos, Senior Editor

Tracy Brown, and Assistant Editor Justin Daniels helped to shape, hone, and sharpen every chapter; as always, the work is incalculably better for their efforts. Managing Editor Brent Kallmer seamlessly orchestrated the book's production and layout; he has a gift for looking ahead and seeing around the corners, and we all benefit from it. The camaraderie and good cheer with which this team approaches each challenge makes the work even more rewarding.

Finally, we must express our appreciation to the National Endowment for Democracy's President and CEO Damon Wilson and the Board of Directors for the unstinting support they have provided to the International Forum for Democratic Studies and the *Journal of Democracy*. We are engaged in a colossal contest for those who aspire to be free, but as this collective work can attest, we are heartened by the friends, partners, and allies we count among our ranks.

—*William J. Dobson, Tarek Masoud, and Christopher Walker*

Defending Democracy in an
Age of Sharp Power

Introduction: The Hidden War on Democracy

WILLIAM J. DOBSON *and* TAREK MASOUD

ALTHOUGH THERE MAY BE A DEBATE over the true extent to which democracy is in danger in this third decade of the twenty-first century, there can be no debating that the world's autocrats are doing their level best to gain the upper hand. Rather than viewing democracies as mere competitors, autocrats see them as an existential threat—whether by actions or example—to their grasp on power and their legitimacy at home and abroad. Dictators are no longer content to shore up their own rule, they are now reaching across borders to prevent democracy where it does not yet exist, and to undermine it where it does.

This new, muscular, outward-looking authoritarianism finds its most horrific expression in Vladimir Putin's bloody invasion of Ukraine (which, as of February 2023, had cost the lives of roughly 200,000 Russian and Ukrainian soldiers and more then 7,000 civilians) or, quieter and more effectively, Xi Jinping's hollowing out of the last vestiges of free speech and the rule of law in Hong Kong. But it also finds less sanguinary—though no less dangerous—expression in the form of widespread propaganda that extols authoritarianism as somehow more able than democracy to cope with global challenges from climate change to economic underdevelopment to pandemics. In this new narrative, autocracy is decisive, forward-looking, and oriented to the long term, while democratic governments are feckless, navel-gazing, and barely able to think beyond the next election.

If authoritarianism's challenges to democracy came only in the form of tanks and appealing stories, that would be threatening enough, but recent years have seen the world's autocrats open an entirely new front in their war on liberal, representative government. This new attack on democracy takes advantage of democracy's very openness to weaken it from within.

While autocracies are able to raise up the proverbial drawbridge against ideological incursions from the free world, the commitment of democracies to the open exchange of ideas renders them vulnerable to a novel form of asymmetric warfare called "sharp power." In contrast to hard power, which compels behavior through the use of force, or soft power, which influences behavior through suasion and seduction, sharp power "pierces, penetrates, or perforates the political and information environments in the targeted countries."[1] The aim is not to change the behavior of leaders or to win the hearts and minds of citizens or even to sap the vitality of democracies and thereby render them less able to confront dictatorship: It is to undermine the idea of democracy itself.

Thus the Kremlin invests in propaganda efforts such as its RT satellite television channel (whose motto, "Question More," does not extend to the activities of Vladimir Putin), fake news sites such as the Crimea-based News-Front and the Bulgaria-based Zero Hedge, and troll farms such as the St. Petersburg–based "Internet Research Agency," which seeks to sow chaos and stoke political polarization by spreading disinformation, sowing online discord, and encouraging Twitter and Facebook fights to spill over into the real world.[2] Similarly, the Chinese Communist Party (CCP) walks through the open doors of Western media and academic institutions, using its cash and promises of access to sway journalists, buy off scholars, and set the boundaries of what is permissible to write, think, and say. And neither country is shy about using sharp power's "harder" edge when necessary. Russia is famously accused of trying to upend U.S. democratic institutions by hacking into the computer systems of "state boards of elections, secretaries of state, and U.S. companies that supplied software and other technology related to the administration of U.S. elections," according to a 2018 grand jury indictment of a dozen Russian intelligence officers.[3] And China deploys its tech companies, from TikTok to Huawei, to hoover up data, surveil entire societies, and undermine democratic citizenship by keeping us glued to our screens.

Although Russia and China are perhaps the most adept at wielding sharp power, the world's dictators are fast learning their dark arts. Autocracies such as Iran, Saudi Arabia, and the United Arab Emirates routinely weaponize social media and are increasingly penetrating Western cultural and academic institutions in an effort to legitimize their regimes, drown out critics, and distort narratives. They display little hesitation in using their sharp-power tools to snip any green shoots of democracy that appear in their immediate environs.

This book brings together a leading group of analysts to help us understand and respond to this challenge. The chapters that follow describe what sharp power is, how it is being used around the world, and how it can be parried. The book is divided into two parts. Part I, "Grasping Sharp Power," records the ways in which the world's autocracies are employing sharp power to advance their interests and attack the foundations of democratic government. In the opening chapter, "The Authoritarian Assault on Knowledge," Glenn Tiffert describes how authoritarian regimes—and particularly Beijing—have exploited the revenue pressures that bedevil Western knowledge-sector institutions to directly influence the workings of those institutions and inhibit them from generating ideas that these regimes find challenging. Western universities hungry for Chinese students' tuition dollars, publishers seeking access to China's vast market, and researchers eager to land new sources of funding for their research all begin to self-censor and otherwise act in ways that are at odds with their fundamental responsibility to tell the truth, no matter how inconvenient. A secondary effect of this feeding at the authoritarian trough is that these institutions become ripe targets for would-be authoritarians at home, who seize on such behaviors to "sharply question the legitimacy of many bodies of knowledge, the experts and organizations behind them, and the interests they serve."

Autocrats are waging a similar assault on our media. In chapter 2, "How Autocrats Undermine Media Freedom," Edward Lucas describes how our unregulated media markets are particularly vulnerable to sharp-power influence campaigns. There are currently no barriers to entry for nefarious actors who seek to spread disinformation and fake news. The revenue pressures confronting cash-strapped media companies mean that they willingly hold their tongues in order to secure advertising and access to markets. Similarly, reporters who face an increasingly grim job market sometimes allow themselves to be swayed by press junkets and access to officials. And when these carrots do not work, out come the sticks—which range from pulling advertisements to denying journalist visas to launching coordinated cyberattacks. And when those sticks fail, autocrats are not above using the aggressive libel laws that exist in many of the world's democracies to keep damaging information out of the public eye.

In chapter 3, "How Beijing Runs the Show in Hollywood," Aynne Kokas chronicles how this same depressing story plays out in the entertainment industry. China is "the world's largest market for theatrically distributed films," and Western companies are lining up not just to sell their movies but also to build movie theaters, theme parks, and other entertainment facilities for a Chinese population hungry for diversions. Beijing, therefore, is often in a position to call the shots. These entertainment firms, Kokas writes, "have billions of reasons to make sure that all their platforms—films, streaming programs, video games, and beyond—observe Beijing's content rules and avoid carrying material that will anger [Chinese] authorities." It would be one thing if these restrictions were limited to media intended for consumption in the Chinese market. But, as Kokas shows, they are increasingly shaping what is said and shown everywhere.

Although much of the attention to sharp power has focused on China's deployment of it, chapter 4, "The Kremlin Playbook for Latin America," shifts our attention to how Putin has used his country's (admittedly more limited) leverage to interfere with the relatively fragile democracies of Latin America. In that chapter, Ruslan Stefanov and Martin Vladimirov describe how the Kremlin wields "state-owned and nominally private corporations as political instruments" in an effort "to achieve outsized global influence." The Russian playbook includes sweetheart deals, outright bribes, and other corrupt practices that allow it to buy the loyalty of local political elites. That playbook also includes "the deployment of massive tech-enhanced disinformation and propaganda campaigns" that enable the Kremlin "to exploit governance gaps and other societal vulnerabilities."

A common theme of the chapters thus far is how money permits sharp power to operate. It is the insatiable appetite for resources on the part of academic institutions, filmmakers, and politicians that allows Russia and China to secure compliance. The final two chapters of this section depart from this narrative by focusing not on what makes Western societies and institutions vulnerable, but on what makes China especially dangerous.

In chapter 5, "China's Tech-Enhanced Authoritarianism," Samantha Hoffman chronicles how China's export of technologies such as big-data tools and the urban-management systems behind so-called smart cities serves as a kind of technological Trojan horse, allowing Beijing unprecedented access to the sinews of modern liberal societies. These technologies, billed as providing smart solutions to everyday problems, in reality provide the CCP with vast data-gathering and surveillance capabilities that allow it "to know and manipulate its international audiences." The result, Hoffman writes, is China's enhanced capacity to "disrupt democratic processes and create a more favorable global environment for its own power and security."

In chapter 6, "China's Pandemic Power Play," Nadège Rolland describes how China has used the sharp-power tools detailed in previous chapters to advance traditional, soft-power aims: showcasing the regime's competence, creating an impression of unstoppable forward momentum, and communicating that "resistance is futile." As the world reeled from a global pandemic that in some accounts was credibly of China's making, the CCP made its "successful" handling of that pandemic a central focus of its "propaganda work." In this telling, the Chinese people's selfless compliance with strict government lockdowns and mask mandates demonstrated the superiority of the Chinese model, which state media contrasted with the laxer efforts of most Western democracies. To deflect scrutiny or blame by the Chinese people or the outside world, the CCP regime simultaneously launched an assiduous disinformation campaign employing "distortions of fact, statements made in bad faith, accusations of inappropriate behavior and racism, *ad hominem* attacks, economic retaliation, and even . . . wild conspiracy theories." False narratives of China's superior handling of the covid-19 pandemic not only served Beijing's main goal of "building a new order in which other states are drawn into its orbit," but they may also have shaken faith in democracy within the world's democracies themselves.

If Part I sounds the alarm, Part II of the book, "Blunting Sharp Power's Edge," provides the beginnings of a plan of action. These chapters describe how some of the world's democracies have begun to fight back against sharp-power challenges and the lessons that can be learned by societies just waking up to those threats.

In chapter 7, "Transparency Wins in Europe," Martin Hála describes how the Czech Republic has resisted a concerted Chinese campaign to coopt, subvert, and hollow out its democracy from within. He concludes that democracies, though vulnerable to sharp power, possess their own "magic weapon," namely, their "openness." Hála argues that in open societies, citizens "can freely research, analyze, and publicize CCP sharp-power manipulations," which is a necessary step toward resisting them. Openness is only a liability, he writes, "if we stop being vigilant and remain passive, complacent, and ignorant." How can we keep from falling back into the passivity, complacency, and ignorance that allows the wielders of sharp power to win? This is where civil society comes in. "It is the role of civil society," Hála writes, "to wake up the people and the politicians by channeling reliable yet easy-to-understand information and analysis into the public discourse."

The book's remaining chapters describe what this looks like in practice. In chapter 8, "Taiwan's Democracy Under Fire," Ketty W. Chen both catalogues China's aggressive influence operations in her country and describes how Taiwan's "robust and vibrant" civil society—with its "commitment to defending the island nation's democracy"—fought back. Thus when China targeted Taiwan with an information-warfare campaign during its 2018 local elections, Taiwanese civil society organizations "began working systematically to study, track, and raise awareness of Beijing's sharp-power efforts in Taiwan and elsewhere." The result is that when Taiwan's 2020 general elections rolled around, "Beijing's political warfare was not only falling flat, but backfiring."

Further evidence of civil society's ability to serve as democracy's immune response to sharp power is offered in chapter 9, "How Australia's Civil Society Led the Way." Here John Fitzgerald attributes the recent freeze in Chinese-Australian relations to a civil society that "was ten years ahead of the government and its agencies" in exposing sharp power, and which through steady work "finally succeeded in alerting authorities" to the extent of those operations, and in "strengthen[ing] the government's resolve to deal with them." Particularly vital, writes Fitzgerald, were groups formed by Australians of Chinese heritage, who were uniquely targeted by China's influence and disinformation operations, and deeply motivated to ensure "the welfare of Chinese-Australians who were being bullied and spied on, the integrity of civic institutions vital to democracy, and the preservation of the values and principles that undergird the Australian way of life."

In chapter 10, "Countering Beijing's Media Manipulation," Sarah Cook describes "a growing accumulation of advocacy, expertise, policymaking, legislation, and activities aimed at countering Beijing's media influence and protecting democratic institutions." At the forefront of these efforts, she reports, are civil society groups, media organizations, and private-sector firms often working together, as when social-media companies partnered with academia and civil society groups to "put in place new measures to track inauthentic activity linked to China, expose emerging disinformation campaigns, take down problematic accounts, and implement labeling that clearly designates Chinese state-funded or state-affiliated accounts."

Despite the notes of optimism sounded in these chapters, Christopher Walker reminds us in his concluding chapter that, these encouraging stories of democratic resistance to corrosive authoritarian influence notwithstanding, most of the world's democracies remain dangerously vulnerable.

Summarizing the lessons of the volume, he identifies six components of what he calls a "democratic countermobilization" against sharp power: 1) thwarting autocrats' preference for secrecy by "incorporat[ing] nongovernmental voices into key forums, discussions, and decisionmaking processes" relating to work with foreign partners; 2) reducing "vulnerability to elite capture" by foreign agents "through a combination of tighter investment rules . . . economic deterrence, . . . and standardized procedures for screening foreign investments and tracking the resulting ties that form with local elites"; 3) defending free speech and expression; 4) endowing the targets of sharp power with the "deeper understandings of how sharp-power tactics and Chinese and Russian influence" present themselves, so that they might be more able to recognize and resist them; 5) incentivizing journalists and analysts to further uncover, conceptualize, and measure sharp power so that we will know it when we see it; and finally 6) adopting technological standards "that embrace transparency and accountability."

All these measures assume a society that possesses a commitment to democratic values, and the intellectual and organizational wherewithal to act on their behalf. Sharp power can only succeed where people are indifferent to democracy's survival, incapable of recognizing when it is under threat, or unwilling to act in concert to resist that threat. Wherever sharp power has faltered—in Australia, the Czech Republic, Taiwan, and elsewhere—it was because the citizenry was too committed to democracy, too critical, and too organized to be penetrated. This suggests that, as we think about how to resist sharp power, and how to strengthen democracy generally, we would do well to attend to the educational, cultural, and social institutions that transmit basic values and endow citizens with the skills necessary to uphold free and representative government.

* * *

The essays in this volume, in recording the aggressive campaigns of the world's autocrats to erode democracy from within, should serve as a call to action. For much of the last twenty years, the received wisdom held that, as ripe fruit falls from a tree, authoritarian political systems would gradually and peacefully give way to democratic ones. All that was needed was the salutary passage of time. Time for a middle class to take hold in authoritarian countries. Time for globalization to bind their elites (in finance, law, and commerce) to our own. Time for the internet to expose their citizens to new ideas and diverse sources of information. Time for their children to study in our universities, imbibe our values, and spread them back home.

Of course, there were many signs along the way that this transformation was not taking hold, but we either ignored them or convinced ourselves that we just needed more time. We can no longer afford this illusion. It should be clear by now that instead of becoming more like us, Russia, China, and their emulators have been busily devising new ways of waging war on freedom. Time is not on our side. The longer we wait to address the sharp-power challenge, the more that the world's most hardened autocracies will continue working the seams of our universities, media, technology, industries, and culture—leveraging them against us. What we did not understand, but we now cannot fail to appreciate, is that authoritarian regimes view democracy as a fundamental and unrelenting threat to their rule. No longer satisfied with keeping democracy at bay, they now seek to snuff it out at the source. It is this aim that drives the autocratic machinations, stratagems, and tactics that this book chronicles. And it is for this reason that the chapters which follow should be of the utmost concern to all who are committed not just to keeping democracy alive but to ensuring that it grows and thrives.

Notes

1. Christopher Walker and Jessica Ludwig, "From 'Soft Power' to 'Sharp Power': Rising Authoritarian Influence in the Democratic World," in *Sharp Power: Rising Authoritarian Influence* (Washington, D.C.: National Endowment for Democracy, 2017), 6.

2. Nomaan Merchant, "US Accuses Financial Website of Spreading Russian Propaganda," Associated Press, 15 February 2022, *https://apnews.com/article/ russia-ukraine-coronavirus-pandemic-health-moscow-media-ff4a56b7b08bcd c6adaf02313a85edd9*; Adrian Chen, "The Agency," *New York Times*, 2 June 2015; Claire Allbright, "A Russian Facebook Page Organized a Protest in Texas. A Different Russian Page Launched the Counterprotest," *Texas Tribune*, 1 November 2017, *www.texastribune.org/2017/11/01/russian-facebook-page-organized-protest-texas-different-russian-page-l.*

3. "Most Wanted: Russian Interference in 2016 U.S. Elections," Federal Bureau of Investigation, *www.fbi.gov/wanted/cyber/russian-interference-in-2016-u-s-elections.*

PART ONE

Grasping Sharp Power

CHAPTER ONE

The Authoritarian Assault on Knowledge

GLENN TIFFERT

IN LATE JULY 2019, with tensions high over a proposed extradition law that threatened to strengthen Beijing's grip on Hong Kong, a protester donned a face mask to guard against retaliation by the authorities. The demonstration he attended, however, was not in Hong Kong, but rather at Australia's University of Queensland, where successive protests challenged first the extradition law, then the university's own ties to the People's Republic of China (PRC). As the masked demonstrator explained: "Even in Australia now we cannot be seen here at a protest. We are not out of sight of China's government."[1]

Under Chinese Communist Party (CCP) general secretary Xi Jinping, a coercive campaign to intensify ideological discipline—the most sweeping in more than forty years—is constricting not just the narrow space for expression within the PRC, but also its exercise abroad.[2] Overseas students from the PRC and their families are especially vulnerable, but universities, publishers, and researchers based in democracies are also coming under the campaign's influence. In August 2020, another Australian institution, the University of New South Wales, embroiled itself in controversy by deleting from its official Twitter account a tweet about Hong Kong that quoted an adjunct lecturer who is also the director of Human Rights Watch Australia. PRC students at the university had heavily criticized the tweet and reportedly appealed to the local consulate for intervention. A Chinese state-media outlet amplified the case. Compounding the imbroglio, university administrators issued divergent statements about the incident in English and Chinese: Both cited concerns that the tweet seemed to conflate the university's views with those of the speaker, but only the former emphasized a commitment to free expression and called the deletion a mistake.[3]

These examples cast a spotlight on an urgent new class of challenges to independent intellectual inquiry. More diffuse than traditional state censorship and repression, which are also surging around the world, these challenges stem primarily from the vulnerabilities that economic and technological change have introduced into the knowledge sectors of open societies, including both mature and developing democracies. Observers have been slower to recognize the significance of these diffuse threats, but when combined with the artful exploitation of globalization by authoritarian regimes, they make for a toxic brew.

In recent years, intensifying marketization has placed ever-greater financial and competitive pressures on publishers, universities, and other knowledge-sector institutions critical to the functioning of democracies. Changes to the incentive structures, performance benchmarks, and funding models of these entities threaten to erode their autonomy—and with it, their resistance to external influence. Faced with tighter budgetary constraints and growing intrasectoral inequalities, institutions have grown less tolerant of controversy.

These economic pressures have been aggravated by the rise of powerful online platforms, which have in some cases come to exercise quasi-governmental authority over their respective domains. As these platforms assume a central role in aggregating and repackaging knowledge, they are creating unparalleled opportunities not only to profit healthily from information flows, but also to manipulate our information space and globalize surveillance, propaganda, and disinformation.

Finally, for better or worse, populist critics are seizing on the tension between intellectual freedom and public accountability to sharply question the legitimacy of many bodies of knowledge, the experts and organizations behind them, and the interests they serve.

These developments have profound ramifications for the robust competition of ideas on which democracies depend. Independent intellectual inquiry, particularly as supported by publishers and universities, supplies public goods that are essential to good governance: high-quality data, reliable and pluralistic feedback mechanisms, and creative insights into problems. It serves as a check on poorly performing governments and political processes, and a balance against their capture or corruption by parochial interests. More broadly, it provides a channel through which individuals can express the diverse meanings they attach to their lives. By bringing unmet needs and marginal voices to the fore, forestalling ideological ossification, and facilitating the negotiation of competing interests, free inquiry can enhance the quality and legitimacy of policy making. Conversely, the more obstacles there are standing in the way of such inquiry, the more difficult it will be to realize democracy's promise and to reverse growing popular discontent with democratic systems.

Authoritarian regimes grasp these connections, and they are exploiting vulnerabilities in open knowledge economies to quash critical voices and subvert the independence of intellectual inquiry.[4] Money is the common solvent. Resisting its corrosive effects on democratic values and practices requires a communal awakening, heightened regulatory and institutional standards, major commitments to employee training and compliance, robust monitoring, and the fortitude simply to say "no."

Thinking Locally, Acting Globally

While a number of authoritarian regimes are investing in efforts to coerce and coopt knowledge-sector institutions in democracies, Beijing's global reach stands out. At times, the PRC exerts its influence openly, through acts designed to send a public message. For instance, on the eve of the 2014 annual meeting in Portugal of the European Association of Chinese Studies, personnel from Confucius Institute Headquarters (which supports a network of foreign-university–based cultural and educational centers with PRC funding) provoked a confrontation by seizing the printed conference programs. Following a standoff, the programs were returned with several pages torn out, including one highlighting sponsorship by a Taiwanese foundation.[5] Beijing was similarly open in expressing its displeasure when, in 2019, Sweden's minister of culture and democracy awarded a PEN Prize to Gui Minhai, a Hong Kong–based author and publisher of books critical of the CCP, who is now imprisoned in the PRC. Undeterred by the fact that Gui is a Swedish citizen, the PRC retaliated by canceling major trade delegations, denying journalist visas, and leveling public threats through media and diplomatic channels.[6]

Foreign scholars researching the PRC have encountered a range of repressive tactics. Only a small minority suffer physical coercion, and the risk to foreigners of imprisonment for scholarly pursuits is generally greater elsewhere, most notoriously in Iran and the United Arab Emirates. However, in one recent case, a visiting Japanese historian was arrested in Beijing by officers of the Ministry of State Security, and then deported several weeks later after confessing to "collecting inappropriate historical materials"—reportedly sources on twentieth-century history that he had purchased openly at a bookstore.[7]

Usually, the pressure is more subtle. PRC diplomats stationed abroad monitor scholarly research output and engagements, including petitions, public lectures, and comments on social media and email lists. Some over-seas Chinese Students and Scholars Associations (CSSAs) and individual students from the PRC reputedly assist with this collection. If the findings regarding a given scholar are not to Beijing's liking, letters of invitation and access to sources and research sites in the PRC are sometimes withdrawn. Outright visa denials remain infrequent, but visas are commonly delayed right up to the edge of their dates of validity or beyond, or simply never issued at all. Once in the country, foreign scholars may encounter surveil-lance, and their local informants and associates may be questioned and intimidated by the authorities. These tactics are meant to induce scholars, left to guess for themselves where the red lines might be, to err on the side of caution; and while the degree of self-censorship among China watchers is a subject of debate, the phenomenon is real. Its burden falls most heav-ily on those who have family in the PRC or who depend on access to the country for their research and professional advancement.

Faustian Bargains

When institutions such as universities and publishers partner with enti-ties based in authoritarian states, they expose themselves to perils that traditional due-diligence and risk-management frameworks were not designed to handle.[8] Most fundamentally, institutions based in autoc-racies may actually be indifferent or hostile to the core values espoused by their democracy-based counterparts, and exempt from transparency and accountability standards comparable to those in democratic societ-ies. Democracy-based institutions must therefore be prepared to shoul-der responsibility for defending and upholding their values alone. If they are not, considerable damage may ensue simply as a result of local organizational shortcomings, naïveté, conflicts of interest, venality, and parochialism.

Collaborations with autocracy-based partners often appear especially feasible and alluring in the spheres of business, science, and technology. Here shared priorities are easier to identify, and joint endeavors can be framed in ways that minimize or set to the side ethical and political sensitivities. Business, science, and technology are global, the argument goes, and so senior administrators are incentivized to strike deals, not to throw obstacles in the way. Laudable goals such as combatting climate change and disease can make these proposals especially compelling. Yet the officials responsible for signing off on foreign engagements may be unaware of the specific hazards they present. Thus, the Computer Science and Artificial Intelligence Laboratory at the Massachusetts Institute of Technology (MIT), the Business School at Rutgers University, and the School of Engineering at York University in Canada accepted sums adding up to millions of dollars from iFlytek, a PRC artificial-intelligence firm. The U.S. Department of Commerce later placed this company on a restricted-entity list over connections to human-rights abuses and state repression in Xinjiang.[9] Collaborations in the biomedical sciences raise their own particular concerns, as observance of fundamental norms governing human-subjects research has been a persistent problem in the PRC.

The humanities and social sciences are no less prone to blunders. In 2014, after a sensational scandal involving the Libyan government of Muammar al-Qadhafi, the London School of Economics adopted an ethics code that champions integrity and intellectual freedom. However, administrators soon shifted key provisions on working with outside parties to a subsidiary document—easing consideration in 2019 of a multimillion-dollar gift from Beijing-boosting venture capitalist Eric Li, which was slated to support an academic program that would have been overseen by "distinguished individuals from China."[10]

In 2011, Griffith University in Australia signed an agreement with Confucius Institute Headquarters (known as Hanban) to open a Confucius Institute on the university's campus. The title of the agreement contains an obvious typographical error, and Article 12, on dispute resolution, ends abruptly with a nonsensical sentence. By all appearances, the English text was prepared by the PRC side and translated poorly from a Chinese original, and the university could not be bothered to perform a basic proofreading before its vice-chancellor signed.[11] Worse, in 2017, the Free University of Berlin signed a contract with the Hanban worth roughly half a million dollars to endow a professorship in Chinese language and literature. Under the terms of the agreement, PRC law would govern interpretation and enforcement; the Hanban retained the right to reduce or terminate funding in the event of a violation of PRC law; and a PRC tribunal was to arbitrate any disputes. In effect, a prestigious German university bound itself to the PRC's illiberal norms.[12]

External funding is essential to the modern research enterprise but, even when it comes with no formal strings attached, it can erode integrity and independence. At the very least, it generates constituencies within research institutions that are invested in keeping their sponsors satisfied, which becomes awkward if those sponsors are prone to assert preferences about matters of intellectual substance. Worse, it can encourage self-dealing and corruption. In the Czech Republic, faculty members at Charles University ran a sideline business that took undeclared payments from the PRC embassy to organize conferences through a university center.[13] At the H. Lee Moffitt Cancer Center and Research Institute in Florida, the president, vice-president, and four researchers "resigned abruptly" after internal investigators identified compliance violations stemming from undeclared participation in the PRC's "Thousand Talents" recruitment program.[14] In early 2020, the FBI arrested a Harvard chemistry-department chair researching medical applications of nanotechnology for allegedly lying to investigators about his undisclosed participation in the same recruitment scheme. The arrangement reportedly entitled him to a "[US]$50,000 monthly salary, $150,000 in annual living expenses and more than $1.5 million for a second laboratory" in the PRC.[15]

As these examples indicate, transparency is a pressing concern. Section 117 of the U.S. Higher Education Act requires universities to report foreign gifts and contracts valued at $250,000 or more to the federal government. Yet in 2019, a preliminary investigation found that six U.S. universities failed to report a total of $1.3 billion in foreign funds, whose sources included the PRC, Russia, and Qatar.[16] Fortunately, regulatory changes and closer government scrutiny are compelling universities to strengthen their compliance protocols. Between July 2019 and February 2020, American universities belatedly disclosed at least $6.5 billion in previously unreported foreign gifts, grants, and contracts.[17] In response to pointed questions about its own funding sources and research collaborations, MIT announced a new review process for "elevated-risk" international proposals from the PRC, Russia, and Saudi Arabia.[18]

Anecdotal evidence suggests that faculty who raise uncomfortable questions about potential high-value foreign partnerships risk marginalization by their administrators and exclusion from future consultations.[19] And that is just the minority with secure, tenured employment. In a sharply competitive higher-education sector where contingent and part-time appointments are ever more prevalent, academics whose careers may already be hanging by a thread have even stronger incentives not to risk challenging potentially lucrative deals, losing visa access to their countries of study, or provoking retaliation against their employers.

Tuition revenue represents another potential lever of authoritarian influence. In the 2018–19 academic year, 35 percent of international students in the United States hailed from the PRC, with no other country of origin coming close to that share. Unlike most domestic students, Chinese students generally pay full tuition, adding approximately $15 billion to the U.S. economy in 2018.[20] Australian, Canadian, and U.K. universities are even more reliant on the contributions of students from the PRC. In all of these systems, foreign tuition plugs budgetary holes left by shrinking state support.[21] On average, an international student in Canada pays about four times the tuition of a domestic student; at the University of British Columbia, international students contributed nearly $100 million more in tuition revenue in 2019–20 than Canadian students.[22]

A major disruption to that revenue would plunge these schools into financial distress. In 2018, the University of Illinois purchased insurance against this contingency.[23] In New Zealand in early 2020, universities cited the prospect of close to $100 million in lost tuition revenue to appeal for a student exemption from the temporary entry ban that their government, in response to the covid-19 pandemic, had imposed on travelers from the PRC.[24]

PRC authorities have been keen to test the leverage this supply-chain dependence generates. For example, they threatened to withhold students from Oxford University in an unsuccessful bid to force the school's chancellor, Chris Patten, to cancel a visit to Hong Kong, where he had once served as colonial governor.[25] After the Dalai Lama delivered the 2017 commencement address at the University of California, San Diego (UCSD), the PRC government retaliated by prohibiting visiting scholars with China

Scholarship Council grants from attending the university, as well as by reportedly blocking the transfer of funds for a joint research center.[26] Similarly, after the University of Calgary issued the Dalai Lama an honorary degree in 2009, it was stricken from the PRC government's list of accredited foreign universities for one year. That cast a cloud over the value of the university's degrees in China, threw a wrench into its recruitment plans, and prompted matriculating PRC students to transfer to other schools.[27] Most recently, in 2018, the University of Maryland suffered serious disruptions to the executive-training programs run by its Office of China Affairs after the university pushed back against a wave of social-media vitriol targeting a student from the PRC, who had used a graduation speech to compare the conditions for freedom of speech and democracy in her home country unfavorably with those in the United States.[28]

Notably, the PRC is not alone in weaponizing enrollments. In 2017, after Canadian foreign minister Chrystia Freeland used social media to voice support for imprisoned Saudi women's rights activists, Saudi Arabia abruptly expelled the Canadian ambassador from Riyadh and announced that it would withdraw all state-sponsored Saudi students from Canada. In addition to the massive financial impact, it was feared that this move would trigger a staffing crisis in Canadian hospitals, since a large fraction of the students were medical residents or fellows. While the Saudi government ultimately permitted the medical students to stay, the number of Saudi students enrolled in Canadian universities fell by almost half the following year, and the number of new study permits issued to Saudis by the Canadian government has fallen nearly 80 percent since 2017.[29] In 2018, the credit-rating agency Moody's warned that three of Canada's top universities could face financial emergencies if the PRC reacted similarly to the Canadian government's detention of Meng Wanzhou, chief financial officer of the Chinese telecommunications giant Huawei, over alleged violations of U.S. sanctions on Iran.

Campuses Offer No Sanctuary

The PRC Ministry of Education promotes an ethnonationalist curriculum of "patriotic education" that seeks to "teach the essential commonality of love for the country, love for the Party, and love for socialism."[30] This mandate has been pursued to devastating effect in the far-western region of Xinjiang, where the state is detaining vast numbers of people in indoctrination camps in a bid to crush the distinct cultural identities of Uyghurs and other predominantly Muslim ethnic minorities.

As with Xi Jinping's broader campaign to tighten ideological discipline, Beijing is taking a global approach to "patriotic education." A 2019 document calls for patriotic struggle to promote the CCP's unyielding brand of national and ethnic unity (*guojia tongyi he minzu tuanjie*) throughout the Chinese diaspora.[31] While most PRC students abroad approach contentious issues of territory and identity with an open mind, their forbearance is plainly in spite of official policy rather than because of it. The CCP line and the diplomats who amplify it are inciting some students to vehemently rebuke those who hold opposing views, and causing stress and fear among others who opt to self-censor.[32] The Party's reach can be seen in the menacing counterdemonstrations held at overseas institutions in support of Beijing's positions on Hong Kong, Tibet, and Taiwan, as well as in the threats leveled against PRC students who express independent views—and their families back home. This campaign of intimidation, part of a multidimensional strategy "to seize the right to speak" on behalf of the PRC state, is fundamentally incompatible with the tolerance that lies at the heart of genuine intellectual freedom. It aims to censor and dominate rather than to debate and persuade.

Lest there be any doubt, in 2019 the CCP Central Committee published a compilation of Xi's speeches under the title "On Adhering to the Party's Leadership in All Work."[33] In keeping with that message, all members of the CCP and its youth league are required to faithfully execute Party policy, including in their work abroad—and this policy places them in tension with the pluralistic values of liberal-democratic societies. Members are charged with monitoring and reporting back on activities, conversations, and people of interest, and they face personal risks and rewards depending on how well they carry out this mission. PRC students understand this well, with many modulating their behavior accordingly.[34] One such student observed that a U.S. classroom "isn't a free space," and political expression by PRC students in the United States can in fact have consequences when the speaker returns home.[35] In November 2019, a young man from Wuhan was sentenced by a PRC court to six months in prison for posting a series of "comments denigrating a [PRC] national leader's image and indecent pictures" on Twitter "while he was studying at the University of Minnesota."[36] (Twitter is blocked in the PRC.)

The CSSAs that many universities rely on to help students from the PRC acclimatize to campus life merit special attention in this regard. Although the associations provide valuable social and cultural services, some also serve as a surveillance apparatus and mobilizational arm of the local PRC consulate. In 2017, the UCSD chapter openly coordinated with the local consulate its protest against the university's invitation to the Dalai Lama to deliver the commencement address. In 2019, the student union of McMaster University in Canada rescinded accreditation of its campus CSSA chapter for reporting to the local consulate about a talk on Xinjiang. In short, CSSAs are a principal route through which Beijing projects its influence not only over PRC citizens abroad, but also over the foreign institutions and personnel with whom those citizens engage. Online Chinese-language media and messaging platforms such as WeChat reinforce this influence by tethering students abroad to state-controlled information spheres.

The Business of Censorship

Beyond universities, Beijing has likewise flexed its market power in an often successful bid to outsource its censorship to institutions that are integral to open knowledge economies. In part, this means enlisting foreign entities to help circumscribe the information available to citizens in the PRC. For instance, LinkedIn, a Microsoft company, reports to users in the PRC that this author's profile "is not available," because the profile quotes from the abstract of a scholarly publication about the bloody suppression of the 1989 Tiananmen Square protests. In June 2020, the videoconferencing platform Zoom complied with a request from the Chinese government to terminate online commemorations of the Tiananmen massacre, and briefly canceled the accounts of Chinese dissidents living in the United States.[37]

The question of whether Western universities can teach such sensitive subjects to students in China via online platforms remains open, but the signs are not encouraging. Four leading U.K. universities have accepted the constraints of Chinese censorship in order to deliver online courses to students in the PRC via a pilot project with Alibaba Cloud. The project, designed in response to worries that the PRC's "Great Firewall" would keep students from consulting online resources needed for their coursework, will grant access only to a predefined list of materials placed on a "security 'allow' list."[38] Prompted by a confluence of factors—the problem of teaching students in the PRC, Beijing's recent enactment of a harsh Hong Kong national-security law with global reach, and fears that online course delivery may lend itself to recording—other universities are contemplating a range of precautionary measures. These include warning notices for courses covering topics likely to incur the wrath of PRC authorities; at Princeton, the anonymous submission of coursework on China; and, at Harvard Business School, possible student exemptions from discussing matters that raise political sensitivities.[39]

Publishers have made similar compromises. In 2017, Cambridge University Press (CUP) created a special sanitized edition of the U.K.-based *China Quarterly* when, at the behest of its PRC importer, CUP quietly removed approximately 315 articles and book reviews from the online archive it offers users in that country. It reversed course only after media exposure sparked intense criticism and put the press's reputation in jeopardy. By contrast, Springer Nature, which bills itself as the largest academic publisher in the world, continues to censor more than a thousand of its articles for PRC subscribers. The publisher Taylor and Francis sells subscription packages in the PRC that omit entire journals, largely in the humanities and social sciences.

The PRC projects its censorship into foreign information markets through many of the same channels. For instance, well-funded PRC institutions subsidize the publication of an array of "internationally refereed academic journals" by prestigious foreign presses that effectively globalize PRC narratives among English-speaking audiences, with CCP authorities holding fast to editorial control.[40] In 2020, Springer Nature announced that it could not accept manuscript submissions for the medical journal *Eye and Vision* that did not refer to Taiwan as "Taiwan, China."[41] In a notorious example from 2019, the PRC co-publisher of *Frontiers of Literary Studies in China* clumsily censored an entire article from an issue of the journal while it was in production, and the U.S.-based editor not only declined to intercede but rationalized the deletion.[42] Similarly, in 2016, the American Bar Association (ABA) rescinded an offer to publish in the United States a book by the exiled human-rights lawyer Teng Biao. The decision was reportedly driven by concern that the book would upset Beijing, complicating ABA activities in the PRC and putting staffers in the country at risk.[43]

The PRC has cornered the market for high-quality color book printing, which allows it to police even the content of books written by foreign authors in foreign languages for foreign markets. In 2019, the intensification of this vetting caused major production delays for publishers around the world. Some publishers reportedly received from their Chinese printers lists of words to avoid, including the names of political dissidents. Victoria University Press in New Zealand opted to remove reference to Mount Everest in a book after its Chinese printer objected to the term; the mountain is known by another name in China. Harsh economic logic may keep books that defy the preferences of PRC censors from being published at all. A regulation introduced in 2018 requires all maps printed in China to pass government vetting. An Australian publisher was forced to abandon a children's atlas meant for its home market when censors objected to its labeling of Tibet and Taiwan, and a suitably priced printer outside of China could not be found.[44]

So-called lawfare—the use of legal tools to wage political battles—is another increasingly prominent strategy employed by authoritarians who seek to project their censorship abroad, especially in jurisdictions that follow British legal norms. For instance, political figures in Singapore have long resorted to libel actions to intimidate critics, including international media outlets such as the *International Herald Tribune,* the *Financial Times,* and the *Far Eastern Economic Review.* In 2006, the country banned the latter publication over an article that quoted at length an opposition politician's critical remarks about the government. In 2014, Penguin withdrew from the Indian market an academic book that it had already published rather than defend itself in court against charges that the text was offensive to Hindus. In the same year, CUP declined to publish a book by the late Russia expert Karen Dawisha that documented how Vladimir Putin's inner circle had accumulated immense wealth and power. A letter from CUP explained that it had no appetite for the "disruption and expense" of libel suits that might result from publishing her book.[45] In 2017, Allen and Unwin cited similar grounds for canceling its publication of *Silent Invasion,* a book detailing PRC influence on media and politics in Australia. (All three of these volumes were later picked up by other publishers.) More recently, a Taiwanese media group friendly to Beijing filed a libel action against a journalist from the *Financial Times* who reported on alleged PRC meddling in the editorial division of a Taiwanese daily newspaper.[46] And in France, Huawei filed defamation suits against a respected think-tank scholar, a broadcast journalist, and a wireless-networking expert over claims that the telecommunications firm is controlled by the PRC government and involved in acts of espionage.[47]

Authoritarian regimes are using technology as a devastating force multiplier. The PRC is widely reputed to operate the most sophisticated regime of online surveillance and censorship on the planet, and it is exporting this model to interested governments, with offers of financing through Chinese loans to sweeten the deal.[48] While the CCP's efforts to restrict free expression in the present are legion, its attempts to manipulate the historical record are less well known. Reaching deep into the specialized databases and online publication archives used by scholars of China around the world, Beijing has worked to erase inconvenient facts and stealthily globalize its own preferred narratives. Artificial intelligence promises to automate such campaigns at colossal scales, further subjecting our information space and our perceptions to the whims of the powerful.

The Way Forward

Engagement with authoritarian partners was never going to be a one-way street, and the failure to anticipate and prepare for the foreseeable ways in which they might use collaborations to advance their own interests at democracies' expense was a blunder born of hubris. When disciplined authoritarian regimes with deep pockets meet fragmented liberal societies subject to the logic of the marketplace, the encounter can be an unbalanced one. Over time, a succession of discrete decisions and compromises, often made with good intentions—to facilitate this undertaking or smooth that wrinkle—have grown into a systemic threat to the freedom and independence of intellectual inquiry in the places that profess to value them most.

The financial shock of covid-19 has plunged many institutions central to the knowledge economy into crisis, leaving them more vulnerable than ever to coercion and cooptation by authoritarian actors. But in other ways, the environment has grown more favorable. Authoritarian regimes and their surrogates have themselves been disrupted by the pandemic, which has eroded goodwill and sharpened geopolitical rivalries. This will constrain their future freedom of action. Awareness of how easily engagements with them can corrode the integrity and democratic values of institutions in open societies is also rising, and leading to the adoption of heightened safeguards and vigilance.

Research institutions in democracies are rising to this challenge; they are strengthening their internal processes, motivated by the threats of damaged reputations, loss of state funding, and stern regulatory or legislative action.[49] In the United States, Purdue University, Virginia Tech, and Texas A&M University have led with robust programs to assess and manage foreign-engagement risk. These programs are distinguished by strong leadership, strategic focus, and a high degree of integration with university operations. Government agencies are demanding higher standards of research integrity and security as a condition of eligibility for funding. Sectoral organizations such as the Academic Security and Counter-Exploitation Program, the Association of University Export Control Officers, and the Council on Government Relations are disseminating and refining best practices. Analysts in the United States, the Netherlands, and Australia have defined roadmaps for assessing risk and building local capacity to manage it.[50]

Maintaining the independence and integrity on which the knowledge economy thrives will require expanding upon these initiatives, and commercial ventures would do well to learn from their example. Upholding democratic values and practices in their traditional strongholds can help to sustain them in places where they are weakly institutionalized. Forsake them cheaply, and the price of recovering them will surely be high.

Notes

1. Naaman Zhou and Ben Smee, "'We Cannot Be Seen': The Fallout from the University of Queensland's Hong Kong Protests," *Guardian*, 3 August 2019.

2. Minxin Pei, "Ideological Indoctrination under Xi Jinping," *China Leadership Monitor* no. 62 (2019); Carl Minzner, "Intelligentsia in the Crosshairs: Xi Jinping's Ideological Rectification of Higher Education in China," *China*

Leadership Monitor no. 62 (2019); Larry Diamond and Orville Schell, eds., *China's Influence and American Interests: Promoting Constructive Vigilance* (Stanford, Calif.: Hoover Institution Press, 2018).

3. Ben Smee, "UNSW Faces Backlash After Deleting Twitter Post Critical of China's Crackdown in Hong Kong," *Guardian,* 2 August 2020; Bang Xiao and Stephen Dziedzic, "UNSW Accused of Dishonesty After Sending 'Completely Contradictory' Statements Regarding China," ABC News (Australia), 7 August 2020.

4. Christopher Walker, "What Is 'Sharp Power'?" *Journal of Democracy* 29 (July 2018): 9–23.

5. Roger Greatrex, "Report: The Deletion of Pages from EACS Conference Materials in Braga (July 2014)," European Association for Chinese Studies, 30 July 2014, *http://chinesestudies.eu/?p=584.*

6. Alison Flood, "China Threatens Sweden After Gui Minhai Wins Free Speech Award," *Guardian,* 18 November 2019; Richard Orange, "Swedish Media Calls for Action Against Attacks from Chinese Officials," *Guardian,* 30 January 2020; Björn Jerdén and Viking Bohman, *China's Propaganda Campaign in Sweden, 2018–2019* (Stockholm: Swedish Institute of International Affairs, 2019), *www.ui.se/globalassets/ui.se-eng/publications/ui-publications/2019/ui-brief-no.-4-2019.pdf.*

7. Sheena Chestnut Greitens and Rory Truex, "Repressive Experiences Among China Scholars: New Evidence from Survey Data," *China Quarterly* 242 (June 2020): 349–75; Shaun O'Dwyer, "China's Growing Threat to Academic Freedom," *Japan Times,* 25 November 2019.

8. John Fitzgerald, "Academic Freedom and the Contemporary University: Lessons from China," *Humanities Australia* 8 (2017): 8–22.

9. Madhumita Murgia and Christian Shepherd, "US Universities Reconsider Research Links with Chinese AI Company," *Financial Times,* 13 June 2019; Alexandra Harney, "Risky Partner: Top U.S. Universities Took Funds from Chinese Firm Tied to Xinjiang Security," Reuters, 12 June 2019.

10. *The Woolf Inquiry: An Inquiry into the LSE's Links with Libya and Lessons to Be Learned* (London: London School of Economics, October 2011), *www.lse.ac.uk/News/News-Assets/PDFs/The-Woolf-Inquiry-Report-An-inquiry-into-LSEs-links-with-Libya-and-lessons-to-be-learned-London-School-of-Economics-and-Political-Sciences.pdf;* Primrose Riordan, "London School of Economics Academics Outraged by Proposed China Programme," *Financial Times,* 27 October 2019.

11. "Agreement Between Confucius Institute Headquarters of China and Griffith University, Australia on the Establishment of Tourisam [sic] Confucius Institute at Griffith University," 2011, *www.griffith.edu.au/__data/assets/pdf_file/0036/836964/establishment-agreement-griffith-university-confucius-institute-headquarters-of-china.pdf*.

12. Hinnerk Feldwisch-Drentrup, "Wie sich die FU an chinesische Gesetze bindet" [How the FU binds itself to China], *Der Tagesspiegel* (Berlin), 29 January 2020; David Matthews, "China Influence Scandal Rocks Berlin University," *Times Higher Education*, 4 February 2020, *www.timeshighereducation.com/news/china-influence-scandal-rocks-berlin-university*.

13. Katherin Hille and James Shotter, "Charles University Mired in Chinese Influence Scandal," *Financial Times*, 10 November 2019.

14. Justine Griffin, "Moffitt Cancer Center Shakeup: CEO and Others Resign over China Ties," *Tampa Bay Times*, 18 December 2019.

15. Ellen Barry, "U.S. Accuses Harvard Scientist of Concealing Chinese Funding," *New York Times*, 28 January 2020.

16. Jerry Dunleavy, "'Scratching the Surface': Education Department Uncovers $1.3b in Foreign University Funding," *Washington Examiner*, 10 December 2019.

17. Kate O'Keefe, "Education Department Investigating Harvard, Yale over Foreign Funding," *Wall Street Journal*, 13 February 2020.

18. "Elevated-Risk Review Process," Massachusetts Institute of Technology, *https://icc.mit.edu/elevated-risk-review-process*; Michael Sokolove, "Why Is There So Much Saudi Money in American Universities?" *New York Times*, 3 July 2019.

19. "Autocracies and UK Foreign Policy HC 1948," House of Commons Foreign Affairs Committee, 3 September 2019, 10–11, *http://data.parliament.uk/writtenevidence/committeeevidence.svc/evidencedocument/foreign-affairs-committee/autocracies-and-uk-foreign-policy/oral/105583.pdf*.

20. "Leading Places of Origin," Open Doors Data, Institute of International Education, *https://opendoorsdata.org/data/international-scholars/leading-places-of-origin*; "2019 Fact Sheet: China." Open Doors Data. Institute of International Education, *https://opendoorsdata.org/fact_sheets/china*.

21. "Credit Agency Warns Big Risk to Canadian Schools if China Pulls Students," *Montreal Gazette*, 7 February 2019.

22. Dorothy Settles, "UBC Quietly Changes References to Taiwan Amid Sensitive Political Climate," *The Ubyssey*, 4 July 2020, *www.ubyssey.ca/news/taiwan-references-changed*.

23. Ellie Bothwell, "Insuring Against Drop in Chinese Students," *Inside Higher Ed,* 29 November 2018, *www.insidehighered.com/news/2018/11/29/university-illinois-insures-itself-against-possible-drop-chinese-enrollments.*

24. Eleanor Ainge Roy, "Exempt Chinese Students from Coronavirus Travel Ban, New Zealand Universities Urge," *Guardian,* 17 February 2020.

25. Charles Parton, *China–UK Relations: Where to Draw the Border Between Influence and Interference?* (London: Royal United Services Institute for Defence and Security Studies, 2019), 17.

26. Anastasya Lloyd-Damnjanovic, *A Preliminary Study of PRC Political Influence and Interference Activities in American Higher Education* (Washington, D.C.: Wilson Center), 60–62.

27. Elizabeth Redden, "Is China Punishing a U.S. University for Hosting the Dalai Lama?" *Inside Higher Ed,* 20 September 2017, *www.insidehighered.com/news/2017/09/20/china-punishing-american-university-hosting-dalai-lama.*

28. Simon Denyer and Congcong Zhang, "A Chinese Student Praised the 'Fresh Air of Free Speech' at a U.S. College. Then Came the Backlash," *Washington Post,* 23 May 2017.

29. Steven Chase, "Saudi Arabia Withdrawing Students from Canadian Schools, Suspending Flights," *Globe and Mail,* 6 August 2018; "Canada—Study Permit Holders by Country of Citizenship and Year in Which Permit(s) Became Effective, January 2015–October 2019," Immigration, Refugees and Citizenship Canada, *https://open.canada.ca/data/en/dataset/90115b00-f9b8-49e8-afa3-b4cff8facaee.*

30. "Opinion of the CCP Party Group of the Ministry of Education on the Implementation of Deepening Patriotic Education in the Educational System" [in Chinese] Ministry of Education, 26 January 2016, *www.moe.gov.cn/srcsite/A13/s7061/201601/t20160129_229131.html.*

31. "The CCP Central Committee and the State Council Release the 'Implementation Plan for Patriotic Education in the New Era'" [in Chinese], Xinhua, 12 November 2019, *www.gov.cn/zhengce/2019-11/12/content_5451352.htm.*

32. Peter C. Perdue, "Reflections on the 'Visualizing Cultures' Incident," *MIT Faculty Newsletter* May–June 2006, *http://web.mit.edu/fnl/volume/185/perdue.html;* Darren Byler, "Responses to Unanswered Questions at UC Berkeley," *The Art of Life in Chinese Central Asia,* 10 May 2019, *https://livingotherwise.com/2019/05/10/responses-unanswered-questions-uc-berkeley.*

33. Xi Jinping, On Adhering to Party Leadership in All Work [in Chinese] (Beijing: CCP Central Committee Documents Press, 2019).

34. Eric Fish, "How Strained US-China Relations are Playing Out in American Universities," *South China Morning Post* (Hong Kong), 4 July 2020.

35. "China: Government Threats to Academic Freedom Abroad," Human Rights Watch, 21 March 2019, *www.hrw.org/news/2019/03/21/china-government-threats-academic-freedom-abroad#.*

36. Bethany Allen-Ebrahimian, "University of Minnesota Student Jailed in China over Tweets," *Axios,* 23 January 2020, *www.axios.com/china-arrests-university-minnesota-twitter-e495cf47-d895-4014-9ac8-8dc76aa6004d.html.*

37. Paul Mozur, "Zoom Blocks Activist in U.S. After China Objects to Tiananmen Vigil," *New York Times,* 11 June 2020.

38. Sean Coughlan, "UK Universities Comply with China's Internet Restrictions," BBC, 9 July 2020, *www.bbc.com/news/education-53341217.*

39. Lucy Craymer, "China's National-Security Law Reaches Into Harvard, Princeton Classrooms," *Wall Street Journal,* 19 August 2020.

40. Ma Sha, "The 'China Quarterly' Affair Uncovers the Tip of the Iceberg: How Is Chinese-Style Academic Censorship Exported to the World?" [in Chinese] *Initium,* 3 September 2017, *https://theinitium.com/article/20170904-mainland-The-China-Quarterly.*

41. William Yang, "International Journals Undergo Political Review Again, Academics Worry About Taiwan's Shrinking Academic Space" [in Chinese], *Deutsche Welle,* 26 August 2020, *https://tinyurl.com/y4djzxbf.*

42. Elizabeth Redden, "Censorship in a China Studies Journal," *Inside Higher Ed,* 19 April 2019, *www.insidehighered.com/news/2019/04/19/another-case-censorship-china-studies-journal.*

43. Issac Stone Fish, "Leaked Email: ABA Cancels Book for Fear of 'Upsetting the Chinese Government,'" *Foreign Policy,* 15 April 2016.

44. Linda Lew, "Chinese Censorship Laws Could Prompt Foreign Book Publishers to Look Elsewhere for Printers," *South China Morning Post,* 25 August 2019; Michael Bachelard, "Chinese Government Censors Ruling Lines through Australian Books," *Sydney Morning Herald,* 23 February 2019.

45. E. L., "A Book Too Far," *Economist,* 3 April 2014, *www.economist.com/eastern-approaches/2014/04/03/a-book-too-far.*

46. "Taiwan: Abusive Libel Suit Against Financial Times Correspondent," Reporters Without Borders, 24 July 2019, *https://rsf.org/en/news/taiwan-abusive-libel-suit-against-financial-times-correspondent.*

47. Helene Fouquet, "Huawei Sues Critics in France over Remarks on China State Ties," *Bloomberg,* 22 November 2019, *www.bloomberg.com/news/arti-*

cles/2019-11-22/huawei-sues-critics-in-france-over-remarks-on-china-state-ties.

48. Paul Mozur, Jonah M. Kessel, and Melissa Chan, "Made in China, Exported to the World: The Surveillance State," *New York Times*, 24 April 2019; Tom Wilson and Madhumita Murgia, "Uganda Confirms Use of Huawei Facial Recognition Cameras," *Financial Times,* 20 August 2019.

49. "University Actions to Address Concerns about Security Threats and Undue Foreign Government Influence on Campus," Association of American Universities, May 2020, *https://www.aau.edu/sites/default/files/AAU-Files/ Key-Issues/Science-Security/2020-Effective-Science-Security-Practices- Summary.pdf.*

50. *Global Engagement: Rethinking Risk in the Research Enterprise,* ed. Glenn Tiffert (Stanford: Hoover Institution Press, 2020); Ingrid d'Hooghe and Brigitte Dekker, *China's Invloed op Onderwijs in Nederland: Een Verkenning* [China's Influence on Education in the Netherlands: An Outlook] (The Hague: Clingendael Institute, 2020), *www.clingendael.org/sites/ default/files/2020-07/Rapport_politieke_beinvloeding_in_het_onderwijs_ juni_2020.pdf*; Frank Bekkers, Willem Oosterveld, and Paul Verhagen, *Checklist for Collaboration with Chinese Universities and Other Research Institutions* (Hague Centre for Strategic Studies, 2019), *https://hcss.nl/sites/default/ files/files/reports/BZ127566%20HCSS%20Checklist%20for%20collabora- tion%20with%20Chinese%20Universities.pdf*; *Guidelines to Counter Foreign Interference in the Australian University Sector* (University Foreign Interference Taskforce, November 2019), *https://www.education.gov.au/ guidelines-counter-foreign-interference-australian-university-sector.*

CHAPTER TWO

How Autocrats Undermine Media Freedom

EDWARD LUCAS

"TRUTH WILL PREVAIL" was the motto of the Czech and Slovak demonstrators against communist rule in 1989. Once the dead hand of censorship and monopolistic state ownership was lifted, they thought, competition and innovation would do for the media industries what they had done for retail, employment, and other parts of the economy. The ex-communist world would catch up to the "normal" advanced, industrialized countries. The market for information is no different than the market for soap. Leave the media alone, and smart consumers, market pressures, and public-spirited journalists will do the rest. The only people who should fear the power of the free media are wrongdoers.

That was a dangerous, even fatal misapprehension. The soap trade does not attract mischief makers and influence peddlers. The information system does. Information is a weapon—and one that can be used against us. This is an uncomfortable truth for open, democratic societies. Moreover, the media industries—whether in established industrial democracies, in their postcommunist counterparts, or in emerging economies—are far more vulnerable than we realized in 1989.

First, news outlets have faced wrenching changes in their business models, changes that are driven by a technological revolution. Second, features of the media system such as competition, openness, fair-mindedness, and prudence, once seen only as strengths, have also turned out to be weaknesses.

The underlying fallacy here is the idea that the "marketplace of ideas" works well without any externally imposed structure or sanctions. This is not the case even in the market for soap, and is certainly not the case in the market for information. As Joseph Stiglitz, the Nobel Prize–winning economist, noted in the *Financial Times*:

Much of the thrust of economics over the past half century has been to understand what regulations are needed to ensure that markets work. We have tort laws that ensure accountability if someone is injured and we don't allow companies to pollute willy-nilly. We have fraud and advertising laws to protect consumers against deceptions—recognising that such laws circumscribe what individuals may say and publish.[1]

Tobacco companies, for example, cannot say that cigare é ttes are safe. Pharmaceutical companies cannot say that opioids are not addictive. In the financial markets, regulation ensures equal access to information for investors.

All this would apply to soap. But distortions in the marketplace for information are potentially much more damaging. If a consumer buys the wrong kind of personal-hygiene product, the risk and cost fall mainly on the individual. But if someone votes on the basis of misinformation, then the whole of society suffers. Economists call such spillover costs "externalities." Stiglitz argues that "without full transparency, without a mechanism for holding participants to account, without equal ability to transmit and receive information, and with unrelenting intimidation, there is no free marketplace of ideas."

These weaknesses do not result merely in imperfect outcomes. They can be exploited by malign actors ranging from politically motivated tycoons to foreign intelligence services. Indeed, major authoritarian powers, including China and Russia, have invested heavily in such efforts. The perpetrators may not all have the same goals or motives, but they often adopt essentially the same tactics: Buy what you can—and befuddle the rest.

In the space of two decades, from the richest countries to the poorest, barriers to entry have collapsed. To be a force in the media world today, you do not need costly transmitters, studios, office buildings, printing presses, or distribution vans. Not only do you not need a large staff— you do not need *any* staff. You do not need a business model. You can run a national or even global disinformation effort on your wits alone, using a smartphone worth US$50 and a public Wi-Fi connection, at almost zero marginal cost. You do not even need to give up your day job.

While life has become easier for newcomers, it has become harder for the incumbents. Collapsing public trust in the media is not a worldwide phenomenon, but it is a common one. The reasons for this erosion, and its extent, are matters of controversy. Among other factors, political polar-ization makes it harder for media to appear impartial. Lower standards caused by economic stress have harmed quality, meaning more mistakes and worse editorial decisions, which compound the problem. The per-ception of journalism as an elite profession has broadened the social gulf between consumers and producers of news.

In many countries, moreover, the economic rents, or unearned income, that sustained mass media for decades have dried up. You do not need to advertise a job, a car, or a retail sale in the print edition of your local broadsheet newspaper. You can reach your customers online, at a cost that is continuing to fall. Nor do you need to advertise with old-style terrestrial broadcasters. It is true that traditional media continue to thrive in some countries: Newspaper readership remains high in Japan and Germany, for instance, for in those places subscribers are apparently more willing to bear the costs of journalism. But these are exceptions. On the whole, mass media are under serious economic pressure, and this leaves them primed for exploitation.

A Market with Few Safeguards

A central principle of the market economy is that unfettered competition is good. It raises standards, punishing the mediocre and rewarding the innovative and efficient. Only narrow exceptions apply, such as antidump-ing rules in international trade, or laws meant to ensure consumer health and safety. Assuming these legal thresholds are met, the market is free to work its will.

Limits on market forces are especially rare in the media world. Some countries have rules about foreign ownership. Libel and other defamation laws can also apply. Broadcast regulators may restrict nudity and obscene language, and require that paid commercial content be properly identified.

But these rules chiefly apply to "old" media and are lightly enforced. There is no counterpart to antidumping rules that would prevent for-eign-subsidized news outlets from competing unfairly with domestic, prof-it-driven enterprises. And there is no equivalent of the U.S. Food and Drug Administration to examine media content for any risks to consumers.

This creates the first vulnerability in the media systems of democracies, what might be termed *faux*-commercial competition. News outlets that need to make a profit struggle against competitors that are bankrolled by someone else, be it a tycoon or a government. The subsidies can be delivered directly or in disguised form, such as through advertising or clandestine payments to journalists.

A related weakness is openness to financial intimidation. An independent, for-profit media outlet operates on the basis of prudence. If you habitually offend your big advertisers, you can lose revenue. If you annoy the government, you may find that your journalists are denied access to decision-makers, which also carries a commercial cost. If you print official secrets, you may be prosecuted; not only does the editor then risk jail, but the burden of legal fees can be crippling. These are the normal concerns that constrain editorial judgment. But they are all open to abuse. Pressure placed on advertisers by the government of the People's Republic of China (PRC), for example, can lead to de facto boycotts that cripple or undermine critical coverage.

In Singapore, the authorities exert pressure on independent media through costly lawsuits.[2] In Hong Kong, corporate advertisers were withholding business from *Apple Daily* (which was eventually raided by police and shuttered) and other prodemocracy outlets to avoid the displeasure of PRC authorities. Jimmy Lai, the strong-willed tycoon who founded *Apple Daily*, has been jailed under Hong Kong's National Security Law, which the territory adopted at Beijing's behest in 2020. The authorities attacked Lai's paper so harshly and directly because he did not mind losing money for a good cause, and because *Apple Daily* enjoyed substantial support from likeminded readers.[3]

In common-law jurisdictions, including England and Ireland, that lack U.S.-style First Amendment protections, losing a libel case means not only printing an apology, but also paying damages and the plaintiff's legal fees. Even if the plaintiff's case fails, the defendant news outlet must still spend large sums on its own legal fees, which in most jurisdictions it cannot recover. The typical complainant does not care. His aim is to harass and bully his critics until they decide that writing about his business activities, personal life, or political affiliations is no longer worth the effort.

In some cases, the economic weakness may prove transient. At least for media outlets working in big-language markets, in rich countries, and appealing to high-information consumers, new business models are emerging. As the market fragments, it is easier to see where profits lie, and to chase them. Media outlets such as the *Economist,* the *New York Times,* and the *Washington Post* are showing how the high-quality news business can thrive, not just survive, in the twenty-first century. If the PRC, or the government of Vladimir Putin in Russia, tried to finance rivals to these outlets, they would probably fare poorly. The sort of people who read upmarket news are less likely to be fooled by imitations.

But that is little comfort elsewhere in the media ecosystem. Some well-known outlets looking to buttress their revenues have resorted to licensing their brands abroad, where they may become vehicles for propagandistic content. The *Independent,* a British newspaper, entered into such an arrangement with the Saudi Research and Marketing Group, a company that is closely linked to the Saudi monarchy.[4] Britain's Sky News has licensed its brand to the Abu Dhabi Media Investment Corporation, owned by the brother of the de facto ruler of the United Arab Emirates (UAE). The resulting Sky News Arabia became a vehicle for smears aimed at regional rival Qatar.[5]

If the information systems in well-resourced, established democracies are struggling, the vulnerabilities are all the greater in societies where capacity is weaker, the financial picture is bleaker, and institutional roots are shallower. The greatest exposure to *faux*-competition is among media that cater to low-information consumers in the smallish markets of poor countries. Three European countries that have faced Russian subversion and information operations are North Macedonia (population 1.8 million), Montenegro (620,000), and Moldova (2.6 million, and Europe's poorest country).[6] It is hard to see how, in such circumstances, a media outlet can make money by producing responsible, high-quality news. You cannot sell your product outside your country's borders. Your consumers cannot pay much in subscriptions and are not rich or numerous enough to attract much in the way of advertising. Your *faux*-competitors have none of these worries.

Exploitable Gaps in Journalistic Ethics

A second and much deeper weakness in the media systems of open societies lies in their moral and conceptual foundations. Journalism rests on the ethical instincts, usually unstated and uncodified, of the editors and reporters who select and publish stories. What counts as fair? What counts as relevant? What counts as true? These are questions that ultimately lead back to philosophy classes, where the final answers are elusive. But they are the warp and weft of the fabric produced in our news factories.

Fair-mindedness is easily abused. One source says that it is raining, while another says that it is not. The lazy and ostensibly fair-minded approach is to report both assertions. The readers can draw their own conclusions. In fact, this approach is profoundly unfair to readers. The journalist's job is to go and see whether the rain is falling. Is the sidewalk wet? What do passers-by say? The veracity of the contradictory sources can be assessed and explained. What qualifications do they have in meteorology? Have their past predictions and reports been accurate? But this sort of work costs time and money, both of which, outside the rarefied world of high-end journalism, are scarce. It is easier to report "both sides" of the story and move on.

Similar dereliction can affect an outlet's screening of outside contributors, allowing authoritarian actors to disseminate propaganda through writers who conceal their financial ties and affiliations. Gulf states such as the UAE and Qatar, for example, have been known to use lobbying firms and contractors to spread their messages in op-eds and other media content without the appropriate disclosures.[7]

An associated vulnerability stems from decisions about what is news in the first place. News agendas are notoriously tricky to pin down. Topics go in and out of fashion, based on perceptions of what media consumers will find interesting. "Man bites dog" is news; "dog bites man" is not. Human tragedies close to readers' own experience are more interesting than distant ones. Plane crashes matter more than automobile accidents. One life lost nearby is more newsworthy than a dozen elsewhere, or thousands on the other side of the world. Controversy, however meaningless, is typically more newsworthy than agreement. Human psychology, and editorial perceptions of it, create a natural drift toward sensationalist news. This is exacerbated by competition. If your rivals are chasing the most attention-grabbing news and you are not, you may lose out.

At the top end of the market, new outlets can build their brands by cultivating a measured, even aloof, approach to the news. The BBC World Service newsroom, where this author worked in the mid-1980s, built its reputation on broadcasting news only when it had at least two reputable sources. It was better to miss stories than to get them wrong. But in other segments of the news business, the reverse applies. It is better to be first than to be right. Memories are short, and appetites are strong.

A particular problem involves the reporting of perceived wrongdoing. Journalists have a strong, even overwhelming instinct to pursue stories that imply misconduct. The line between private hypocrisy, rudeness, and extravagance on the one hand and serious criminal or unethical behavior on the other is blurry, and can easily be blurred further. A clandestine recording of a public figure using obscene language, or saying unpleasant things about supposed friends and allies, is instantly newsworthy. How dare Politician X pretend in public to be cozy with Politician Y, and then say mean things about him in private?

That approach is eminently open to abuse. The right to have a private conversation is a fundamental element of a free society. Even the most zealous advocate of transparency in public life does not argue that politicians should wear body cameras recording their every deed and word.

Once you accept that public figures have the right to private behavior, you should then accept that this will on occasion differ from what they say and do in public. The difference—call it privacy arbitrage—becomes newsworthy only when it is genuinely scandalous, calling into question the politician's fitness for office. Potentially criminal or treasonous behavior, for example, would qualify.

This was illustrated by the *afera taśmowa*, or tape scandal, in Poland in 2014.[8] Government ministers were clandestinely recorded in Warsaw restaurants. In one case, two were eating an expensive meal (featuring octopus) at taxpayers' expense and badmouthing other members of the government as well as the Barack Obama administration in the United States. The Polish media—rightly, in a narrow commercial sense—published the recordings, which appalled the Polish public. One of the parties to the "octopus" conversation, Foreign Minister Radosław Sikorski, was moved to another position and suffered substantial damage to his political career. It could be argued that some wrongdoing—namely, lavish spending and ugly, hypocritical language—was exposed. But the Polish media skated over the difficult aspects of the story. Are ministers allowed to meet and talk privately? Are they allowed to use swear words in private? If they are to live in a digital panopticon, when was this decided, by whom, and with what exceptions, punishments, and other rules?

The media largely missed the most important questions pertaining to material that reaches journalists through unorthodox means. Is it genuine? Are the inferences drawn from it correct? What were the motives of those who obtained and provided it? Were the means used legal? If they involved trickery or even lawbreaking, is that proportionate to the purported wrongdoing exposed? Grzegorz Rzeczkowski, an investigative reporter for the weekly magazine *Polityka,* has described the Polish entrepreneur who organized the covert taping, Marek Falenta, as a Russian intelligence asset. Rzeczkowski has said that he found evidence of links between Falenta and Poland's populist-conservative Law and Justice party (then in opposition), as well as links between Falenta and Russians that go beyond a publicly known business connection involving coal imports.[9] This seems far more scandalous than the content of the recordings, and raises the possibility that the Polish media were manipulated into serving the political interests of an authoritarian power.

It is notable that this sort of story has played out in similar ways again and again. The most notorious case may have been the Russian leaks of hacked Democratic Party emails during the 2016 U.S. presidential election,[10] but other actors have also used the bait of enticing leaks to instrumentalize mass media in democracies. Figures on both sides of the diplomatic rift between Qatar and other members of the Gulf Cooperation Council have been targeted by such leaks since 2017, including a prominent U.S. lobbyist and the UAE ambassador to the United States.[11]

Another instructive example of inadequate journalistic rigor concerns the 17 July 2014 surface-to-air–missile shootdown by Russian-backed rebels in eastern Ukraine of Malaysian Airlines Flight 17, a Boeing 777 with 298 people aboard. The perpetrators' culpability for the loss of all those lives was fairly clear at the time, and has since been proven beyond all reasonable doubt by the open-source investigators at Bellingcat.[12] Prosecutors in the Netherlands, where the flight originated, have endorsed these conclusions.[13] But Russian state-controlled media and their allies in Western Europe continue to insist that the story is not so simple. They focus on minor details in the evidence and possible failures of procedure by the investigating authorities to cast doubt on the obvious version of events. No single alternative explanation is adduced. Instead, the Russian side produces a blizzard of possible scenarios ranging from the superficially plausible to the outlandish. One proposes that the Ukrainian government shot down the plane by mistake and is covering that up with help from Western intelligence services.[14]

The responsible reaction to this behavior would be to treat it like flat-earthism—as a phenomenon rather than as a theory in viable competition with other accounts of the truth. It is interesting that the Kremlin is putting forward these stories. But the stories are not themselves interesting. Adopting this approach would require journalists and editors to consciously set aside their natural instincts toward fair-mindedness and take on the more difficult but more valuable task of distinguishing what is true and important from what is merely noteworthy nonsense.

Russia's Sharp-Power Media Strategy

To appreciate the danger posed by the vulnerabilities described above, one must understand that propaganda efforts like those surrounding the downing of the Malaysian jetliner are not isolated Russian responses to particular events. Instead, they are manifestations of a comprehensive strategy using "sharp power" to disrupt, subvert, and essentially hijack the information systems of targeted countries and regions. The Kremlin's ambitions are evident in the scale of its financial investments and the global reach of its activities.

There are three main parts to Russia's sharp-power strategy in the media sphere. The first is to reach media consumers through the Kremlin's own state-media outlets. The state-owned newspaper *Rossiyskaya Gazeta* produces a paid supplement, *Russia Beyond,* which is inserted into local papers in some 27 countries using sixteen different languages. The external television broadcaster RT and the *soi-disant* news agency and external radio broadcaster Sputnik are even more widely available, producing content in dozens of languages. When their material is accessed directly from the source, the ownership and the agenda of these outlets are concealed scarcely, if at all. The selling point is "balance." You have heard what the mainstream media have to say. Now here is another view. If you pride yourself on your open-mindedness, should you not at least try to understand the Kremlin's point of view? Do you really trust your own media to tell you the truth? This approach is epitomized by the RT motto "Question more."

The second part of the Russian media strategy is to use financial and other means to influence mainstream media in target countries. Sputnik content, for example, is free for use, whereas Reuters and other international news agencies charge client outlets for their services. Much of Sputnik's reporting is not overtly political, and includes otherwise-expensive categories such as foreign news. It is, therefore, tempting for cash-strapped media outlets in poor countries, like those of the Western Balkans, to rely on Sputnik to fill pages and airtime. In this case, the media consumer, and indeed the editors and reporters involved in repackaging and disseminating Sputnik content, may have little idea that they are dealing with material produced by a Kremlin-financed propaganda outlet. What they notice is that it is free and interesting.

Along with these carrots come sticks. If a foreign outlet offends the Kremlin, it risks punishment. The lucrative paid supplements may be withdrawn. Outlets that report critically about Moscow's activities may face libel actions or cyberattacks.

The third part of the strategy is clandestine or indirect pressure. This can take the form of secret financing of competitors, disguised mergers and acquisitions, and the bribery of key staff. Or it can involve news outlets that have no overt connection with Russia. Examples of these include *Baltnews* in the Baltic states,[15] or the infamous *DCLeaks* and *USAPoliticsToday* websites, which published the material stolen from the Democratic Party and the Hillary Clinton campaign computers in the run-up to the 2016 U.S. presidential election.[16] Clandestine pressure tactics also include the direct provision to mainstream media of material obtained through intelligence operations, as in Poland's *afera taśmowa*, cited above. Although these methods should set off journalistic alarm bells, all too often they do not.

China's Strategy for Media Influence

The PRC, the other major player in global sharp-power influence activities, employs many of the same media strategies as Russia, but with some differences. For example, in addition to the paid newspaper supplements put out by the state-run *China Daily* and the free news content distributed by the official Xinhua News Agency, the external broadcaster China Global Television Network (CGTN) engages in co-productions with mainstream outlets in target countries, which then air the resulting programs to their own viewers.[17] As with Russia, the state affiliation and political agendas of Chinese media outlets and content are often veiled in various ways to avoid raising the suspicions of foreign news consumers.

Beijing uses the nonmedia business interests of media owners as economic leverage. If a U.S. media giant hopes to distribute its entertainment programming in China, or a Taiwanese conglomerate wishes to maintain its snack-food empire on the mainland, they will learn not to let their news-media assets offend. Some pressure and outright threats are conveyed directly—particularly via PRC diplomats abroad and state-security agents within China. Disfavored media and critical journalists face visa denials, blocked websites, and harassment or even detention of family members in China. Outside the country, not only are advertisers warned to avoid certain outlets, but foreign institutions and government agencies are enlisted to bar critical outlets' access to newsworthy venues, or to launch prosecutions of key staff.[18]

Meanwhile, many positive incentives draw journalists and media owners into Beijing's fold: prestige, junkets of various kinds, or the prospect of access to Chinese state media and its vast audience. Like Russia's state media, official Chinese outlets frame collaboration as a way to challenge Western media dominance and provide an alternative perspective on global events. This does not necessarily mean casting doubt on rival outlets' reporting. Rather, foreign media are urged to partner with China to better reflect the views of the developing world or the global South.[19]

Lastly, the Chinese government and its favored private companies, which have far greater resources than their Russian counterparts, are seeking to become the "gatekeepers" of news and information in other countries via influence and control over key content-dissemination platforms and infrastructure. This is already beginning to play out in the digital-television sector in several African countries and on social-media platforms such as the Tencent-owned WeChat and ByteDance's TikTok.[20]

While Russia's efforts to expand its international media influence and weaken its geopolitical adversaries are certainly ambitious, China's sprawling activities amount to a bid for outright dominance of the world's information systems.[21] Together, and combined with similar engagement by lesser authoritarian powers in the Middle East and elsewhere, they present a formidable challenge to the survival of press freedom and freedom of expression in democracies.

Responding to the Challenge

An effective response to authoritarian media influence requires an array of normative, legal, and practical changes.

Norm-building is a common feature of governmental and nongovernmental efforts to pursue the public good in democratic societies. When it comes to road safety and public health, for instance, people are urged to be considerate (by washing their hands frequently, let us say) and not primarily to fear the sanctions of the criminal law. We need to apply this to the information space. Encouraging people not to spread rumors or malicious gossip would be a good place to start. This does not point toward any kind of statutory licensing system for journalists. Many professions self-regulate in ways that do not involve the legal system. Journalists can do the same.

A blueprint for action on norm-building is overdue. The first step should be the creation of a charter of responsible practice with input from professional associations and trade unions, journalism schools, and industry bodies. Diversity of opinion would be accepted and welcome. But media outlets that sign up to the charter should commit to the following:

- Transparency of ownership and commercial relationships;
- Clear and visible acknowledgment of franchising, sponsorship, and "advertorial" deals;
- Publication of "real-world" location and contact details;
- Naming of editors-in-chief and other senior staff;
- Public display of editorial policy regarding the use of anonymous sourcing; and
- Provision of means for the public to complain about inaccuracies or distortions, development of a procedure for dealing with these complaints, and the issuance of print apologies, clarifications, and corrections where appropriate.

It should be noted that none of these requirements would constrain editorial freedom. A media outlet that adopts this charter could have a highly partisan editorial stance, but would still distinguish itself from willful and clandestine purveyors of disinformation and rumor.

A related norm-building effort involves discretion in interactions with problematic media. Considerations of both ethics and national security suggest that there are outlets unworthy of cooperation. State-owned propaganda outlets such as RT and CGTN know that they can exploit the egos of public figures, authors, academics, and others who like being seen on television. We cannot ban people from appearing on these channels, but we can increase the social cost. Publishers could discourage their authors from accepting invitations. Universities could issue guidance through their press offices to faculty and students. Public bodies could decline to provide quotes. Starved of reputable contributors, these outlets' dependence on cranks, axe-grinders, and propagandists would become embarrassing—and damaging.

In the long term, media-literacy education offers the best hope of improving the "immune system" of democratic media environments. Children and young people are often less naïve about online information than are their elders; teaching the young how to assess the veracity and origins of news is easier. Curriculum development in rich countries offers plenty of scope for cross-fertilization.

Finnish media-literacy projects, for instance, are already attracting attention.[22] In poor countries with less-developed education systems, media literacy needs to be part of development policy.

Statutory regulation has its place too. Laws need to require that media outlets have transparent ownership, including state affiliation. Terrestrial broadcast frequencies should be available only to media enterprises that make clear who or what owns and runs them. Separately, we should encourage the numerous private and nongovernmental initiatives that are developing systems for ranking and signaling in online news. Does this site have a street address? Does it have a phone number? Does it publish corrections and apologies? Does it carry dissenting viewpoints? Do its journalists have professional backgrounds? Has its coverage ever won a journalistic prize? All these questions, and others, provide the grounds for scoring a news site in terms of its credibility and integrity. A site that does poorly should not be banned, but we should find ways of letting visitors know what kind of online neighborhood they are entering.

The next major issue is media resilience in the face of intimidation, which similarly requires a combined statutory, normative, and civil society effort. The aim is to make authoritarian pressure tactics so ineffective that they are no longer used.

The first thing to do is to make institutions more resilient by persuading them to cooperate in response to threats. News outlets should compete against one another, but there may be times when bad actors exploit competitiveness, tempting people and organizations with commercial or professional advantages in order to play divide-and-rule. Journalists and editors already display some solidarity in response to threats, through trade unions, editors' associations, press clubs, and media-ethics programs. The proposals outlined above could play a role in strengthening cohesion.

For maximum resilience, however, we need to add a specific threat-related dimension. We need to think strategically about the allocation of resources, research, and outreach. We need to study manipulative tactics in order to counter them. Imagine if news outlets pooled their efforts to bring in heavyweight legal support for investigative journalism. A hostile oligarch or autocrat would think twice before trying to intimidate a small media organization if he knew it could call on a multimillion-dollar legal-defense fund. Another form of collective action would involve editors agreeing to reject advertorials from hostile-state actors, and to ostracize those outlets that do. Information-technology staffs could collaborate across media outlets to strengthen the cybersecurity of newsrooms, reporters, and sources. Outlets could even agree to host one another's content as a way of defeating distributed denial-of-service attacks. Media organizations could also teach editors to band together against pressure from embassies or threats of visa bans. The best response to targeted intimidation by, say, the Chinese authorities might be collective action—a warning that no Beijing-based correspondent will attend a press conference unless *all* accredited foreign journalists are allowed to attend it.

Cooperative behavior needs to include support for individual journalists, too. The case of Jessikka Aro, the Finnish journalist who in 2016 helped to uncover Russia's online "troll factory" in St. Petersburg, is illustrative here. She was the subject of targeted, state-sponsored harassment, ranging from the unearthing of irrelevant but embarrassing personal information to vindictive pranks, such as the sending of a spoofed text message purporting to be from her deceased father. The Finnish system let her down, and she had to leave Finland for an undisclosed location abroad.[23]

Since then, Finnish officials and media figures have tried to provide journalists, activists, and other victims of state-sponsored harassment with support and redress, both private and public.

Ideally such a system, applied more broadly, would include the following:

- A hotline offering the victim a single point of high-level contact;
- Speedy intervention by the criminal-justice system;
- The attention of counterintelligence authorities;
- A diplomatic protest lodged with the culprit country;

- Liaison with other countries whose nationals may be involved in the harassment;
- Psychological and other support;
- Assistance with legal fees;
- Physical security at home and at work (panic buttons, security cameras); and
- Cooperation of other media, for example in boycotting leaked personal material.

When the components of support are listed like this, the need for it becomes clear. At the moment, a journalist (or activist, think-tank researcher, academic, or author) who is targeted by Russia or China is largely dependent on his or her employer, if there is one. This employer may or may not be supportive, or may even be under pressure to refuse involvement. The police may not grasp the political significance of what looks like harassment that falls short of criminal behavior. Counterintelligence and security agencies typically only protect state employees. Governments may be unwilling to sour trade or diplomatic relations on behalf of an individual. There is, therefore, a need to quickly assess the merits of the case—is the victim indeed suffering real harassment because of genuine journalistic or similar activity? If so, there must be systematic support backed with planning, funding, and high-level official actions—not just improvisations by whichever actors might choose to "step up."

The biggest and most difficult vulnerability, of course, is the economic weakness of the mainstream media, coupled with the political polarization mentioned above. For these problems, no easy solutions exist. State subsidies to the media would inevitably come with political strings. Some forms of philanthropic support can encourage editors to pander to their donors, rather than to serve the public, and can place the outlets that try to make a living on purely commercial grounds at a certain disadvantage. One solution may be to subsidize individual journalists through prizes, fellowships, and other grants. A reporter who knows that his or her income is secure for the next five years will be harder to bully or bribe than one who worries about how to feed the family month to month.

No single or simple solution will blunt the impact of sharp power on the information systems of our democracies. But remedies, preventive measures, and deterrents are all available. The problem is not one of principle, or of means, but of will. We need to accept that in a world where hostile state actors have great market power and no accountability, free speech is too important to be left to the free market. If we allow commercial pressure alone to dictate the information flows in our societies, we are in effect selling political decisionmaking to the highest bidder.

This does not mean that we must adopt the top-down information controls that our adversaries favor. We do not want governments or intelligence agencies deciding what information is "safe" and what is "unsafe." It would be a perverse outcome if we responded to the threat of Putinism by "Putinizing" our own societies.

But distaste for state intervention in the media is no excuse for apathy or complacency. We need to create a commercial environment in which authentic, responsible media outlets can thrive without being drowned out by propagandists. Media practitioners need to change how they think about competition, openness, fair-mindedness, and prudence so that authoritarians cannot exploit these as weaknesses. Seen from the perspective of high-end media in rich, big countries with strong institutions, these problems can look less daunting. For this reason, remedial efforts should focus on small-language and poor countries, and on nonelite parts of the media landscape.

We need to accept the bleak truth that we are losing the battle of ideas with authoritarian regimes, not because our ideas are weak, but because we have let the battlefield be skewed against us. If we fail to rise to this challenge, our information systems will cease to be a bulwark against hostile sharp power, and will instead become a vector for its transmission. Our other public institutions—justice systems, elected officials, the civil service, and the armed forces—and ultimately democracy and freedom themselves will be gravely, and eventually fatally, weakened if the information system falls into the hands of our adversaries.

Notes

1. Joseph Stiglitz, "Facebook Does Not Understand the Marketplace of Ideas," *Financial Times,* 17 January 2020.

2. John O'Callaghan, "Lawsuit Threat Reminds Critics of Caution in More Open Singapore," Reuters, 11 January 2013, *www.reuters.com/article/*

us-singapore-lawsuits/lawsuit-threat-reminds-critics-of-caution-in-more-open-singapore-idUSBRE90A05920130111.

3. Jenni Marsh, "Why Pro-Democracy Troublemaker Jimmy Lai Is the Only Hong Kong Multi-Millionaire Standing Up to China," CNN, 28 August 2019, *www.cnn.com/2019/08/27/media/jimmy-lai-hong-kong-protests-intl-hk/index.html.*

4. Jim Waterson, "Court Blocks Inquiry Into Independent and Standard's Links to Saudi Arabia," *Guardian,* 16 August 2019, *www.theguardian.com/media/2019/aug/16/independent-evening-standard-links-to-saudi-arabia-inquiry-blocked;* Jim Waterson and Saeed Kamali Dehghan, "Independent's Deal With Saudi Publisher Back Under Spotlight," *Guardian,* 19 October 2018, *www.theguardian.com/media/2018/oct/19/independent-deal-with-saudi-publisher-back-under-spotlight.*

5. Adam Taylor, "UAE Touts Film Linking Rival Qatar to 9/11 Attacks," *Washington Post,* 25 July 2017.

6. Editorial Board, "Macedonia Is a Tiny Country With a Giant Russia Problem," *Washington Post,* 20 September 2018; Heather A. Conley and Matthew Melino, "Russian Malign Influence in Montenegro: The Weaponization and Exploitation of History, Religion, and Economics," Center for Strategic and International Studies, 14 May 2019, *www.csis.org/analysis/russian-malign-influence-montenegro;* Madalin Necsutu, "Moldova Highly 'Vulnerable' to Russian Propaganda, Study Says," *Balkan Insight,* 26 July 2018, *https://balkaninsight.com/2018/07/26/moldova-the-most-vulnerable-country-to-russian-propaganda-07-26-2018.*7. Richard Lardner, "Qatar, UAE Spend Heavily on Lobbyists Amid War of Words," Associated Press, 30 March 2018, *https://apnews.com/b2d5003280e343a88985d784e9060586/Qatar,-UAE-spend-heavily-on-lobbyists-amid-a-war-of-words.*

8. Jan Cienski, "A Polish 'Game of Tapes,'" *Politico Europe,* 10 June 2015, *www.politico.eu/article/a-polish-game-of-tapes.*

9. Grzegorz Rzeczkowski, "Kto Stoi za Falenta" [Who is behind Falenta?], *Polityka* (Warsaw), 17 June 2019, *www.polityka.pl/tygodnikpolityka/kraj/1796928,1,kto-stoi-za-falenta.read.*

10. Ellen Nakashima and Shane Harris, "How the Russians Hacked the DNC and Passed Its Emails to WikiLeaks," *Washington Post,* 13 July 2018.

11. Zaid Jilani and Ryan Grim, "Hacked Emails Show Top UAE Diplomat Coordinating With Pro-Israel Think Tank Against Iran," *Intercept,* 3 June 2017, *https://theintercept.com/2017/06/03/hacked-emails-show-top-uae-diplomat-coordinating-with-pro-israel-neocon-think-tank-against-iran;* Kevin Collier, "How Two Persian Gulf Nations Turned the US Media Into Their Battleground,"

BuzzFeed News, 10 May 2018, *www.buzzfeednews.com/article/kevincollier/ qatar-uae-iran-trump-leaks-emails-broidy.*

12. "Identifying the Separatists Linked to the Downing of MH17," Bellingcat, 19 June 2019, *https://www.bellingcat.com/news/uk-and-europe/2019/06/19/ identifying-the-separatists-linked-to-the-downing-of-mh17.*

13. "Dutch Prosecutor Names Four to be Tried for Murder in Downing of MH17," Radio Free Europe–Radio Liberty, 19 June 2019, *www.rferl.org/a/jit-name-suspects- charges-mh17-ukraine- malaysia-russia-shootdown/30007817.html.*

14. "MH17 Crash Four Years On: Probe Continues, While No Solid Proof Presented So Far," Sputnik International, 17 July 2018, *https://sputniknews. com/20180717/investigation-mh-17-plane-crash-results-1066428305.html.*

15. Holger Roonemaa and Inga Springe, "This Is How Russian Pro- paganda Actually Works in the 21st Century," *BuzzFeed News*, 31 August 2018, *https://www.buzzfeednews.com/article/holgerroonemaa/ russia-propaganda-baltics-baltnews.*

16. Scott Shane, "The Fake Americans Russia Created to Influence the Elec- tion," *New York Times*, 7 September 2017.

17. Sarah Cook, "Beijing's Global Megaphone: The Expansion of Chinese Communist Party Media Influence Since 2017," Freedom House, 2020, *https:// freedomhouse.org/report/special-report/2020/beijings-global-megaphone.*

18. Cook, "Beijing's Global Megaphone."

19. Andrew Jacobs, "Pursuing Soft Power, China Puts Stamp on Africa's News," *New York Times*, 16 August 2012.

20. Yaqiu Wang, "How China's Censorship Machine Crosses Borders—and Into Western Politics," Human Rights Watch, 20 February 2019, *www.hrw.org/ news/2019/02/20/how-chinas-censorship-machine-crosses-borders-and-west- ern-politics.*

21. Shanthi Kalathil, *"Beyond the Great Firewall: How China Became a Global Information Power,"* Center for International Media Assis- tance, Washington, D.C., 7 March 2017, *www.cima.ned.org/publication/ beyond-great-firewall-china-became-global-information-power.*

22. Emma Charlton, "How Finland Is Fighting Fake News— in the Classroom," World Economic Forum, 21 May 2019, *www.weforum.org/ agenda/2019/05/how-finland-is-fighting-fake-news-in-the-classroom.*

23. Andrew Higgins, "Efforts to Expose Russia's 'Troll Army' Draws Vicious Retaliation," *New York Times*, 30 May 2016.

CHAPTER THREE

How Beijing Runs the Show
in Hollywood

AYNNE KOKAS

IN 2017, ACTION-ADVENTURE STAR AND DIRECTOR Wu Jing released a movie called *Wolf Warrior 2* that became the highest-grossing Chinese feature film made up to that time. Continuing the saga of Chinese special-forces veteran Leng Feng, hero of *Wolf Warrior* (2015), and detailing his exploits battling pirates and Western mercenaries while saving lives in an unnamed African country wracked by pestilence and civil war, WW2 became an instant runaway hit. It played largely in the People's Republic of China (PRC), but the Chinese movie market is so large that this meant the film grossed hundreds of millions of dollars.

Since then, more Chinese-made blockbusters have followed, including the science-fiction film *Wandering Earth* (2019), the time-travel comedy *Hi, Mom* (2021), and the Korean War epic *Battle at Lake Changjin* (2021). Also starring Wu Jing, *Battle* passed WW2 to become the highest-grossing Chinese film ever made. Its sequel, *Battle at Lake Changjin II*, was released on 1 February 2022 to coincide with Chinese New Year celebrations. As of mid-March, according to the entertainment-industry publication *Variety*, it had made US$635 million, making it the highest-grossing current-release film not just in China, but worldwide.

In 2020, as this wave of major movie hits was gathering force, the PRC surpassed the United States to become—as many had long predicted it would—the world's largest market for theatrically distributed films. The PRC kept this status in 2021. Twenty years ago, the Chinese movie market was worth only a few million dollars annually, but the PRC had joined the World Trade Organization in 2001, and things were about to change. Chinese authorities decided to direct heavy investments into movie theaters and the modernization of the domestic film industry. Hengdian World Studios, founded a few hours south of Shanghai in 1996, expanded to become the largest film- and television-production facility on the planet. China pursued coproductions with Hollywood (infusing the PRC film industry with U.S. and international cinematic expertise) while also limiting the content and quantity of foreign films that could be shown in PRC theaters. In 2019, according to Box Office Mojo, the PRC film market was worth about $9.1 billion, a figure that slid to a pandemic-constricted $6.2 billion in 2021 but which still towers over the number from two decades ago. Observers are forecasting more and stronger Chinese-government assertions of control over cinematic content, with overseas film companies thirsty for access to the world's biggest movie audience expected to comply. Using opaque practices, Beijing limits entry into the PRC's media market, lays down rules about content, and passes extraterritorial laws designed to control content and distribution even beyond the PRC's borders.

China's growing clout in global media extends beyond movies to the entertainment industry generally. Capital investments by U.S. firms in ventures such as the Shanghai Disney Resort and the Universal Beijing Resort (which opened in 2016 and 2021, respectively) give Chinese officials still more levers with which to control U.S. media conglomerates. Companies that have sunk vast sums into Chinese theme parks have billions of reasons to make sure that all their platforms—films, streaming programs, video games, and beyond—observe Beijing's content rules and avoid carrying material that will anger PRC authorities.

Chinese-owned platforms in the United States follow a similar trajectory. The financial interests of users, brands, and advertisers eclipse well-founded concerns regarding freedom of expression and privacy. In 2020 and 2021, Chinese social-media platform TikTok became the most downloaded app in the United States despite worries about the amount of data that it was collecting from users and what it was doing with the information. In August 2020, a White House threat to ban the platform unless its ownership changed hands ran into a massive backlash from U.S.-based influencers and advertisers who were making money off the short videos in which TikTok specializes. At about the same time, opposition to a similar Donald Trump administration order banning the Chinese social-media platform WeChat revealed how heavily U.S. companies had come to rely on it. Since then, both platforms have only become more prominent on the U.S. social-media scene and in the commercial promotion of brands worldwide.

The relationship between PRC content rules, the Chinese entertainment industry (broadly defined), and U.S. media conglomerates such as AT&T (which owns WarnerMedia), Comcast, Discovery, Paramount Global, and the Walt Disney Company underscores a transition in the role of entertainment in politics. The shift is from "soft power,"[1] a term coined three decades ago to describe a form of noncoercive cultural currency most prominently associated with Hollywood's global influence from 1945 through the 2010s, to what has more recently been called "sharp power."[2] The type of sharp power that is of interest here weaponizes technology and corporations' dependence on political authorities for market access to control content. Beijing deploys sharp power to constrain content by bringing PRC laws and market pressures to bear on U.S. corporate interests.

In my 2017 book *Hollywood Made in China*, I argued that the financial interests of Hollywood studios drove them to collaborate with Chinese regulators for the sake of gaining access to the Chinese market.[3] Desire to retain access to that enormous market has changed what Hollywood produces. Now I am seeing a PRC approach that relies less on the attractive power of Chinese media corporations as partners than on threats to cut off access to the Chinese market. This minatory approach, moreover, has become increasingly pervasive as U.S. media conglomerates and brands run into Chinese-government restrictions across multiple sectors, from theme parks and consumer products to films and streaming platforms. The threats work. Brands, corporations, and influencers in the United States limit what they say about topics that Beijing deems sensitive for fear of having content barred from China. These U.S. interests now think of China less as a place where they can look eagerly for Chinese partners in a mutual pursuit of riches, and more as a thorny thicket of "forbidden subjects" (including Falun Gong, Hong Kong, Taiwan, the 1989 Tiananmen Square protests and their brutal suppression, Tibet, and the Uyghurs) that must be navigated with care and circumspection lest costly hits to revenues, profits, and share prices follow.

Controlling Market Access

Much has been made of the soft power that U.S. media products exert. Already influential by the 1930s, Hollywood emerged from the Second World War intact while other national film industries were ravaged. With their domestic market the world's largest, U.S. movie studios turned out decades of international hits. The attractiveness of U.S.-made entertainment spread U.S. cultural influence—helped, no doubt, by U.S. economic advantages and even the far-flung U.S. military presence in Germany, Japan, South Korea, and other places.[4] The economic and military predominance of the United States played a role in promoting U.S. soft power, but that power did not derive from control over access to the U.S. domestic media and entertainment markets.

As China's film market grew, Beijing began tightening controls on the domestic movie industry, with repercussions that were felt abroad. Existing subject-matter controls are considerable. They cover expected areas such as excessive violence, political critique, and sexual content. In addition, they can also be more idiosyncratic, with bans on supernatural content and images of Winnie the Pooh, who has become well known (and unwelcome in government eyes) as the meme stand-in for China's President Xi Jinping. The Film Industry Promotion Law of 2016 also requires cast and crew members to exhibit "core socialist values." The law's vague language and inconsistent application make specific instances of its use difficult to trace. But it has been associated with the internet exile of Chinese actor and director Zhao Wei, whose entire digital footprint regulators deleted in August 2021. The idea of making the display of such values mandatory came from Xi Jinping's notion of what he termed China's "cultural soft power."[5] The law enables limits on market access according to these "soft" values.

In 2018, China reinforced the link between media oversight and state goals by raising the main media-regulation agency—now called the National Radio and Television Administration—to cabinet rank and putting it under the control of the Propaganda Department of the Chinese Communist Party (CCP). The next year brought updated digital-content rules that laid out civil and criminal penalties for producing, distributing, and even consuming content deemed to violate China's national security, regardless of one's location. In 2020, the National Security Law that Beijing imposed on Hong Kong claimed extraterritorial enforcement power against perceived violations of PRC national security occurring outside that city and outside the PRC altogether. In 2021, the Data Security Law formally required national-security audits of data generated by Chinese firms anywhere in the world.

Hollywood studios that hope to sell tickets to PRC moviegoers must follow these increasingly strict media-content rules even as Beijing clamps an annual lid on the theatrical distribution of foreign movies within China. Examples of Hollywood films undergoing PRC censorship come from as early as 2006 with J.J. Abrams's *Mission: Impossible III*. The film's Chinese release was delayed for months because one sequence shows laundry hanging on clotheslines as Tom Cruise runs past buildings in Shanghai (the government felt this suggested that electric clothes dryers are scarce in China). In early 2022, the Chinese streaming platform Tencent issued the first official Chinese release of David Fincher's raw, anarchic *Fight Club* (1999) with a huge deletion. The excised material included the film's apocalyptic closing images of bombs causing tall city buildings to collapse in flames. What viewers saw instead was onscreen text stating that "the police rapidly figured out the whole plan and arrested all criminals." After general online ridicule and a public outcry from Chinese users well aware of the movie's real ending from pirated DVDs that have circulated in the PRC for decades, Tencent restored eleven of the twelve minutes cut (still left out were scenes with nudity).

Beijing's content control goes beyond what can or cannot be seen by audiences within China. The 2013 Hollywood film *World War Z* originally featured a fictional virus of Chinese origin, but the originating country was changed to North Korea in the final version of the film for fear of offending the PRC.[6] The 2014 Sony hack revealed that the 2015 Adam Sandler film *Pixels* ditched a scene in which space aliens demolish the Great Wall of China.[7] Instead, the celluloid interplanetary hostiles destroy India's Taj Mahal, the Washington Monument, and parts of Manhattan—a fitting metaphor for the studio's cooperation with Chinese regulators and the impact on freedom of expression in democratic nations around the world.

The long-in-the-works sequel to *Top Gun* (1986), titled *Top Gun: Maverick*, is slated for release late in May 2022, on the Friday that is the eve of Memorial Day weekend in the United States. This Tom Cruise movie best embodies in one product the tension between U.S. and Chinese political interests. Support for the production came from both China's Tencent Pictures and the United States military.[8] The movie features U.S. military hardware, including F/A-18 Super Hornet fighter jets and a pair of real U.S. Navy aircraft carriers. Viewers of the movie's trailer, however, noticed that the Republic of China on Taiwan flag, which had appeared on a patch sewn on the leather flight jacket of Cruise's character in the original film, had disappeared. In its place was a rectangle with the same blue and red colors but representing no country—presumably a concession to Beijing's insistence that Taiwan is merely a province of China.

Even before the 2012 U.S.-China Film Agreement expired in 2017, studios could never be sure whether their films would be allowed access to the PRC market. The financial stakes are huge—being released in China can double a film's global box-office total—and the uncertainty fuels intense anxiety to avoid any possible misstep regarding content.

In recent years, uncertainty regarding access to the Chinese market has only increased. In 2020, PRC authorities banned coverage of Disney's release in China of the live-action version of *Mulan* following international protests sparked by the filmmakers' collaboration with officials in the Xinjiang Uyghur Autonomous Region (a filming location) who were associated with the PRC's Uyghur internment camps—that is to say, with Chinese policies that the U.S. State Department describes as "genocide and crimes against humanity."[9] In 2021, three Marvel Cinematic Universe films appeared but none secured a Chinese release. Two of them had characteristics designed to appeal to the Chinese market: Chloe Zhao's *The Eternals* had a director from mainland China, while *Shang Chi and the Legend of the Ten Rings* relied on Chinese source materials and popular Chinese actors.

Among the things that set soft power apart from sharp power are the time and location at which the power is exercised. In the case of soft power as exerted through the media, the power makes itself felt as the audience reads, hears, or watches the media product. Sharp power, by contrast, is more likely to be exerted as the media content is being produced or distributed. Unlike consumption, production and distribution are the province not of individuals but of corporate and government interests. Responding to sharp power requires learning how businesses and governments exert content control during production and distribution. This is so even though businesses and governments typically want to avoid sharing such information, preferring as they do to remain inconspicuous while "calling the shots."

If Hollywood depends heavily on access to the Chinese market, Chinese film studios that operate in the United States, including Tencent Pictures and Alibaba Pictures, depend on it completely—unlike Hollywood, they literally have no business model without it. Chinese studios, moreover, are also subject to Chinese-government audits and other forms of direct PRC oversight (under China's national-security laws, for example).

Bricks, Mortar, and Beijing's Leverage

The streaming giant Netflix, based in Los Gatos, California, has tried to enter the Chinese market while passing off PRC censorship as involving nothing more serious than the routine practice of making "airplane cuts" to versions of films that are shown on passenger jets (where the message "edited for content" typically precedes the movie on the small seat-back screen).[10] In 2017, Netflix received approval to distribute content on China's iQiyi streaming platform and even developed Chinese-language shows, but the partnership failed because so many Netflix originals could not make it past PRC censors. In mid-2017, Chinese regulators pulled Netflix's animated comedy *Bojack Horseman* a mere two days after it began streaming.

The physical investments that U.S.-based media conglomerates have made in Chinese facilities make these businesses even more vulnerable to pressure from Chinese officials. Disney, DreamWorks Animation, and Universal all have bricks-and-mortar entertainment venues in China. While local partners are the majority stakeholders, the studios' exposure remains substantial. Losing favor in the PRC is bad business indeed if it threatens to tank visits to your costly theme park in Beijing or shutter your production studio in Shanghai.

The firms like to use their media content to draw crowds to their physical venues. The Shanghai Disney Resort urged fans of *Mulan* to visit for "World Princess Week," to enjoy a ride and sculpture gardens featuring characters from the film, or to watch a live performance of the story in "Mickey's Storybook Adventure" theater. There was even a *Mulan*-themed dining room in the Royal Banquet Hall restaurant.

Yet these promotional efforts (known in trade jargon as "cross-platform synergies") gloss over the suspect things that media firms do to gain and keep access to the Chinese entertainment market. As noted above, Disney shot parts of *Mulan* in Xinjiang with the support of, among other entities, the Turpan Municipality Public Security Bureau. This police agency—

thanked by Disney in the movie's closing credits—is closely associated with the PRC's "vocational centers" (forced-labor internment camps) for Xinjiang's Uyghurs. At the time Disney was extending it "special thanks" onscreen, Turpan's Public Security Bureau had already been placed on the U.S. Commerce Department's "Entities List" for "acting contrary to the foreign policy interests of the United States."[11] Disney had little to say in response to protests other than "it's common to acknowledge in a film's credits the national and local governments that allowed you to film there," and did not even offer this until after the PRC—eager to quiet the controversy—had banned all mention of *Mulan* from Chinese media.[12]

Like Disney, Universal has studiously ignored human-rights issues in China. Universal Beijing Resort, whose corporate parents are the state-owned Beijing Tourism Group and the NBCUniversal media conglomerate (headquartered at 30 Rockefeller Plaza in Manhattan and owned by Comcast), opened in September 2021. The estimated cost to build it was $6.5 billion. NBCUniversal also owned the rights to stream the 2022 Winter Olympics from Beijing via the Peacock streaming platform. The Olympics were shown with all pomp and circumstance, even when a skier from China's persecuted Uyghur Muslim minority was one of two athletes lighting the opening flame on February 4. In a sense, NBC had made Olympics viewers complicit as spectators of a Chinese-government propaganda campaign that tries to paint the mass detentions in Xinjiang as something not to be criticized or even brought up. One of the NBC announcers on hand, Mike Tirico, did weigh in to describe the Uyghurs as "people from the region of northwest China that have attracted so much attention in the conversation of human rights." His colleague Savannah Guthrie called the choice of a Uyghur flame bearer "quite provocative," and "a statement from the Chinese president, Xi Jinping, [that]. . . . is an in-your-face response to Western nations, including the U.S., who have called the Chinese treatment of that group genocide."[13] NBCUniversal's interest in the Chinese market involved consistent access to the Olympics, stability for the Universal theme park, and access to the world's largest market for films.

DreamWorks Animation, which NBCUniversal acquired in 2016, was involved in the initial stages of production for *Abominable* (2019), a Chinese animated film that displayed the PRC's contested "nine-dash line," a feature on certain maps that marks most of the South China Sea as belonging to China. DreamWorks Animation transferred ownership of its Chinese subsidiary to a Chinese corporation before *Abominable* was released, yet only after making sure that the subsidiary would have all the animation capabilities of DreamWorks itself.

In each of these cases, uncertainty surrounding the broader investment environment in China constrained firms' behavior. As in the case of the film industry and related investments, U.S. digital-media content creators face constraints from the entwined business interests of Chinese social-media platforms and the Chinese government.[14]

By closing so many places of in-person socializing and entertainment, the covid-19 lockdowns made social media more prominent than ever. Tik-Tok, owned by the Chinese company ByteDance and made available on the internet worldwide in 2018, became one of the fastest-growing brands of 2020 as its main offering (user-created short videos) became wildly popular. Despite claims of an intention to avoid political speech, TikTok has blocked posts concerning the Tiananmen Square protests and crackdown, Tibetan independence, and other subjects that Beijing deems sensitive.[15]

While TikTok's content-control and data-security practices have fed credible concerns, the service's immense popularity with users has made it a key venue for advertisers (including social-media influencers whom brands pay because of their large followings). TikTok, in short, has become so vital to so many advertising and brand-marketing campaigns that businesses which rely on it to reach the U.S. consumer now feel that they cannot live without it. The speed and intensity with which influencers, brands, and users rallied behind TikTok when the Trump administration threatened to shut it down were telling.

With the pandemic, online gaming has grown beyond being purely a means of entertainment and become also a "public square" in which many topics are discussed. Here too, however, we have seen China's content-control practices at work. In October 2019, the gaming company Blizzard Entertainment—headquartered in California but partly owned by Tencent—shut down speech in support of Hong Kong democracy protesters. When professional gamer Chung Ng Wai (who goes by Blitzchung) repeated in a public interview a slogan used by Hong Kong demonstrators against the new security law that Beijing was then trying to impose on Hong Kong, the company cited a competition rule against any act that the company at its "sole discretion" deemed would cause public disrepute, offend a portion of the public, or damage the company's image. Blizzard threw Blitzchung out of its Hearthstone Grandmasters tournament, took back a year of his winnings, and suspended him for a year going forward.[16] After days of controversy, Blizzard's chief executive J. Allen Brack allowed that "our process wasn't adequate, and we reacted too quickly" while reducing the punishments, a response that both failed to acknowledge what the company had done and diminished its seriousness.[17] While the company had to deal with immediate public-relations blowback, Brack kept his job until August 2021, when he was ousted due to a lawsuit alleging persistent sexual harassment and sexism under his leadership.[18]

In early 2022, Microsoft, which already has substantial stakes in China, acquired Blizzard Entertainment's partly Tencent-owned parent company for almost $69 billion. The Chinese market already hosts Microsoft's most comprehensive subsidiary firm and its largest research and development facility outside the United States. The firm touts its close ties to the Chinese market on its website, noting that *Fast Company* magazine identified Microsoft as one of "The Companies Remaking the Chinese Economy" along with Chinese concerns such as Alibaba, Baidu, and Tencent.[19]

Chinese media companies have grown successful enough that they now have loyal foreign publics—with members ranging from celebrities who make money working with these companies to ordinary users—who will defend them. When President Trump issued August 2020 executive orders banning TikTok from the United States unless its Chinese parent company sold it, TikTok influencers brushed aside the claim that the platform's data-handling practices threatened U.S. national security and advocated continued TikTok access for the sake of their individual commercial and entertainment needs. Users of WeChat, the only reliable platform for staying in touch from abroad with residents of China and U.S. businesses operating in China, similarly complained about a Trump ban on that service and took his administration to court in September 2020.

Outspoken, Just Not About China

The 2022 Olympic-champion skier Eileen Gu, who was born in California to parents who, respectively, had been born in the United States and had immigrated from the PRC, began her career skiing internationally for the United States. In mid-2019, she asked the International Ski Federation to be recognized as a competitor on behalf of the PRC, and skied for China in the Beijing games. Gu speaks out regarding U.S. social issues, denouncing anti-Asian violence and supporting Black Lives Matter. When asked about PRC human-rights abuses in Xinjiang, however, she shifts to anodyne topics that will never disturb a Chinese censor, such as promoting snow-sports participation by women and girls. The asymmetry is startling. Similarly, NBA star LeBron James, in contrast to his activism in the United States, has been silent about China's human-rights record despite—or perhaps because of—the substantial financial interest that he has in promoting his brand within China. Indeed, James even dismissed the activism of former Boston Celtics center Enes Kanter Freedom that painted China in a critical light, and suggested that behind it lay nothing but a drive for self-promotion. In November 2021, after a game between the Celtics and James's Los Angeles Lakers, James said: "He's definitely not someone I would give my energy to. He's trying to use my name to create an opportunity for himself. I definitely won't comment too much on that."[20]

Freedom, who in February 2022 was traded to Houston and then waived by that club, had worn in National Basketball Association (NBA) games shoes bearing such slogans as "Free Tibet," "Free Uyghur," "Taiwan belongs to the Taiwanese people," "Stop organ harvesting in China," "No Beijing [Olympics] 2022," and (on a single pair of Nikes) "Hypocrite Nike" and "Made with slave labor." He had expressed solidarity with Uyghur Muslims and other minorities suffering abuses at the hands of Chinese authorities in Xinjiang. His shoe slogans, which were not against NBA regulations, gestured at the lucrative deals that NBA players have with sports-apparel companies accused of complicity in Chinese rights abuses. In response, Beijing banned broadcasts of Celtics games in China.

It may be worth noting that the Houston Rockets, the franchise which cut Freedom, was the same team that in October 2019 had swiftly distanced itself from its own general manager, Daryl Morey, when he tweeted "Fight for Freedom. Stand with Hong Kong." The next day, Rockets owner Tilman Fertitta publicly emphasized that Morey did not speak for the club, while the NBA called it "regrettable" that Morey had "deeply offended many of our friends and fans in China."[21] Morey deleted his tweet and said that he had meant no offense. A year later, he left the Rockets and became president of the Philadelphia 76ers. The cases of Gu and the NBA provide yet more evidence of how deeply the urge to preserve access to China's market affects brands and content producers in the United States.

Chinese regulators' most potent tool is their ability to threaten a brand's bottom line. Media companies that depend on access to the Chinese market will not be strong advocates for freedom of expression. Before criticizing China, brands will think of how much it will cost to be barred from the giant Chinese market that the CCP so assiduously gatekeeps.

When it comes to freedom of expression and China, civil society's main challenge has to do with the structure of the U.S. economy. Firms from the United States benefit from access to the Chinese market while in the U.S. context, they face few constraints on what they do with content. Civil society advocacy is uniquely vulnerable to sharp power. Civil society groups in the United States also draw upon the commercial power of brands and influencers to push the groups' messages.

Ideas for U.S. Civil Society

What can be done to improve the way U.S. civil society responds to Chinese-government content control? One idea is to reestablish not-for-profit content production and distribution options in the United States. This could bring new voices not driven by social-media "likes" and profitability into U.S.-made content. It would mean a U.S. media system less driven by a globalized pursuit of profits. Valuable as this would be, it is difficult to imagine it happening in the current U.S. media environment, especially at a time when the U.S. political system is so highly polarized.

A second idea is to rebuild community organizations that operate independently of corporate interests. From service organizations to religious institutions to sports leagues, the erosion of independent community groups has, as political scientist Robert Putnam argues, deeply affected U.S. society.[22] With independent civil society so much thinner on the ground than it used to be, there is less to counterweigh the influence of media conglomerates whose financial interests now shape so much of what is said and shown about China.

A third idea is to increase education about contemporary China in U.S. schools. Most U.S. students today at the primary and even secondary levels have little access to even rudimentary knowledge about contemporary

China. Enhanced education at all levels up to and including college will prepare young people in the United States to ask hard questions of the brands whose content they consume, questions about these brands' financial investments and how those affect what the brands say or refrain from saying.

A fourth idea is the most dramatic. This would be to reduce the Chinese market's influence on Hollywood and U.S. media corporations by wholesale decoupling. This is a bad suggestion, however, for two reasons. First, cutting business ties between the two countries would tend to make their overall relationship less stable, especially at times of high tension. Second, a U.S.-China media-market decoupling would not reduce the pressure that other markets bring to bear. China is the best-known example of pressure to change or censor content, but it is not the only one. Netflix, for example, has removed content from its platform in Germany, New Zealand, Singapore, and Vietnam in response to government complaints. A notable instance occurred in early 2019, when Netflix pulled a 2018 episode of the comedy show *Patriot Act* starring American Muslim comic Hasan Minhaj from the Saudi Arabian version of the Netflix streaming platform. Unlike the Chinese market, the Saudi market is not so large that those who control access to it can dictate global trends. But the *Patriot Act* case, in which Netflix censored an unflattering discussion of Saudi Arabia's Crown Prince Muhammad bin Salman, underscores the complicity of the U.S. entertainment sector in global suppression of critical speech.

China's ability to exert sharp power on the U.S. media and entertainment industries does not exist in a vacuum. True, Beijing's stringent rules control access to China's huge market and limit the content that can be distributed in it. Yet conditions in the United States—where many civil society groups depend on corporate donations, and where corporations seeking constant growth and rising share prices are driven to cater to ever more contentious markets—provide the environment in which China's assertions of sharp power over U.S. media conglomerates can thrive.

Notes

1. Joseph S. Nye, Jr., "Soft Power," *Foreign Policy* 80 (Fall 1990): 153–71; Maria Repnikova, *Chinese Soft Power* (Cambridge: Cambridge University Press, 2022).

2. Christopher Walker, Shanthi Kalathil, and Jessica Ludwig, "The Cutting Edge of Sharp Power," *Journal of Democracy* 31 (January 2020): 124–37.

3. Aynne Kokas, *Hollywood Made in China* (Oakland: University of California Press, 2017).

4. Kyung Hyun Kim, *Hegemonic Mimicry: Korean Popular Culture of the Twenty-First Century* (Durham: Duke University Press, 2021); Jennifer Fay, *Theaters of Occupation: Hollywood and the Reeducation of Postwar Germany* (Minneapolis: University of Minnesota Press, 2008); Hiroshi Kitamura, *Screening Enlightenment: Hollywood and the Cultural Reconstruction of Defeated Japan* (Ithaca: Cornell University Press, 2010).

5. "Core Socialist Values," *China Daily* (Beijing), 12 October 2017, *www.chinadaily.com.cn/china/19thcpcnationalcongress/2017-10/12/content_33160115.htm.*

6. Lucas Shaw, "Fearing Chinese Censors, Paramount Changes 'World War Z' (Exclusive)," *The Wrap,* 31 March 2013, *www.thewrap.com/fearing-chinese-censors-paramount-changes-world-war-z-exclusive-83316.*

7. Clare Baldwin and Kristina Cooke, "Special Report: How Sony Sanitized Adam Sandler Movie to Please Chinese Censors," Reuters, 24 July 2015, *www.reuters.com/article/us-china-film-specialreport-idUSKCN0PY1OJ20150724.*

8. Tom Secker, "'Weave in Key Talking Points'—Pentagon Contract for Top Gun: Maverick," *Spy Culture,* 21 June 2019, *www.spyculture.com/weave-in-key-talking-points-pentagon-contract-for-top-gun-maverick.*

9. U.S. State Department, "2021 Report to Congress Pursuant to Section 5 of the Elie Wiesel Genocide and Atrocities Prevention Act of 2018 (P.L. 115-441)," 12 July 2021, *www.state.gov/2022-report-to-congress-pursuant-to-section-5-of-the-elie-wiesel-genocide-and-atrocities-prevention-act-of-2018.*

10. Aynne Kokas, "Chilling Netflix: Financialization, and the Influence of the Chinese Market on the American Entertainment Industry," *Information, Communication and Society* 23, issue 3 (2020): 407–19.

11. Industry and Security Bureau, U.S. Commerce Department, "Addition of Certain Entities to the Entity List," *Federal Register,* 9 October 2019, *www.federalregister.gov/documents/2019/10/09/2019-22210/addition-of-certain-entities-to-the-entity-list.*

12. Rebecca Davis, "Disney CFO Admits Filming 'Mulan' in Xinjiang Has 'Generated a Lot of Issues,'" *Variety,* 10 September 2020, *https://variety.com/2020/film/news/disney-cfo-filming-mulan-in-xinjiang-problematic-1234766342.*

13. Erik Brady, "NBC Coverage of Winter Olympic Games Open-

ing Ceremony Put Spotlight on China's Treatment of Uyghurs, But More Must Be Done," *USA Today,* 4 February 2022, *https:// www.usatoday.com/story/sports/olympics/beijing/2022/02/04/ nbc-coverage-china-uyghur-flame-lighter-genocide/6666757001.*

14. Aynne Kokas, *Trafficking Data: How China Is Winning the Battle for Digital Sovereignty* (Oxford: Oxford University Press, 2022).

15. Alex Hern, "Revealed: How TikTok Censors Videos That Do Not Please Beijing," *Guardian,* 25 September 2019, *www.theguardian.com/technology/2019/ sep/25/revealed-how-tiktok-censors-videos-that-do-not-please-beijing.*

16. "Hearthstone Grandmasters Asia-Pacific Ruling," Blizzard Entertainment, 8 October 2019, *https://playhearthstone.com/en-us/news/23179289.*

17. J. Allen Brack, "Regarding Last Weekend's Hearthstone Grandmasters Tournament," Inside Blizzard blog, 12 October 2019, *https://news.blizzard.com/en-us/ blizzard/23185888/regarding-last-weekend-s-hearthstone-grandmasters-tournament.*

18. Todd Spangler, "Blizzard President J. Allen Brack Exits amid Sexual Harassment and Discrimination Lawsuit Against Company," *Variety,* 3 August 2021, *https://variety.com/2021/digital/news/ blizzard-j-allen-brack-exits-sexual-harassment-lawsuit-1235033387.*

19. Microsoft, "About Microsoft's Presence in China," news release, *https:// news.microsoft.com/about-microsofts-presence-in-china.*

20. "LeBron James Reacts to Enes Kanter's Political Criticism After Celtics Blow Out Lakers," Celtics Wire blog, *USA Today,* 20 November 2021, *https://celticswire. usatoday.com/2021/11/20/nba-boston-celtics-kanter-vs-lebron-james.*

21. "Rockets' General Manager's Hong Kong Comments Anger China," Associated Press, 7 October 2019, *https://apnews.com/article/asia-pacific-tx-state-wire-china-daryl-morey-houston-rockets-0a660e9e10664e31bf6ee359c 22058cf.*

22. Robert Putnam, *Bowling Alone: The Collapse and Revival of American Community* (New York: Simon and Schuster, 2000).

CHAPTER FOUR

The Kremlin Playbook
for Latin America

RUSLAN STEFANOV AND MARTIN VLADIMIROV

IN THE WAKE OF RUSSIA'S INVASION OF UKRAINE, former Bolivian president Evo Morales took to Twitter to demand an end to the "interventionist expansionism of NATO and the United States." This was an expected response from someone whom Russian president Vladimir Putin had lauded as a "partner, friend, and ally of Russia" during his official visit to Moscow in July 2019. During Morales's visit, Putin hailed the construction of a US$300 million nuclear-research facility in Bolivia by the Russian state nuclear giant, Rosatom. Yet the investment, facilitated by a 2017 agreement between the two countries, had never been approved by the Bolivian legislature, nor had a feasibility study been conducted.[1] And another of Rosatom's Bolivian "investments" remained undisclosed: The firm had hired spin doctors and propagandists to boost Morales in the lead-up to the presidential election in October 2019.[2]

The Rosatom deal is but one of many large infrastructure deals that Russian firms close to the Kremlin have proposed to Bolivia and neighboring Argentina. These deals, often of questionable economic value, have a highly specific goal: to create structural economic dependencies to give the Kremlin greater political leverage. Although Russia has a larger financial footprint in other parts of Latin America, Moscow's outreach to Argentina and Bolivia illustrates the early stages of how authoritarian states use large investments to interfere in the politics of host countries.

The invasion of Ukraine and the resulting international sanctions have pushed Russia to redouble its influence efforts outside Europe. The Kremlin has strengthened ties with its traditional Latin American allies such as Cuba, Nicaragua, and Venezuela, who have directly and indirectly supported Russia in line with their anti-American leanings. Argentina, Brazil, and Mexico have been ambivalent about the Kremlin's war of choice as their governments have continued deepening cooperation with Russia in agriculture, defense, and energy.[3]

The methods that the Kremlin employs to expand its influence in Latin America were tried and tested first in Central and Eastern Europe. There, Putin's regime has gained dominant positions in strategic markets by locking governments into long-term, expensive infrastructure deals (particularly in the energy sector) and creating structural trade dependencies. To these ends, the Kremlin and its surrogates forge corrupt relationships with local elites and exploit gaps in the rule of law and regulatory oversight in target countries. In Latin America and elsewhere, Russia has amplified its influence by reactivating Cold War–era security networks and launching aggressive media disinformation campaigns.[4]

The Kremlin's ability to wield state-owned and nominally private corporations as political instruments, swiftly and without visible deliberation, has allowed it to achieve outsized global influence—still short of Soviet stature, but beyond what modern Russia's modest resources would suggest. The Kremlin's influence efforts began in the former Soviet Union, and then extended into Central and Eastern Europe and the Western Balkans. Then they were rolled out globally, as Putin's regime sought to reengage with former Soviet channels of influence in the Middle East, Latin America, and Africa, and to undermine Western unity in countering Russia's revisionist objectives. The deployment of massive tech-enhanced disinformation and propaganda campaigns has enhanced the Kremlin's ability to exploit governance gaps and other societal vulnerabilities at a fairly low cost around the world.

While the People's Republic of China is clearly the larger and more potent authoritarian power, Russia has been surprisingly adept at leveraging its more modest resources to advance its priorities, and its activities have received less attention from analysts. China has typically placed major loans and public debt at the center of its strategy, while Russia has generally developed business relationships with local oligarchic networks with the aim of promoting large-scale projects for its state-owned energy conglomerates. The Kremlin has also offered political support to governments that share its desire to counter U.S. influence.[5]

The Kremlin's Influence Playbook

At the heart of the Kremlin's international-influence strategy lies a mastery of "state capture" techniques. State capture is the process by which private interests (known as "captors") exploit critical vulnerabilities in public governance systems, effectively privatizing public functions in order to extract undue advantages and key assets for personal or political gain. This process could turn captors into "free riders"—exempt from or in control of the rules that apply to other actors in a given field or sector.[6] But from the outside, captured institutions may still appear to be part of formal, legal economic or political systems, providing captors with a veil of legitimacy that they can then use, for example, to enter the international financial system as a nominally independent player.

Coming to power in 2000, Putin pioneered state capture in order to assert control over the emerging post-Soviet Russian elite, enriching cronies and punishing critics. Now his regime employs these techniques abroad: In targeted countries, the Kremlin engages with existing or aspiring captors in the hopes of dominating local strategic markets in energy, telecommunications, and banking. Having gained an economic foothold, the regime's networks employ opaque financial flows or "corrosive capital" to further exploit governance weaknesses (particularly gaps in the rule of law and nonindependent oversight of state finances and decisionmaking), break down democratic institutions, and entrench themselves in the power centers of the host country.[7] These vulnerabilities are then sustained through the purposeful debilitation and partial enforcement of anticorruption, antitrust, and public-procurement laws.

Corrosive capital can take the form of ostensibly private investments or purchases that appear detached from any political motive or government involvement. In order to inject corrosive capital into a target country, authoritarian governments employ three main methods: 1) intergovernmental or commercial loans that mimic traditional development assistance but are the product of opaque negotiations and include hidden terms; 2) large infrastructure projects; and 3) foreign direct investment (FDI) facilitated by corporate entities based in offshore tax havens. These entities may have unclear ownership structures to mask ties to state enterprises or politically connected business magnates. When employing these tactics, authoritarian powers and their surrogates seek out strategic or high-profit sectors, particularly those with high entry barriers (such as licensing requirements), natural monopolies (such as regional power, heating, and gas distribution), or a high dependence on state subsidies. Once corrosive capital has been injected into the host country, it becomes a powerful tool for state capture and the exercise of sharp power. For instance, funds may be directed to specific companies with high profit margins, providing cash to support the reelection campaigns of the incumbent political leadership.

The Kremlin's Reach into Latin America

Russian influence in Latin America has followed this pattern despite the Kremlin's more modest reach and overall success when compared to other regions, namely Central and Eastern Europe.

With the exception of Venezuela—and to a lesser degree Cuba and Nicaragua—Russia has not penetrated strategic economic sectors, nor has it implemented many large-scale projects. Its efforts in the region are dwarfed by China's in terms of trade and investment, and its influence pales in comparison to the old Soviet Union's. But the Kremlin has taken advantage of state-capture vulnerabilities, political corruption, and a fusion of political and economic power to advance large deals of questionable economic value, gaining outsize political influence in the process.

For much of the two decades after the Cold War, Russia's interest in Latin America appears to have declined steadily; although the Kremlin does maintain close political ties with former Soviet allies, including Cuba. Russia's trade with the region, at roughly $13.5 billion per year, is relatively small; it represents only 2 percent of Russia's external trade and roughly 0.7 percent of Latin America's. Its most important trade partners in the region have been Brazil, Mexico, Argentina, Chile, and Ecuador, which are major exporters of food products to Russia. In terms of imports, some countries, including Venezuela, Nicaragua, and Peru, are heavily dependent on Russian military equipment.[8]

Russia is not a major source of FDI for Latin America. Excluding the Caribbean-island tax havens, Russian investment in the region totaled less than $3 billion from 2000 to 2019, and sharply declined to just $157 million by the end of 2021. China, in comparison, invested more than $160 billion from 2000 to 2020, most of which went to the extractive, transportation, energy, and finance industries. FDI from the United States was much greater at roughly $264 billion. But determining the true size of Russian capital inflows is difficult, as the details of investment agreements are often confidential. Some investments are channeled through offshore shell companies, obfuscating the ultimate beneficial ownership.

Russia has been especially active in deepening ties to the Bolivarian Alliance for Peoples of Our America, a regional organization led by Cuba and Venezuela. Bilateral ties with Venezuela improved during Hugo Chávez's rule (which ended with his death in 2013), particularly around the time of the 2008 Russian invasion of Georgia; Venezuela, along with Nicaragua, recognized the Russia-backed separatist republics of South Ossetia and Abkhazia. Chávez purchased billions of dollars of Russian arms and military equipment and allowed Russia to penetrate deeper into the economic fabric of Latin America. Bolivia, a member of the Bolivarian Alliance from 2006 to 2019, rejoined in 2020 following the election of Luis Arce to the presidency that year.

In the past ten years, Russia's economic activity in Bolivia and Argentina has grown as political relations have improved: Both countries came to be dominated by left-populist governments that sought to push back against U.S. influence in the region, finding common cause with the Kremlin. In pursuing these partnerships, Putin's regime relied heavily on state-owned energy companies to establish an economic presence in the target countries and attempt to influence their domestic and international policies.

We analyze cases of Russian corrosive capital and sharp power directed at Argentina and Bolivia, two Latin American democracies with recurring governance challenges that are common to many other countries in the region. The Economist Intelligence Unit calls Argentina a "flawed democracy" and Bolivia a "hybrid regime." Both countries feature polarized political environments where illiberal practices have flared over the last two decades. Despite the overall competitive nature of their electoral systems, powerful political factions have often captured decisionmaking processes for the benefit of specific regional, ethnic, or private interests. Greater understanding of Russian activities in Argentina and Bolivia could inform efforts to detect and prevent much more comprehensive authoritarian-influence efforts, such as those seen in Venezuela.

While the Kremlin has used similar strategies in Argentina and Bolivia, the success of its techniques also depends on local conditions. In Argentina, where political decisionmaking is more dispersed and transfers of power between rival political factions have been more frequent, the implementation of large-scale, long-term projects has been extremely difficult. Moreover, the scale of the proposed projects requires financial resources that Russia simply does not have in its own era of domestic economic retrenchment. By contrast, in Bolivia, the Kremlin benefited from close ties to President Evo Morales and his Movement Toward Socialism (MAS) party during his tenure from 2006 to 2019. Morales's concentration of power in Bolivia enabled Russian state-owned companies to push through projects without significant resistance or oversight from independent democratic and regulatory institutions. After the one-year interim presidency of Jeanine Áñez, who tried to suspend several Russia-backed projects, MAS candidate Luis Arce's 2020 victory has reinvigorated economic relations with Russia—even amid the invasion of Ukraine. Arce's government has reopened a giant lithium-mining concession and is negotiating with several international firms to handle extraction. Among the bidders are Rosatom and its subsidiary Uranium One—the same firms involved in the development of the aforementioned nuclear-research facility in Bolivia.[9]

All major Russian investment initiatives in Bolivia and Argentina involve the use of local political and business intermediaries as well as other techniques associated with state capture. Russia's deals are typically signed at the intergovernmental level—benefiting political incumbents—and are then carried out by close associates, to the economic advantage of specific regime-favored private actors. The blurring of the line between public, private, business, and political interests creates conflict-of-interest vulnerabilities that the Kremlin can easily exploit.

(Mis)adventures in Argentina

Argentina's relationship with Russia has deep roots in the Cold War. Soviet support for the country during the 1982 Falklands War led Argentina to reorient its large agricultural-export sector toward the Soviet Union.[10] After nearly two decades of relative decline in economic ties following the 1991 Soviet collapse, ties between Russia and Argentina improved under the left-populist presidency of Cristina Fernández de Kirchner (2007–15). She shared Putin's desire for change in the international order and wanted to find alternate economic partners in the aftermath of the 2008 global financial crisis. Russia and Argentina signed a 2008 strategic partnership document that has since led to 180 bilateral agreements in numerous economic and political areas.[11]

Trade between the two countries has grown by roughly 350 percent in the past decade and now hovers between $1.2 billion and $1.5 billion annually, making Argentina Russia's third-largest trading partner in Latin America.[12] Argentina remains a major exporter of food products and grains to Russia, which in turn exports fuels and energy equipment. The Kremlin has leveraged Argentina's dependence on agricultural exports to overcome political obstacles. For instance, in response to President Mauricio Macri's 2015 decision to pull the Russian state-owned propaganda channel RT from Argentina's public-television platform, the Kremlin threatened to ban Argentine beef exports and suspend investment in infrastructure projects. Several weeks later, Macri reversed the decision and allowed RT to continue operating on the platform, where it can reach Argentine viewers free 24 hours a day.[13]

Infrastructure projects have played an important part in Russia's efforts to build up its economic and political presence in Argentina. As president, Kirchner signed a series of agreements with Moscow envisioning roles for Russian state-owned companies Rosatom and Inter RAO in the construction of nuclear and hydroelectric power plants in Argentina. But as in European countries such as Bulgaria and the Czech Republic, Russian entities face competition from China. In 2015, during Kircher's presidency, Nucleoeléctrica Argentina SA and Rosatom signed an agreement for the construction of Argentina's fourth nuclear plant. Yet Rosatom's participation has not yet materialized, as the Macri administration signed agreements with China to construct a plant at the Atucha III site. Rosatom nevertheless kept its prospects alive by reaching a new agreement with Macri during the 2018 G20 summit in Buenos Aires. Since then, the Russian government has continued to discuss nuclear-power collaboration, but has not received a firm commitment from President Alberto Fernández, who defeated Macri in the 2019 election.

Russian state-owned companies Gazprom, Rosatom, and Inter RAO have all sought to develop large-scale energy-infrastructure projects with Argentine counterparts. To ensure that Russian companies obtained preferential access to lucrative assets, the Kremlin leveraged its existing connections with powerful business networks close to the Argentine government and political insiders. Even though most of these projects ultimately did not materialize, they showcase the Kremlin's international-influence playbook.

The most well-documented example was the unsuccessful attempts of the privately owned but Kremlin-friendly oil giant Lukoil to enter the Argentine market. In 2008 and again in 2017, the company tried and failed to acquire a share in fuel distribution by using intermediaries close to the Kirchner government. The Kirchner family had long been involved in the country's petroleum sector: The state-owned oil and gas company, then known as Enarsa, was founded by President Kirchner's late husband, former president Nestor Kirchner (2003–2007) and his planning minister, Julio de Vido, who managed public funds for state-led projects. (In 2020, de Vido was charged with money laundering.)

In 2008, Lukoil planned to invest $500 million in the construction of a fuel-storage plant and pipeline; in return, Enarsa would buy Lukoil's liquid fuels for five years to supply the new Manuel Belgrano power plant in Campana, a city in Buenos Aires Province.[14] Enarsa and Lukoil also planned to jointly explore for hydrocarbons in the Argentine marine shelf. The deal, signed on the sidelines of Cristina Kirchner's 2008 Moscow visit, was facilitated by de Vido. At the same time, however, he was allegedly assisting Horacio Sambucetti, one of the owners of the Argentine oil-storage firm Rhasa and one of Kirchner's closest business-sector allies.[15] Rhasa, which was financially afloat only because of government contracts linked to de Vido, was to store the fuel from the Enarsa-Lukoil deal. The proceeds from that deal would have benefited an obscure Sambucetti-linked firm called Pobater. It had previously partnered with the Venezuelan state oil company PDVSA and Enarsa in an attempt to buy Rhasa.[16] Although Pobater was represented by Sambucetti in the Lukoil-Enarsa agreement, he denied both owning the firm and its connections to Rhasa. (The head of Enarsa at the time, a Nestor Kirchner appointee and de Vido ally, was prosecuted in 2021 for fraudulent contracts that distributed funds to Pobater.[17])

This deal shows how Russian businesses can leverage an existing state-capture network involving politically well-connected private interests in a strategic sector of the Argentine economy. Capital-investment agreements can become corrosive instruments with the participation of state institutions or companies and parasitic intermediary firms. The purpose of these obscure intermediaries could be to layer and distribute hidden profits or to mask the disbursement of corrupt funds for political activities—a tried-and-tested strategy straight from the Kremlin playbook.

In 2017, a Lukoil subsidiary tried to buy into Oil Combustibles, which owned more than three-hundred gas stations across Argentina and operated the San Lorenzo refinery.[18] As in the 2008 deal, Lukoil worked with businesses close to the government, which was then led by Macri. Lukoil pledged to invest $300 million in partnership with OP Investments, which operates in the Latin American asset-management sector. Its owner, Ignacio Rosner—an alleged Macri ally—was charged in 2019 with extortion and coercion in connection to the sale of Oil Combustibles' owner, Grupo Indalo.[19] Indalo's owners had been detained on tax-evasion and embezzlement charges involving about 8 billion pesos in unpaid taxes. They were released in October 2019, allegedly due to the intervention of President Fernández, who at the time was perceived to be under the influence of his vice-president, former president Cristina Kirchner.[20]

The next year, Lukoil tried and failed to buy Oil Combustibles directly. Had the deal with the Russian company gone through, it would have given Lukoil access to Oil Combustibles' entire regional fuel-distribution business. Lukoil could have then implemented a strategy similar to the one it has pursued in Southeastern Europe, where it has taken over a significant share of the refining, wholesale, and retail-fuels markets. Regional dominance there has allowed Lukoil to charge monopoly prices and to meddle in the strategic decisions of national governments—including through the funding of political activities in a bid to expand Russia's sway.

Buying Support in Bolivia

Although Russia's economic footprint in Bolivia, as in Argentina, is relatively small in terms of trade, investment, and corporate presence, the Kremlin has tried to maximize its political influence by focusing on strategic markets and long-term infrastructure deals. Russian exports to Bolivia stood at $88.3 million in 2020—an increase from a mere $2.4 million a decade prior. For comparison, imports from China, Bolivia's most important trading partner, were nearly fifteen times greater. Exports to Russia are also miniscule, valued at around $3.7 million in 2020. While official Russian FDI in Bolivia is practically nonexistent, Russian capital may be channeled through third countries with preferential tax regimes. For example, two of the most important Russian businesses operating in Bolivia, Lukoil and Gazprom, are both registered in the Netherlands. As a result, their investments appear as FDI from the Netherlands, which contributes about 8 percent to Bolivia's total FDI inflows, making the Dutch among the five largest foreign investors in the country.

Gazprom entered the Bolivian energy market, joining a rush for natural-gas exploration and production. It holds a 20 percent stake in a $130 million project for the development of the Incahuasi gas field inside the Ipati and Aquio hydrocarbon reserves. Under agreements signed in 2008 and 2013, Gazprom is participating in the Azero Exploration Project with YPFB (the Bolivian state oil and gas company) and Total (a major French energy company). YPFB holds a 55 percent stake and the other two firms control 22.5 percent each. Drilling of exploration wells began in 2016. Gazprom's biggest investment in Bolivia is a planned $1.2 billion contract for the development of the hydrocarbon reserves in the Vitiacua area. The agreement has yet to pass through the Bolivian legislature, as the end of Morales's presidency put many Russia-backed projects on hold. The Arce administration could have revived the project, but the covid pandemic has stalled the development of many flagship Russian-led energy projects around the world.

A key intermediary between Russia and Bolivia emerged in the figure of Juan Ramón Quintana, who as Morales's Minister of the Presidency was the architect of numerous policies concerning the country's strategic economic sectors. He is also believed to have called the shots at YPFB, and to have made his cronies—including many relatives of army officers—employees of the firm in order to ensure the approval of specific, controversial deals.[21] During a 2019 visit to Moscow, Quintana declared that Russia's presence in Latin America was "essential." He argued that Russia, unlike the United States, was contributing to the creation of a responsible international order in which state sovereignty would be respected.[22]

After Morales resigned and fled to Argentina, Quintana may have worked with the Maduro regime in Venezuela to move funds out of Bolivia for his in-exile operations. In January 2020, Quintana's former secretary, María Palacios, was found at a Bolivian airport carrying $100,000 in cash en route to Argentina. She claimed to be working for PDVSA in Bolivia and said that the money was for the company's Argentine offices. But investigators noted that the money had not been declared and that its origins were unclear. She had made more than forty trips between September 2019 to January 2020.[23]

Moreover, the PDVSA office in Bolivia had been inactive since 2018.[24] Morales's interim successor, Jeanine Áñez, alleged that the money was destined to finance the activities of Morales and his political party in Argentina.

Russian state-owned companies also took advantage of the close political ties between the Kremlin and Morales's government to become more active in Bolivia's defense and infrastructure sectors. Rostec, an infrastructure-development company, partnered with the Italian holding firm Azimut in 2019 to respond to a tender for the construction of an international transportation hub at Santa Cruz's Viru Viru airport. Rostec also expressed interest in building medical facilities and supplying medical equipment, and sought to grow its military exports. This followed Morales's repeated statements expressing his intention to replace Bolivia's U.S. or European weapons systems with Russian alternatives. In 2009, Russia extended a $100 million credit line to Bolivia to purchase Russian helicopters.[25] In 2018, the Kremlin pushed for the sale of Russian transport helicopters and Yak-130 fighter jets,[26] but it never materialized.

Because the Kremlin's business and political interests in Bolivia were so closely intertwined with Morales's presidency, Russia did not hesitate to offer support when his decision to run for a fourth term in 2019 met with pushback. In January, Rosatom dispatched political strategists in an effort to boost Morales's fading popularity. These spin doctors, trained in the management of local political campaigns in Russia, weaponized social media, amplifying Morales's campaign messages and attempting to smear or discredit his opponents.[27]

The Russian regime's political preferences grew particularly evident after the October 2019 election. After results showed that Morales won by a large enough margin to avoid a runoff, large street protests and violence broke out over signs of fraud and other irregularities. Security forces refused to back Morales, forcing him to resign in November. His departure was met with fury from Russian state media outlets and Russia-linked social-media users in Bolivia.[28] The U.S. State Department revealed that following the election, social-media accounts supporting Russian interests in Bolivia had become extremely active, publishing more than a thousand posts a day.[29] The Kremlin continues to call the episode a coup d'état, even as it recognized the interim Áñez government as essential for a peaceful transition in Bolivia and signaled that it would expand economic cooperation with the country.[30]

How to Respond

Although the Kremlin has failed to implement many of the large-scale projects that it has pursued in Latin America, its efforts in Argentina and especially Bolivia have exposed serious governance vulnerabilities and state-capture risks. Many countries in the region lack strong legal safeguards and public institutions that could ensure transparency and independent oversight of foreign investment. Without these protections, there is a high risk of state capture and asymmetrical economic relationships, which could lead to political dependency.

Weaknesses in public governance and society, including strategic corruption and state capture, make the strategies of corrosive authoritarian influence viable in Latin America and elsewhere in the first place. There is still very little understanding among Latin American policymakers and civil society leaders about the mechanics of authoritarian influence, and the links between state-capture vulnerabilities and sharp power. There is also a dearth of knowledge about campaign-finance laws and legislation regulating intergovernmental agreements. Addressing these deficits will require a range of interventions from civil society, politicians, and other actors. But democratic backsliding, economic uncertainty, and shifting geopolitical priorities hamper these efforts. Thus combating authoritarian influence means strengthening Latin American democracy as well.

The most effective check on corrosive capital is civil society–led efforts to expose domestic and foreign state-capture practices and to flag high-risk deals. Civil society should scrutinize intergovernmental agreements with Russia and other authoritarian states, and in particular deals related to large-scale infrastructure projects or to strategic mergers and acquisitions in key sectors such as energy, healthcare, and the media. As such, civil society, investigative journalists, and media need more advanced means to conduct investigations of corporate ownership and foreign investments; they must also closely and continuously track money flows and business-political relationships.

More global and regional approaches to authoritarian investment would strengthen the ties between local civil society groups across Latin America and with international peers, increasing their capabilities. On several occasions, the Russian and Chinese regimes have employed influence strategies in Latin America involving multiple countries along with various private and state entities in order to find and exploit the weakest link. Pushing back against these schemes thus requires regional approaches for monitoring state-capture vulnerabilities, identifying common legal loopholes that allow corrosive capital to enter, and institutionalizing the enforcement of democratic-governance standards.

National-security agencies, antitrust authorities, and market regulators should strengthen their capacity to investigate money-laundering activities in cooperation with civil society and whistleblowers. It is crucial that government agencies remain insulated from political meddling in order to avoid state-capture vulnerabilities. These authorities should aim to locate the ultimate beneficial ownership of FDI inflows in order to prevent the acquisition of critical assets by unknown actors who could be furthering the strategic agendas of authoritarian governments.

By increasing transparency and competition in Latin American economies, governments can minimize entry points for corrosive-capital investments and increase economic growth. Governments should strengthen anti–money-laundering legislation and establish independent financial-intelligence and tax-collection agencies. Adequate controls must be introduced to limit cross-border currency smuggling and to prevent use of offshore destinations for international money laundering. Proposed intergovernmental agreements should be assessed in independent cost-benefit analyses and governed by strict transparency guidelines.

But reducing the appeal of authoritarian investment—particularly as Latin America is still struggling to secure sustainable economic development and manage the pandemic's economic impact—requires strategic investment from the United States and other democratic countries. Greater economic involvement by democratic countries would increase competition and allow Latin American governments to prioritize financial transparency and economic reform.

Corrosive investments often operate in tandem with authoritarian efforts to distort the information environment. Social media are easily abused for political ends, including by foreign powers. This manipulation often includes the exploitation of existing geographic, socioeconomic, and racial divides to shape public discourse and promote authoritarian interests. Civil society and public institutions must work together not only to combat online manipulation but also to address these underlying social vulnerabilities. Policies preventing the capture of influential media outlets and methods to detect disinformation campaigns early are critical to countering election meddling and attempts to sow social unrest.

The invasion of Ukraine is a rude wakeup call to liberal democracies, underscoring the critical need for a democratic response to the Kremlin's full-spectrum assault on the rules-based international order. Outside Eurasia, Latin America is one of the most vulnerable regions to Russian attempts to augment its economic and political influence, particularly through the use of corrosive capital and long-term investment deals. Addressing the region's persistent governance challenges will not only prevent corrosive capital from capturing strategic economic sectors, but will also improve the health and independence of democratic institutions in Latin America.

Notes

1. Boris Miranda, "En que consiste el plan de Evo Morales y Vladimir Putin para construir la central nuclear mas alta del mundo en Bolivia," BBC News, 12 July 2019, *www.bbc.com/mundo/noticias-america-latina-48959233*; "Bolivia Set to Build Nuclear Research Centre," World Nuclear News, 30 October 2015, *www.worldnuclear-news.org/NN-Bolivia-set-to-build-nuclear-research-centre-3010155.html*; "El Alto: Vecinos se declaran en estado de emergencia por la paralizacion de centro nuclear," *Estado Digital*, 14 February 2020, *www. elestadodigital.com/2020/02/14/el-alto-vecinos-se-declaran-en-estado-de-emergencia-por-la-paralizacion-de-centro-nuclear*.

2. "Coca & Co.: How Russia Secretly Helps Evo Morales to Win the Fourth Election," Proekt, 23 October 2019, *www.proekt.media/en/investigationen/ morales-rosatom-eng*.

3. Even though Brazil and Argentina tried to play neutral when former president Bolsonaro and President Fernández visited Putin a few days before the invasion started, high-level officials condemned it once the war started. See Sandra Weiss, "Putin Has Few Friends Left in Latin America," *Deutsche Welle*, 8 March 2022, *www.dw.com/en/ putin-loses-allies-in-latin-america-after-invading-ukraine/a-61045133*.

4. See Heather A. Conley et al., *The Kremlin Playbook: Understanding Russian Influence in Central and Eastern Europe* (Washington, D.C.: Center for Strategic and International Studies, 2016); and Heather A. Conley, et al., *The Kremlin Playbook 2: The Enablers* (Washington, D.C.: Center for Strategic and International Studies, 2019).

5. See Vladimir Rouvinski, "Understanding Russian Priorities in Latin America," *Kennan Cable* (February 2017): 1–8.

6. Ognian Shentov, Ruslan Stefanov, and Martin Vladimirov, eds., *The Kremlin Playbook in Europe* (Sofia, Bulgaria: Center for the Study of Democracy, 2020).

7. John Morrell et al., *Channeling the Tide: Protecting Democracies Amid a Flood of Corrosive Capital* (Washington, D.C.: Center for International Private Enterprise, 2018).

8. Mira Milosevich-Juaristi, "Rusia en América Latina: repercusiones para España," working paper, Royal Institute Elcano, March 2019.

9. Joseph Bouchard, "Why Russia Should Not Win the Bid for Bolivia's Lithium," Mongabay, 7 June 2022, *https://news.mongabay.com/2022/06/why-russia-should-not-win-the-bid-for-bolivias-lithium-commentary.*

10. "Argentina y el gigante euroasiatico," *DEF Online,* 19 December 2015, *https://defonline.com.ar/argentina-gigante-euroasiatico.*

11. Juan Pablo Cardenal, "Navigating Political Change in Argentina," in Christopher Walker and Jessica Ludwig, eds., *Sharp Power: Rising Authoritarian Influence* (Washington, D.C.: National Endowment for Democracy, 2017), 54.

12. Data are from the United Nations Conference on Trade and Development.

13. Cardenal, "Navigating Political Change in Argentina," 55–57.

14. "Inversión energética de Rusia en Argentina," Office of the Argentine Presidency, 10 December 2008, *www.casarosada.gob.ar/informacion/archivo/20340.*

15. "Lukoil Intends to Launch New Projects in Latin America," Lukoil, 10 December 2008, *www.lukoil.com/api/presscenter/exportpressrelease?id=49068&dl=1;* "La carta de intencion que De Vido firmo con la petrolera rusa Lukoil tiene como 'socia' a una empresa fantasma," *Perfil* (Buenos Aires), 15 February 2009.

16. "Rhasa, una empresa que vivio de todos los gobiernos," *Perfil,* 15 February 2009.

17. Fernando Krakowiak, "La trama que llevó al procesamiento y embargo del ex presidente de Enarsa Exequiel Espinosa por administración fraudulenta agravada," EconoJournal, 19 July 2021, *https://econojournal.com.ar/2021/07/la-trama-que-llevo-al-procesamiento-y-embargo-del-ex-presidente-de-enarsa-exequiel-espinosa-por-administracion-fraudulenta-agravada.*

18. Felix Grandet, "Otra vez los rusos," *Energia y Negocios,* November 2017, *www.energiaynegocios.com.ar/2017/11/otra-vez-los-rusos.*

19. Irina Hauser, "Dos imputados tras la denuncia de Cristóbal López contra Macri," *Página12* (Buenos Aires), 7 November 2019; Agustino Fontevec-

chia, "The Russian Connection: Lukoil to Invest in Grupo Indalo," *Buenos Aires Times,* 18 November 2017.

20. "Alberto Fernández defendió a Cristóbal López: 'Aplicaron una doctrina vergonzosa para tenerlo detenido,'" *Perfil,* 23 July 2019.

21. Wilson Garcia Merida, "Personal involucrado en corrupcion de YPFB tuvo aval politico de Quintana," *Sol de Pando,* 24 April 2017, *www.soldepando.com/personal-involucrado.*

22. Quoted in Victor Ternovsky, "Juan Ramón Quintana: 'La presencia rusa en América del Sur es imprescindible,'" Sputnik Mundo, 8 February 2019, *https://mundo.sputniknews.com/20190208/rusia-bolivia-relaciones-cooperacion-1085343201.html.*

23. "Bolivia detuvo a una mujer que viajaba a la Argentina con US$ 100 mil sin declarar: 'Era para financiar a Evo Morales,'" *La Nación* (Buenos Aires), 9 January 2020.

24. Lidia Mamani, "Pdvsa llego a Bolivia con Evo y tras fracasos dejo de operar," *Página Siete,* 10 January 2020, *https://web.archive.org/web/20200110115953/https://www.paginasiete.bo/economia/2020/1/10/pdvsa-llego-bolivia-con-evo-tras-fracasos-dejo-de-operar-243022.html.*

25. Mary Vaca, "Bolivia 'es grande' para comprar armas," BBC News, 11 August 2009, *https://www.bbc.com/mundo/america_latina/2009/08/090811_2244_armas_bolivia_jg.*

26. Julia Gurganus, "Russia: Playing a Geopolitical Game in Latin America," Return of Global Russia blog, Carnegie Endowment for International Peace, 3 May 2018, *https://carnegieendowment.org/2018/05/03/russia-playing-geopolitical-game-in-latin-america-pub-76228.*

27. "Coca & Co."

28. Adam Robinson, "Analysis: Russian Media Come Out in Force Behind Bolivia's Ex-Leader," BBC Monitoring, 15 November 2019, *https://monitoring.bbc.co.uk/product/c2018k31.*

29. See Lara Jakes, "As Protests in South America Surged, So Did Russian Trolls on Twitter, U.S. Finds," *New York Times,* 20 January 2020.

30. Daniel Gomez, "Rusia pone el foco en Bolivia y en unas elecciones en las que el MAS va unido y la oposición dividida," *Alnavío, https://alnavio.es/rusia-pone-el-foco-en-bolivia-y-en-unas-elecciones-en-las-que-el-mas-va-unido-y-la-oposicion-dividida.*

CHAPTER FIVE

China's Tech-Enhanced Authoritarianism

SAMANTHA HOFFMAN

EMERGING TECHNOLOGIES ARE RESHAPING how humans interact with their environment, how businesses deliver services, and how governments solve problems. "Big data" tools, integrated urban-management systems ("smart cities"), the Internet of Things (IoT), and other technologies offer a host of conveniences and practical capabilities, but also carry inherent risks. Even when a technology's creator or owner has no nefarious aims, there is always a danger that bad actors will gain access to data generated by a technology and then use those data for their own purposes. In the absence of democratic oversight, this threat only grows. When authoritarian governments become involved, emerging technologies have the potential to undermine democracy.

The world's authoritarian regimes, while sharing key characteristics, may vary significantly in how they operate and what they want. This essay focuses on the People's Republic of China (PRC) to illustrate the full scope of challenges facing liberal democracies when emerging technologies are wielded by a powerful regime aiming to bend the world to accommodate its authoritarianism. While the national-security implications of China's technological rise have been well documented, and democratic governments have begun to take steps in response, the threat to democratic norms and institutions has yet to be fully examined. China is home to many of the leading companies that export technology products globally, and thus it must be at the center of the global discussion on the political dangers that those technologies pose. Although a number of these PRC-based companies are nominally private, they must be willing to serve the interests of the Chinese Communist Party (CCP) in order to operate and thrive in China.

The CCP regime's use of technology to expand its power and influence is best described as "tech-enhanced authoritarianism." Rather than creating fundamentally new ways of controlling populations, technology augments the party's standard methods of exercising authoritarian dominance. The global repercussions of the PRC's tech-enhanced authoritarianism so far have been vastly underestimated, as analysts tend to focus mostly on overt coercion and direct surveillance while overlooking how the regime uses technologies designed for solving everyday problems and providing public services to expand its power.

Espionage and illicit data mining by bad actors are not the only concerns. There is also a risk that data collected for normal and benign reasons by a vendor thought to be trustworthy could be accessed via everyday business activity or downstream data access by other actors, including governments and companies, for authoritarian purposes or to improve their own information operations. For example, the debate over banning Chinese telecommunications giant Huawei from constructing 5G mobile networks has fixated on the possibility of Huawei's being a vehicle for PRC espionage. But Huawei and companies like it collect data in bulk as part of their routine business activities, and these data can facilitate practices that undermine liberal-democratic interests. The more high-quality data there are, the more accurate facial- and voice-recognition systems, public-sentiment analysis ("opinion mining"), and relationship mapping (seeing how people and groups are connected) will be. Authoritarian governments are not the only ones seeking to develop these capabilities. But effectively policing data collection and usage in liberal democracies is far more difficult when the company in question is based in an authoritarian state.

In terms of geopolitics, some autocracies try to use technology in their wider efforts to expand their global influence and undercut the stability and legitimacy of democracies. Authoritarian regimes use technology both directly and indirectly to project "sharp power." According to Christopher Walker and Jessica Ludwig, sharp power "is not principally about attraction or persuasion; instead, it centers on distraction and manipulation." Unlike soft power, sharp power "pierces, penetrates, or perforates the political and information environments in the targeted countries."[1] It seeks to "limit free expression and to distort political environments."[2] When technology is used for censorship and surveillance or as a platform to conduct information operations, it is serving directly as a tool of sharp power. More indirectly, technology enables authoritarians to better understand the audiences that they seek to influence and to project sharp power more effectively and in more ways. To understand the ramifications, it is important to consider how Beijing is harnessing emerging technologies to protect and expand its power by shaping, managing, and controlling domestic and global environments.

The Hidden Hazards of "Smart Cities"

China's development of smart cities inside its borders and Chinese companies' global export of related products and services show what tech-enhanced authoritarianism looks like in practice. The phenomenon is best understood through the CCP's concept of "social management." This term refers to the CCP leadership's attempts to shape, manage, and control society—and the party's own members—using a combination of cooperative and coercive means. Notably, the same concept can be found in the CCP's approach to global governance. Under party leader Xi Jinping, the phrase "international social management" has been used to describe how Beijing is trying to assert a similar level of control globally.

Smart cities use digital technologies such as "video cameras, social media, and other inputs [to] act as a nervous system, providing the city operator and citizens with constant feedback so they can make informed decisions."[3] The idea behind smart cities—no matter where they are located—is to leverage existing and emerging technologies to improve the efficiency and quality of urban services. In addition to data-collection devices and surveillance cameras, smart cities rely on technologies such as data-visualization platforms, real-time data-processing tools, and cloud-storage platforms.

The benefits of smart-city technologies can obscure their invasiveness and role in advancing political control. Enhanced and streamlined service provision tends to win the cooperation of ordinary people, who understandably focus on immediate and tangible improvements in daily life rather than on the danger lurking down the road. In China, smart cities are the latest in a long series of e-government efforts dating back to the early 1990s and the Golden Projects, which were launched to "build and streamline information systems, and connect agencies to improve their operational capacity."[4] These and other initiatives—such as "grid management," where urban areas are divided into zones for management purposes—were intended not only to enhance public security but also to improve everyday governance, making bureaucracy more efficient and solving problems before they emerged. All were linked more broadly to social management.

Today's smart cities are associated with two related and ongoing public-security projects: Skynet, launched in 2005, and Sharp Eyes, launched in 2015. Skynet is a video-surveillance system with monitoring equipment placed mostly at major intersections, police checkpoints, and other public locations. Skynet relies on the use of Geographic Information System (GIS) mapping, image gathering, transmission, and other technologies to improve real-time monitoring and information recording. Sharp Eyes is a more advanced version of Skynet that builds on Skynet infrastructure, largely by installing government platforms in urban areas for sharing video-image information and establishing rural comprehensive-management centers that streamline government services. Sharp Eyes feeds into work on state security, counterterrorism, enhanced logistics, security supervision, and the prevention and control of criminal activity.[5]

From the CCP's standpoint, the everyday provision of basic public goods, such as traffic safety or the prevention of violent crime, and the projection of authoritarian power, including suppressing dissent, can be fused together. The concept of social management effectively blends the two, while prioritizing regime security over the rights and security of the public. For instance, a smart electricity meter can improve the accuracy, transparency, and reliability of readings, to the benefit of the utility and its customers. For police, the data from that same meter can help to detect "abnormal" behaviors indicative of "illegal" gatherings. Not surprisingly, such technologies are deployed most coercively in the autonomous regions of Xinjiang and Tibet, where the ethnic Uyghur and Tibetan populations, respectively, are victims of gross human-rights violations. According to Human Rights Watch, authorities in Xinjiang are building the Integrated Joint Operations Platform to aggregate data on individual behaviors and flag "those deemed potentially threatening."[6]

Given these abuses, it can be easy to forget that smart-city projects emerged much earlier in other regions of China in a less visibly coercive form. Beyond surveillance, smart cities are supposed to create a more "service-oriented" government. This requires improving intragovernmental coordination with respect to both policies and technical standards, and increasing government efficiency. Like all governments, the CCP regime must solve everyday problems, and smart-city equipment helps it to do that. For instance, to improve traffic management, tech giant Alibaba's "city brain" smart-city architecture brings together information technology, telecommunications, and navigation and positioning technology, and integrates data from different government departments. City-brain systems that monitor traffic flows can even be used to improve response times of the police, paramedics, and firefighters. Services such as geofencing—placing virtual boundaries around physical locations—can be used for everything from targeted advertising to tracking the movements of a person or vehicle.[7] That same technology can be used to help manage natural-disaster responses, public-health crises, and serious civil unrest.

Governments in developing countries are often especially eager to adopt smart-city solutions to both modernize governance and enhance security. To support the development of smart-city projects in Africa, Huawei reportedly set up a US$1.5 billion fund in 2018 to "improve urban traffic and air quality, promote energy efficiency in buildings, improve the management of other flows (including waste and water) and make healthcare and health services intelligent."[8] In some places, Huawei projects have been explicitly linked to surveillance and political security. According to a 2019 *Wall Street Journal* report, Huawei helped to build eleven public-security monitoring centers in Uganda, and Huawei technicians helped Ugandan intelligence agents to surveil prominent opposition politicians.[9] Other smart systems are more explicitly linked to service provision. In Egypt, Chinese media reported in mid-2020 that Huawei was in discussions with the Ministry of Electricity to turn the country's electricity network into a smart grid to optimize power management.[10] Similarly, in 2017, Nigeria's Ministry of Communications announced that it would partner with Huawei on the development of smart cities, and that using open data for government-resource management would improve service provision and increase government revenues.[11] All these technologies, however, could be weaponized against citizens—just as they are in the PRC—if left without effective democratic oversight.

No matter where data are collected, they can support the use of technology for coercion in other settings. Data analytics and artificial intelligence (AI) depend on large inputs of high-quality data. Facial-recognition technology, for example, grows more accurate when it is trained on a larger volume and greater diversity of facial images. In 2018, Zimbabwe's government signed an agreement with the Chinese firm CloudWalk to build a national facial-recognition database and monitoring system. As part of the deal, Zimbabwe agreed to send its own citizens' biometric data to the PRC to improve CloudWalk's ability to recognize faces among different racial and ethnic groups. This will ultimately make the company more globally competitive.

The implications of such PRC-based, globally applicable AI systems are serious, especially if Chinese authorities work with law enforcement in other countries. Huawei has a project in Serbia, for example, that was "inspired" by an incident in which the suspect in a deadly 2015 hit-and-run car accident in Belgrade fled to China. The suspect was identified and arrested in three days thanks to the PRC's advanced facial-recognition technology.[12] Given that the CCP regime already harasses exiles and dissidents overseas and disregards the legal citizenship of Chinese-born or ethnic-Chinese foreign nationals, it is plain to see how law-enforcement partnerships similar to that of Huwei and the Serbian government could, with the aid of smart-surveillance systems, be exploited in other contexts. For instance, Huawei and leading Turkish mobile provider Turkcell have signed numerous agreements, including a smart-city urban-management cooperation agreement. There is already notable law-enforcement cooperation between Turkey and China, and there are many documented cases of Turkish authorities facilitating the forced repatriation of Uyghurs to the PRC.[13] New technical links could further endanger the large Uyghur population living in exile in Turkey.

Even when these technologies are exported to municipalities in established liberal democracies (such as Valenciennes in France or Duisburg in Germany), where the risk of intentional misuse is lower and legal constraints are greater, there are still issues associated with adopting systems designed for use in authoritarian states. There is a genuine risk that any state will not be able to guarantee data security against bad actors who have downstream access to it. Liberal democracies' adoption of smart-city technologies could help to normalize their uptake in countries with weaker legal and regulatory safeguards. These products could also enable the CCP to restrict the freedom of speech of individuals living outside China who might otherwise be protected by democratic institutions because of how Chinese law is applied.

The Motives Behind the CCP's Tech Initiatives

To fully appreciate the scope of the challenge of technology as a tool for projecting sharp power, democratic governments must recognize that intent varies among authoritarians. The CCP's strategy does not mirror Russian disinformation operations or the strategies of other authoritarian regimes, even if they are using similar tools. The Kremlin's efforts are largely designed to create distrust in the states that it targets. The CCP's aim is to shape, manage, and control the international environment so that public sentiment is—or is seen to be—favorable to its interests (that is, the party's interests, not simply China's or the Chinese people's interests). This goal is driven foremost by the CCP's concept of "state security," which in essence is to protect the CCP against the extensive threats that it perceives, regardless of state borders and especially in the realms of ideology and politics.

In a 2018 speech, Xi explained how this conception of state security weaves together all threads of society: "People's security is the purpose of state security, political security is the root of state security, the supremacy of national interests is the criterion of state security, realizing people's happiness, the party's long-term governance, and the country's long-term stability." As one article that was originally published in the *People's Liberation Army Daily* described it, political security "refers to the objective state of state sovereignty, political power, political system, political order, and ideology protected from threats, infringements, subversions, and destruction."[14] State security as a concept is not about protecting China and the Chinese people separate from the party's leadership. State security is about protecting CCP rule above all else.

There is increasingly strong evidence that the regime intends to use bulk data collection in this effort—in part to inform the development of tools for shaping public discourse abroad.[15] The CCP does not compartmentalize its security strategy into domestic and international components, as perceived political and ideological threats can come from anywhere. The regime sees the color-revolution events of the early 2000s as having been provoked in part by "hostile forces" outside the PRC. In a 2000 speech, then–PRC leader Jiang Zemin warned of such forces and argued that China needed to actively combat them with online propaganda.[16] In the years since, the CCP's online and international propaganda apparatuses have greatly expanded, particularly under current leader Xi Jinping.

Effectively shaping public perceptions requires the capacity to understand public sentiment. The CCP's methods of doing so are similar to those used in the global advertising industry. But instead of trying to sell a product, the party is trying to promote authoritarian control and governance beyond the PRC's borders. Party officials such as the head of the State Council Information Office, Jiang Jianguo, have stressed the importance of understanding the minds of non-Chinese audiences to enable the regime to adjust, improve, and better target its messages so that they reach and, ideally, have an impact in all corners of the world.

Emerging technologies, particularly those that utilize big data, are a critical component of the CCP's efforts to know and manipulate its international audiences. Large datasets can reveal patterns and trends in human behavior, enabling the party to better understand public sentiment, which could, among other things, help the party-state to disseminate propaganda more effectively.

The Chinese company Global Tone Communications Technology (GTCOM), which is controlled by the PRC's Central Propaganda Department, provides a good case study. A self-described "cross-language big data" business, GTCOM collects bulk data from all over the world and in more than sixty-five languages. The company then processes the information for use in other products and services, for both government and corporate clients. In terms of scale, the firm claims to collect as much as two to three petabytes of data annually—the equivalent of about twenty-billion photos on Facebook. According to the company's director of big data, Liang Haoyu, "GTCOM is trying to build up its recognition [capability] for objects, settings, and human faces, in conjunction with texts and voices, to provide real-time monitoring of security risks. In the future, [GTCOM] will be able to find the requested facial structure through image recognition and provide technical support and assistance for state security."[17] At a presentation Liang gave in 2017, an image projected beside him read, "90 percent of military-grade intelligence data can be obtained from open data analysis."[18]

It is not immediately clear how all this collected information will be used. To a degree, the CCP amasses data now and decides what to do with the information later, anticipating greater technical capacity to exploit the trove in the future. But beyond Liang's statements about potential security applications, the fact that GTCOM is controlled by the Central Propaganda Department is also telling. The structure suggests an intent to develop new tools—such as fake, AI-generated social-media commentary, images, and videos—that could help to manipulate global public discourse and advance the CCP's sharp-power agenda.

While such data-informed propaganda strategies are still developing, the regime is already ramping up its overall efforts to shape international public opinion, demonstrating a political will that may soon be accompanied by more advanced means of carrying it out. In June 2020, for example, Twitter released information on the removal of accounts that it said were part of a state-backed covert-influence campaign. The company took down numerous PRC-linked accounts that had posted mostly disinformation about the Hong Kong democracy movement, the U.S.-based exiled Chinese billionaire Guo Wengui (and especially his relationship with former White House advisor Steve Bannon), and to a lesser extent covid-19 and Taiwan.[19] Although the Twitter campaign was not highly sophisticated, there are signs that the regime's plans and capacities are becoming more so. Among other indicators, GTCOM has reportedly applied for patents related to a machine-translation method based on generative adversarial networks (GANs)—machine-learning models that can produce new content. GANs can synthesize images based on AI or use visual speech recognition to perform lip-reading and generate speech output. This is the same type of technology used to create synthetic or artificial media, also referred to as "deep fakes."

The Mirage of Neutral Technology

The CCP expects technology to enhance its sharp-power efforts, and it is using capitalism as a vehicle to access data that can help it to disrupt democratic processes and create a more favorable global environment for its own power and security. In addition to accumulating data, the party-state is attempting to pioneer new forms of technology and lay the technical foundations for entire industries, which the rest of the world will have to adopt. Actors in liberal democracies often assume that new technology is essentially neutral, and that they can control any risk associated with adopting it. The CCP appears to understand that a technology's inherent design features cannot be removed by users, and that dominating the initial phases of development can pay dividends long into the future. Thus the regime is working today to reshape the global governance of emerging technologies.

International standards for technology are typically set by countries, corporations, or nongovernmental organizations (such as the International Organization for Standardization) to put in place safety benchmarks and reduce the costs of trade and manufacturing. Governments and corporations alike want to have a voice in setting these standards, as new rules always risk increased costs or other undesirable outcomes. The China Standards 2035 plan calls for the global export of PRC standards for emerging technologies, and for those benchmarks to be accepted by international standards-setting bodies. If the plan succeeds and China's standards—especially for key technical infrastructure—are adopted internationally, PRC-made systems will enjoy greater interoperability and market access in the rest of the world. The problem for democracies is that PRC standards were designed not simply to guarantee the quality and interoperability of various types of equipment, but also to ensure that the technology facilitates Beijing's social-management objectives.

Domestically, technologies are being researched and developed to meet the CCP's needs. Standardization is already taking place at the design level, indicating that seamless interoperability between smart-city systems is possible. Chinese government and research institutes collaborate with companies on national-standards technical committees to regulate equipment development as well as the requirements that companies must meet to successfully bid for a project. For instance, a 2015 document on the technical requirements for facial recognition in security systems was drafted through the cooperation of more than a dozen bodies, including research institutes such as the Chinese Academy of Sciences, the National University of Defense Technology, and the First Research Institute of the Ministry of Public Security; tech companies such as Hikvision and Dahua; and public-security bureaus such as the Shanxi Provincial Public Security Department and Wuhan Public Security Bureau. Documents like these form the basis for technical requirements in government-procurement contracts.

In practice, local governments across the PRC have not yet achieved seamless interoperability internally between government departments or with other local governments that are using smart-city platforms. But that goal may soon be realized. The setting of standards, and requiring project bidders to meet those standards, makes it more likely that plans such as Skynet or Sharp Eyes will be successfully implemented across China, despite their complexities. The same logic applies at the international level. Although the PRC cannot force its standards on other countries, it can help to set standards that become the global norm. Its success in doing so would not only facilitate the international adoption of Chinese technology but also effectively embed the CCP's political values in international standards and increase Beijing's ability to exploit these advantages and project sharp power.

It is tempting to dismiss the feasibility of the Chinese government's plan to use smart-city technology to monitor the movements of large populations. The problems that local governments encountered while trying to leverage these systems in response to the covid outbreak in early 2020 exposed the current limitations in integrating data from different sources. The *Financial Times* reported that some private companies refused to share users' location data, which are believed to be more precise than those held by state telecommunications firms, to support local governments' tracking and tracing of high-risk individuals.[20] Focusing on current flaws rather than on the long-term trajectory would be a mistake, however, not least because the gaps that the covid response revealed could speed up improvements and make the technology more effective. Once the technology catches up with the ideas, enforcement of such demands for data will become increasingly automated.

In the end, private companies do not have any genuine power to refuse Beijing's demands for data. The regime holds that everyone is responsible for preventing and stopping behavior that could compromise state security, no matter where in the world they are located, as the suite of state-security–related legislation enacted under Xi Jinping makes clear. There has been a push inside China for increased data security, exemplified in the 2021 enaction of both the Data Security Law and the Personal Information Protection Law. The former places data security in the context of China's state-security strategy. The latter regulates the power of individuals and entities who handle personal data, and includes clauses suggesting that the government's power can be limited, although exemptions effectively render these clauses meaningless. Given that the party-state describes the law as a tool for ensuring the CCP's political security above all else, Chinese companies can have only limited independence to resist political pressure. As Xi Jinping has said, "comprehensively relying upon the law to rule the country does not at all weaken the party's leadership."[21] Rather, it consolidates the party's hold on power.

These factors will not change as Chinese companies go global, or as foreign companies continue to seek access to Chinese markets. The *Wall Street Journal* reported in November 2020 that a former Airbnb executive had resigned over the company's sharing its user data with Chinese officials. Among the Airbnb data were personal details such as users' email addresses and phone numbers, including those of Americans traveling in China, that could enable Chinese government surveillance of these individuals.[22] Relatedly, U.S. Department of Justice prosecutors issued a complaint and arrest warrant in December 2020 for a Zoom employee who shared user information with Chinese security officials and, at the behest of Beijing, terminated video meetings about the anniversary of the 1989 Tiananmen Square massacre that were organized outside China. If the CCP regime can force foreign companies into sharing data, no one should believe that China-based companies have any real power to push back.

The PRC has actively participated in global bodies that set technical standards for emerging technologies including 5G, IoT, and AI. China's engagement in this space, which is far more coordinated than liberal democracies', gives Chinese companies an edge over competitors and allows Beijing to shape international norms that serve its political interests. The PRC government has a strong presence in the International Telecommunication Union, which it uses to "tilt the standard-setting agenda in Huawei's favor."[23]

China has also played a large role at the International Organization for Standardization (ISO) and the International Electrotechnical Commission (IEC), two of the world's largest technical-standards–setting bodies. The US-China Business Council reported that PRC-occupied secretariat positions on technical committees or subcommittees increased by 73 percent between 2011 and 2020 in the ISO, and by 67 percent between 2012 and 2020 in the IEC.[24] In this way, the PRC is able to shape standards on a range of issues. But Chinese companies are also de facto setting standards simply by exporting their products globally. For example, security-camera companies Hikvision and Dahua enjoy global market dominance, even though sales have recently declined due to U.S. sanctions over the firms' provision of surveillance technologies used to repress Xinjiang's Uyghur population.

The problem becomes clearer when China's tech giants are certified for meeting international standards that they helped to set. For example, YITU, one of China's "AI champions," provides facial-recognition and traffic-monitoring software for Huawei smart-city projects. According to a July 2020 press release, the British Standards Institution (BSI) certified that YITU had met "widely accepted international certification for privacy information management systems (PIMS) that meet best practices outlined in regulations such as the [EU's] General Data Protection Regulation (GDPR)."[25] But YITU is also directly involved in the Chinese system of repression in Xinjiang. According to the Australian Strategic Policy Institute's "Mapping China's Technology Giants" project, YITU supports Xinjiang's public-security work through its Dynamic Portrait System, and it cooperates with other companies on public security in the region.[26] A *New York Times* investigation found that a YITU-generated database included code to identify Uyghurs from public surveillance videos.[27] This suggests that YITU complies with standards that require assigning fields for coding a person's nationality and ethnic identity. Clearly, compliance with regulations such as GDPR does not necessarily mean that companies share the values behind them.

For policymakers, researchers, and civil society alike, it is crucial to develop a sophisticated country-specific understanding of how state actors—including the Chinese government—project sharp power using new technologies. States act differently depending on their interests and goals, and the impact of tech-enabled sharp power will vary. Although "country-agnostic" policy approaches to decisionmaking may feel more objective, they often obscure important realities by poorly defining the nature of the problem. Varying intentions among authoritarian actors also affect different issue areas and require distinct responses.

At the same time, liberal democracies must clearly explain to their citizens why China's tech-enhanced authoritarianism is a direct and major threat that, among other things, undermines individual autonomy and freedom of expression. Liberal democracies must also be clear about why the alternative they offer is better. They should define and promote liber-al-democratic values, and invest heavily in protecting them.

Notes

I would like to thank staff at the National Endowment for Democracy as well as Dave Shullman, Dahlia Peterson, Peter Mattis, and my ASPI colleagues Fergus Ryan and Nathan Attrill.

1. Christopher Walker and Jessica Ludwig, "From 'Soft Power' to 'Sharp Power': Rising Authoritarian Influence in the Democratic World," in *Sharp Power: Rising Authoritarian Influence* (Washington, D.C.: National Endowment for Democracy, December 2017), *www.ned.org/wp-content/uploads/2017/12/Sharp-Power-Rising-Authoritarian-Influence-Full-Report.pdf.*

2. Christopher Walker, "What Is 'Sharp Power?'" *Journal of Democracy* 29 (July 2018): 9–23, *www.journalofdemocracy.org/articles/what-is-sharp-power.*

3. Cisco, "What Is a Smart City?" *www.cisco.com/c/en/us/solutions/industries/smart-connected-communities/what-is-a-smart-city.html.*

4. Samantha Hoffman, "Managing the State: Social Credit, Surveillance, and the CCP's Plan for China," *China Brief,* 17 August 2017, *https://jamestown.org/program/managing-the-state-social-credit-surveillance-and-the-ccps-plan-for-china.*

5. Li Zhen, "'Skynet' Plus 'Sharp Eyes': Both Cities and Rural Areas Are Safe," *People's Daily,* 11 October 2017, *http://archive.fo/uEMVC*; Ruan Zhan-jiang and Shuai Biao, "'*xueliang gongcheng' zhi mi ping'an jianshe fanghu-wang*" ["Sharp Eyes Project" Weaving Security Construction Net], *People's Daily,* 14 February 2019, *http://archive.fo/m6XIB.*

6. Maya Wang, "China's Algorithms of Repression: Reverse Engineering a Xinjiang Police Mass Surveillance App," Human Rights Watch, May 2019, *www.hrw.org/sites/default/files/report_pdf/china0519_web5.pdf.*

7. Sarah K. White, "What Is Geofencing? Putting Location to Work," *CIO.com,* 1 November 2017, *https://www.cio.com/article/288810/geofencing-explained.html#:~:text=Geofencing%20is%20a%20location%2Dbased,location%2C%20known%20as%20a%20geofence.*

8. Jean Marie Takouleu, "Huawei Sets Up a $1.5 Billion Fund to Boost Afri-can Smart Cities," *Afrik 21,* 2 October 2019, *www.afrik21.africa/en/africa-huawei-sets-up-a-1-5-billion-fund-to-boost-african-smart-cities.* See also the

Australian Strategic Policy Institute's Mapping China's Tech Giants project, which documented dozens of smart cities projects around the world, led mainly by Huawei, *https://chinatechmap.aspi.org.au.*

9. Joe Parkinson, Nicholas Bariyo, and Josh Chin, "Huawei Technicians Helped African Governments Spy on Political Opponents," *Wall Street Journal,* 15 August 2019, *www.wsj.com/articles/huawei-technicians-helped-african-governments-spy-on-political-opponents-11565793017.*

10. "Egypt, China's Huawei Discuss Electricity Network's Transformation to Smart Grid," China Global Television Network, 4 September 2020, *https://africa.cgtn.com/2020/09/04/egypt-chinas-huawei-discuss-electricity-networks-transformation-to-smart-grid.*

11. "Nigerian Government and Huawei Partner on Smart Cities Initiative," IT News Africa, 10 August 2017, *https://www.itnewsafrica.com/2017/08/nigerian-government-and-huawei-partner-on-smart-cities-initiative.*

12. "Huawei Safe City Solution: Safeguards Serbia," Huawei, 23 August 2018, *https://archive.vn/pZ9HO.*

13. Can Sezer, "Update 1—Turkey's Turkcell Signs Deal to Use Huawei's Mobile Services," Reuters, 12 February 2020, *https://archive.vn/TYsby;* Asim Kashgarian and Ezel Sahinkaya, "Analysts: Extradition Treaty Between Turkey, China Endangers Uighur Refugees," Voice of America, 7 January 2021, *www.voanews.com/east-asia-pacific/analysts-extradition-treaty-between-turkey-china-endangers-uighur-refugees;* Gareth Browne, "Turkey Sending Muslim Uighurs Back to China Without Breaking Promise," *Telegraph,* 26 July 2020, *www.telegraph.co.uk/news/2020/07/26/turkey-sending-muslim-uighurs-back-china-without-breaking-promise.*

14. Both quotations are from "Zhenghi anquan shi guojiaanquan de genben" [Political security is the root of state security], *Qstheory,* 20 April 2018, *https://web.archive.org/web/20180420123613/http:/www.qstheory.cn/defense/2018-04/20/c_1122716581.htm.*

15. Liza Tobin, "Xi's Vision for Transforming Global Governance: A Strategic Challenge for Washington and Its Allies," *Texas National Security Review* 2 (November 2018): 154–66, *https://tnsr.org/2018/11/xis-vision-for-transforming-global-governance-a-strategic-challenge-for-washington-and-its-allies.*

16. "*Jiang Zemin: zai zhongyang sixiangzhengzhi gongzuo huiyi shang de jianghua*" [Jiang Zemin: Remarks at the Central Ideological and Political Work Conference], China Reform Information Database, 28 June 2000, *www.reformdata.org/2000/0628/5849.shtml* (published in the *Selected Works of Jiang Zemin Vol 3*).

17. "Liang Haoyu: zhongyiyutong 'quanqiu gongkai dashuju' zhu fang anquan fengxian" [Liang Haoyu: GTCOM "global public big data" helps to prevent security risks], Global Tone Communication Technology Co. Ltd., 20 September 2017, *https://archive.vn/FVJHM*; Samantha Hoffman, "Engineering Global Consent: The Chinese Communist Party's Data-Driven Power Expansion," *The Strategist*, 14 October 2019, Australian Strategic Policy Institute, *www.aspistrategist.org.au/engineering-global-consent-the-chinese-communist-partys-data-driven-power-expansion*.

18. "Liang Haoyu: zhongyiyutong 'quanqiu gongkai dashuju' zhu fang anquan fengxian" [Liang Haoyu: GTCOM "global public big data" helps to prevent security risks], Global Tone Communication Technology Co. Ltd., 20 September 2017, *https://archive.vn/FVJHM*.

19. Jake Wallis et al., "Retweeting Through the Great Firewall: A Persistent and Undeterred Threat Actor," Australian Strategic Policy Institute, June 2020, *https://s3-ap-southeast-2.amazonaws.com/ad-aspi/2020-06/Retweeting%20through%20the%20great%20firewall_1.pdf?ZzW5dlyqlOOgG5m9oHj9DWsjgtXD6TCA*.

20. Yuan Yang et al., "China, Coronavirus, and Surveillance: The Messy Reality of Personal Data," *Financial Times,* 2 April 2020, *www.ft.com/content/760142e6-740e-11ea-95fe-fcd274e920ca*.

21. "Xi Jinping tan fazhi zuixin jin ju pouxi gaoji ganbu zoushang fanzui daolu yuanyin" [The latest quotes from Xi Jinping on rule of law, an analysis of the reasons why senior cadres have committed crimes], CPC News, 15 February 2019, *http://archive.fo/gnXxA*.

22. Dustin Volz and Kirsten Grind, "Airbnb Executive Resigned Last Year over Chinese Request for More Data Sharing," *Wall Street Journal,* 20 November 2020, *www.wsj.com/articles/airbnb-executive-resigned-last-year-over-chinese-request-for-more-data-sharing-11605896753*.

23. Melanie Hart and Jordan Link, "There Is a Solution to the Huawei Challenge," Center for American Progress, 14 October 2020, *www.americanprogress.org/issues/security/reports/2020/10/14/491476/solution-huawei-challenge*.

24. "China in International Standards Setting: USCBC Recommendations for Constructive Participation," U.S.-China Business Council, February 2020, *www.uschina.org/sites/default/files/china_in_international_standards_setting.pdf*.

25. Danielle Cave, Fergus Ryan, and Vicky Xiuzhong Xu, "Mapping More of China's Tech Giants: AI and Surveillance," Australian Strategic Policy Institute, 28 November 2019, *www.aspi.org.au/report/mapping-more-chinas-*

tech-giants; "YITU Technology Received ISO/IEC 27701:2019 Certification from BSI, Becomes the First Chinese AI Company to Obtain It," CISION PR Newswire, 1 July 2020, *www.prnewswire.com/news-releases/yitu-technology-received-isoiec-277012019-certification-from-bsi-becomes-the-first-chinese-ai-company-to-obtain-it-301086961.html*; "ISO/IEC 27701:2019 Security Techniques—Extension to ISO/IEC 27001 and ISO/IEC 27002 for Privacy Information Management—Requirements and Guidelines," International Organization for Standardization, August 2019, *www.iso.org/standard/71670. html*.

26. See YITU company overview on the Australian Strategic Policy Institute's Mapping China's Tech Giants website: *https://chinatechmap.aspi.org. au/#/company/yitu.*

27. Paul Mozur, "One Month, 500,000 Face Scans: How China Is Using A.I. to Profile a Minority," *New York Times,* 14 April 2019, *www.nytimes. com/2019/04/14/technology/china-surveillance-artificial-intelligence-racial-profiling.html*.

CHAPTER SIX

China's Pandemic Power Play

NADÈGE ROLLAND

O N 18 OCTOBER 2017, long before the covid-19 pandemic, Xi Jinping stood in Beijing's Great Hall of the People and told the Nineteenth Congress of the Chinese Communist Party (CCP) that China was
entering a "new era." It would be a time, he said, in which all would "see
China moving closer to center stage and making greater contributions to
mankind." While it is common for top officials everywhere to proclaim
confidence in national prospects, Xi's aplomb stood in sharp contrast to
the more ambivalent and low-profile stance that modern Chinese leaders
since Deng Xiaoping have favored when speaking of their country's international role.

Assertiveness and self-confidence are now the order of the day. Xi has
been eager to showcase the economic, military, and technological successes
of the People's Republic of China (PRC), and to signify his regional and
indeed global ambitions, notably through unveiling the Belt and Road Initiative (BRI) not long after coming to power eight years ago.

China's accomplishments are undeniable, but the leadership is keen on
publicizing them for reasons that go beyond natural self-satisfaction. Propaganda and positive publicity are devices that authoritarian regimes, whose
legitimacy does not stem from citizens' votes, tend to use prodigally in order
to help bolster their domestic authority. By showcasing its competence and
appealing to national pride, the CCP seeks to bolster its legitimacy and per-
petuate its rule at home. Creating an impression of forward momentum is
also part of a narrative targeting the rest of the world: If China's ascent is
unstoppable, then resistance is futile. Shaping perceptions both at home and
abroad is a central feature of the CCP's strategic software. During today's
covid-19 crisis, it is yet again Beijing's tool of choice.

In January 2019, Xi Jinping warned senior officials of the Central Party School to watch out for "black swans" and "gray rhinos," but he was thinking more of the potential effects of the trade dispute with the United States and various familiar domestic challenges that could threaten the CCP's survival.[1] The coronavirus—a "black swan" because it was unexpected and a "gray rhino" because it was initially ignored—represents a serious challenge for the CCP. Xi publicly acknowledged this when, on 23 February 2020, he called the epidemic the "largest-ever public health emergency" the PRC had faced, and "a crisis and a big test" for the regime and the country alike.

China now faces an economic slowdown that threatens to be severe and protracted, and which may be accompanied by popular anger and social unrest. Domestic critics of the Party's management of the outbreak found themselves swiftly "harmonized" and "disappeared,"[2] but the gathering international backlash will not be so readily stopped. Rather than seeing the situation as a pure setback, the Chinese leadership appears to understand the covid crisis and its attendant global disarray as a chance to seize new ground in the battle for international influence. As Mao Zedong once said, "There is great chaos under heaven; the situation is excellent."

More often than is generally acknowledged, Beijing's assertive behavior stems from a deep sense of fear. Ambition and insecurity consistently go hand in hand as drivers of China's external behavior. The CCP has long navigated between the two and learned to thrive on both, trying to mitigate threats to its survival while strengthening its international stature. The CCP sees itself as locked in a perpetual struggle against hostile foreign forces, and believes that material strength is key but "discourse power" is needed to back it up. The current pandemic, as big a challenge as it poses, is not a sufficient reason for Beijing to defer, abandon, or scale back its longstanding strategic goals. For a regime that has proclaimed the country's entry into a "new era" of strength and power, there is no turning back to the old posture of low-key patience. The CCP is not changing its tactics, either. If anything, the current crisis has accelerated the use of the "influence operations" that are part of the CCP's regular playbook.

Facing the world, Beijing is advancing a narrative designed to cultivate external perceptions of China as a positive force, centered on themes of selflessness and generosity. The CCP leadership continues to promote its preferred concepts of a "community of shared future" and a China-centric

"Silk Road" that includes cooperation in matters related to global health. At the same time, China maneuvers within international institutions to assert greater influence on the world stage.

Shaping the Narrative

For more than fifteen years, top CCP officials have taken a keen interest in understanding the rise and fall of great powers. They have been especially interested in why and how the Soviet Union collapsed, and—like disciples who dream of surpassing their master—what led to the rise of the United States as a superpower. Among the ingredients they have identified as necessary to become a great power and a world leader, hard power takes a central position, together with "discourse power." Chinese elites define this latter form of power as the ability to voice ideas, concepts, propositions, and claims that are respected and recognized by others and, in the process, to change, without violence or coercion, how others think and behave. Discourse power is about getting others to do the CCP's will through the use not of force, but of words. Chinese elites believe that discourse power has been a crucial instrument in the establishment and maintenance of U.S. global dominance. Confident that its time has come, backed by the prospect of soon surpassing all other countries in quantifiable measures of material power, China is now tempted to follow suit and to engage openly and actively in this form of struggle for influence.

Persuasion, the essential goal of what the Party calls "propaganda work," is at the core of China's efforts to gain and use "discourse power." Under Xi Jinping, it has been given an increasing importance. Words are used to create a narrative and to manipulate the perceptions, behavior, and decisions of others. In the hands of the CCP, propaganda work is characterized by an effort to saturate the bandwidth of others with CCP messages: The Party intends to be the voice that speaks louder and more often, until it becomes the only one that tells China's story. Voices that clash with the preferred official narrative are scorned, slandered, or silenced.

The CCP's narrative contains some enduring themes. Domestically, the CCP presents itself as the only viable option for the country, the best fit for China's specific socioeconomic and cultural conditions, the embodiment of the Chinese people's past and future, and the creator of all things "right" and admirable, whereas other political and social options (especially liberal democracy) can only bring failure, inefficiency, and chaos. The objective is to convince domestic audiences that the CCP's claim to rule is legitimate, and to prevent any alternative from taking shape.

To the world outside China, the CCP strives to present an image of peacefulness, benevolence, harmony, cooperation, and amity. China is depicted as offering opportunities, economic benefits, and a better future. In recent years, Chinese propagandists have also insisted on China's generosity and selflessness as a provider of global public goods to a world in need. Xi Jinping's 17 January 2017 speech at Davos presented China as an emerging leader of worldwide efforts to address wealth gaps, rising protectionism, and environmental sustainability.

Implicit in the outward-facing narrative is the notion that all prior methods for solving the world's problems have failed while China offers a better path, paved with solutions that the country has applied successfully within its own borders. As Xi told the Nineteenth Party Congress in his Great Hall of the People speech, China holds out a "Chinese approach to solving problems facing mankind," which offers a "new option" for countries that want to speed their development and preserve their independence.

Propaganda presenting China as successful, peaceful, and willing to offer contributions to a world in need aims at fostering external perceptions that favor the PRC, while softening or even deterring resistance to its assertiveness whenever necessary. The goal is to steer international focus away from the CCP's real strategic purposes toward opportunities and positive outcomes that China is supposed to deliver. The positive narrative is also accompanied by repeated rebuttals of criticism, denials of wrongdoing or malign intent, and deflections of blame onto others.

By and large, the narrative and tactics that Beijing has been using amid the covid pandemic follow the same patterns. The CCP wants to be seen as a responsible actor standing on the moral high ground; the Party therefore amplifies voices and content that reflect well on its deeds while seeking to silence criticism. In keeping with this, Beijing's propaganda organs are vigorously projecting three main positive tropes: "China sacrificed," "China is helping," and "China is the best." In parallel, the regime is trying to fend off outside criticisms of how Beijing handled the crisis, especially when it was in its first stages. These positive and defensive themes are often interwoven and reinforce each other.

"THE SELFLESS HERO." The official narrative indiscriminately amalgamates the CCP with China as a country and the Chinese people. Thanks to this rhetorical device, the Party's actions become those of China or the Chinese people, and vice-versa, creating an artificial impression of cohesion between the regime and Chinese society at large. In the case of the pandemic, the official narrative praises the "heroic sacrifice" made by the Chinese people and by China as a nation, with which the political leadership associates itself. Foreign Minister Wang Yi has claimed, for example, that in the face of the crisis,

> The Chinese people of all ethnic groups have united as one under the strong leadership of the CPC Central Committee with Comrade Xi Jinping at its core. Together, we have launched a massive, nation-wide response. The heroic acts of the Chinese people in fighting the epidemic have won admiration and support from the international community.[3]

The central government's lockdown of Wuhan as well as subsequent travel restrictions are presented as mature and costly decisions that were made by the political leadership for the greater good.

Included in the nation's sacrifice are fourteen individuals who lost their lives fighting covid in Wuhan, and whom the Hubei provincial government (Wuhan is Hubei's capital) decided to honor as "martyrs" in early April. Among them is Dr. Li Wenliang, whom the Public Security Bureau investigated for "spreading rumors" and "disturbing the social order" after he sent text messages to fellow physicians about a novel virus that he thought was as deadly as SARS. His death from covid-19 triggered a deluge of online grief as well as anger aimed at the PRC government. The outpouring was quickly censored.[4] In the space of a single month, the regime managed to execute a masterful turnaround, deflecting popular anger aimed mostly at the CCP by turning a person whom the authorities had treated as a criminal into a symbol of the whole nation's heroic sacrifice, and then positioning itself to bask in this martyr's glory.

"HELPING A WORLD IN NEED." In addition to highlighting China's heroic sacrifice, the official narrative also emphasizes China's altruism and readiness to help a world in disarray. In typical fashion, China's good deeds are presented as a reflection of the CCP regime's superior moral standing.

The narrative never fails to underline how such generosity shows what a responsible power China is, attempting in this way to legitimize China's great-power status by simply asserting it. On 30 March 2020, for example, Foreign Ministry spokesperson Hua Chunying told the press:

> Although the situation in China is getting better and more stable, [Chinese enterprises] are still working overtime day and night to help other countries in urgent need of them to fight the pandemic. This is China fulfilling its role as a responsible major country and the Chinese people making kind and selfless contribution to the global response. I believe that such efforts are worthy of respect, not disparagement.

Six days previously, the PRC's official news agency had painted in like colors the Chinese offer to assist other countries:

The country has provided assistance to over 80 countries as well as the World Health Organization (WHO) and the African Union, shared its experience combatting the virus with the global community, and sent medical teams to countries in need. These concrete moves have won international praise, including from the WHO and UN chiefs, and demonstrated that China shoulders the responsibility of a major country.[5]

The CCP cites international praise and gratitude to enhance its stature at home and abroad, with the rest of the world presented as cheering in admiration. As the Foreign Ministry's Geng Shuang told the press on 20 April 2020: "China has made tremendous sacrifices, accumulated valuable experience, and made significant contributions to the global response. The international community bears witness to and applauds China's efforts and progress."

"A GUIDING LIGHT." The third narrative from the CCP's persuasion playbook projects the image of China as a superior model. It casts the PRC's response to the pandemic as a successful example for others to follow, contrasting China's performance favorably with those of Western democracies. For example, the CCP-run *Global Times* newspaper published an op-ed denouncing Sweden's "extremely irresponsible" disease-control measures (which involved social distancing and certain closures but stopped short of a mass lockdown) as a "serious violation of humanitarian principles."[6] In the Hong Kong–based *South China Morning Post* (owned by Jack Ma's

PRC-based multinational Alibaba), an "honorary fellow" from China's Academy of Military Science went even further, claiming that the coronavirus had struck a decisive blow to the entire Western world, which was "falling apart."[7]

Such blunt denigrations of the West are usually not relayed by official Chinese figures, but left to social-media and state-owned outlets, in posts and articles that quote foreigners who praise China while discussing their own countries in grim terms. The intention is not to convince other countries that they must replicate China's system, but to buttress the CCP at home. A more subtle aim of this kind of material is to create rifts throughout the West—both between Western countries and within their respective societies—by sowing doubts about Western governments' capacity to tackle the crisis.

A March 17 Global Times article, for instance, urged the United States to "learn from China," quoting several experts including a U.S. population-health scientist who said she felt "afraid" that the United States would be unlikely to control the virus as well as Wuhan had.[8] In late April, China Global Television Network host Robert Lawrence Kuhn—who has received an award for his support of China from Xi Jinping himself—asserted that "China's system of party-led, strong government" would ensure the country's superiority in fighting the pandemic.[9] Even Harvard professor Joseph Nye, speaking to the Global Times, found that China seemed to have "recovered its endurance" whereas the U.S. administration was "still faltering" because of President Donald Trump's "vacillating leadership." Nye's interview perfectly illustrates the lesson he offered that day to his interviewer: "The best propaganda is not propaganda."[10]

An Offensive Turn

In addition to portraying China in a flattering light, Beijing's propaganda campaign has also taken a more offensive (in both senses of the word) turn as it tries to derail growing international criticism of how Chinese authorities handled the early part of the crisis.[11] This attempt to deflect blame and scrutiny has been accompanied by distortions of fact, statements made in bad faith, accusations of inappropriate behavior and racism, *ad hominem* attacks, economic retaliation, and even outright disinformation relaying wild conspiracy theories.

Officials reject external criticism and urge the countries from which it comes to stick instead to fighting the disease at home. Mentioning the origin of the SARS-CoV-2 virus is dismissed as an "improper and immoral" stigmatization, and the result of "ugly political calculations" by countries eager to make China a "scapegoat" to cover their own inability to tackle the problem.[12] Responding to the Australian government's calls for an independent investigation of how Chinese authorities had handled the early stages of the outbreak, the PRC suspended beef imports from four of Australia's largest meat processors and proposed introducing an 80 percent tariff on Australian barley shipments (China buys a quarter of everything Australia exports). Using a style of rhetoric that Pyongyang would envy, Chinese official media lambasted U.S. secretary of state Mike Pompeo—who insists on using the term "Wuhan virus"—as an "enemy of humankind," a "liar," and a "rumor monger" with a "most twisted and ferocious face" whose rhetoric reveals the United States to have a "colossal moral deficit."[13] Even more objectionable, Foreign Ministry spokesman Zhao Lijian used his Twitter account to disseminate conspiracy theories about U.S. soldiers planting the virus in Wuhan.[14]

Such tactics are not new. Beijing has already deployed disinformation and active-interference campaigns in Hong Kong and Taiwan, which the CCP considers core interests. The mounting international criticism of the CCP's early covid mismanagement is now also considered a paramount issue because it strikes at the heart of a key myth the Party uses to bolster its legitimacy at home: that the CCP is efficient, competent, and therefore uniquely capable of leading the nation. The increasing pressure from outside makes the CCP feel threatened at its core, and partly explains why the persuasion campaign has taken such an offensive turn. The perceived need to defend the Party against what seem to be direct attacks on its legitimacy outweighs any concern that an aggressive response will rouse a foreign backlash.

Successful persuasion campaigns rely not only on the message but on the messengers. They give weight and credibility to the narrative. The current campaign uses every available messenger, from Xi Jinping himself to "China-friendly" foreign voices.

Xi Jinping has held telephone calls with foreign heads of state to pledge solidarity with and support for friendly countries. At the G20 summit that was held by videoconference in late March, he suggested confidence-build-

ing measures for the world economy and vowed to put more Chinese supplies, including medicine, on the global market. With most of the borders
closed due to the pandemic, China's public diplomacy has taken a local
turn. Absent the possibility of diplomatic and paradiplomatic engagements
by representatives traveling from Beijing, Chinese ambassadors have played
a growing role in disseminating the official narrative. They have published
op-eds in the Gambia, Nigeria, South Sudan, and the United States; engaged
think tanks in London; and even created new Twitter accounts (trackable
through the German Marshall Fund's Hamilton 2.0 Dashboard) to relay
key CCP themes online using several languages.

In addition, "China-friendly" foreign voices have fulfilled their unspo-
ken purpose of carrying the Party's narrative without revealing any connection to Beijing. Xinhua, China's official news agency, has featured "overseas
experts" praising the Chinese leadership for its "very impressive" antivi-
rus measures.[15] The WHO representative to China praised China's quick
response to the epidemic outbreak, and underlined its self-sacrifice "in order
to win time for the rest of the world to be able to respond."[16]

Inward- and outward-facing propaganda aims to gain respect and admiration for the CCP and China more generally. The recent combative turn is
a puzzle, for it seems to run counter to this key objective. Do not offensive
tactics backfire and hurt rather than help China's image? A large part of this
effort is taking place on social-media platforms that are banned in China, so
who is the intended audience? Maybe the idea is that respect can be earned
by acting strong. After all, this is consistent with Xi's vision of a China that
stands tall and with his call for Party cadres to show more "fighting spirit."
Liberal democracies in North America, Europe, and Oceania have reacted
negatively to such aggressive behavior. But other parts of the world may be
receptive to a China that acts willing and able to stand up to U.S. and Western power and arrogance. Thus far, the bulk of Beijing's effort has been in
the area of "discourse struggle." But the leadership is also trying to use the
pandemic crisis to pursue more concrete objectives.

Shaping the World

While projecting an image of China as selfless, competent, and responsible,
Beijing continues to work toward its main goal: building a new order in

which other states are drawn into its orbit. This vision has been encapsulated since 2013 in the vaporous concept of a "community of shared future for mankind," which was written into the PRC constitution in March 2018. Throughout the pandemic, Beijing has called for the creation of this "community" as essential for meeting a crisis that affects everyone. It has also continued to promote Xi's Belt and Road grand plan, in particular through its "Health Silk Road" component.

The Health Silk Road is China's blueprint for a new form of global health governance with Chinese characteristics. It is still in the early years of its development but, if fully achieved, could become a prominent example of Beijing-led arrangements meant to act as alternatives to existing international arrangements. In the meantime, China's efforts are focused on manipulating existing international organizations to serve CCP interests, as demonstrated by recent controversies surrounding the WHO. This case vividly illustrates the value of Beijing's quest for "institutional power."

Xi's "community of shared future" concept sounds like a call for planetary harmony. The PRC's state media repeat the idea in unison, but always leave out the proviso that Beijing sees itself as sitting at the center of that community, using the reality of growing interdependence to reward or punish as its interests dictate.

Pulling countries more fully into China's orbit may be achieved through demonstrations of good will. On March 20, the PRC announced that it would send more than eighty countries help in the form of surgical masks, testing kits, protective suits, and medical teams. Beijing created an online "covid-19 knowledge center" while Chinese officials videoconferenced with counterparts around the world to share best practices and information about the virus.

Chinese official media trumpet these efforts, but aid from China does not necessarily come for free. In return for medical supplies, Chinese officials have demanded public statements praising China's coronavirus response, or even expressions of gratitude to Xi Jinping.[17] Supplies have sometimes come from Jack Ma's Alibaba Foundation and from telecom giants Tencent and Huawei, prompting questions about their underlying motives.[18] Huawei's offer to let Italian scientists use its WeLink cloud-based platform caused European Parliament member Anna Bonfrisco to officially ask about the implications for data privacy and the protection of critical infrastructure.[19]

The list of countries to which China has dispatched medical teams—

Burma, Cambodia, Iran, Iraq, Italy, Kazakhstan, Laos, Pakistan, the Philippines, Russia, Serbia, and Venezuela—suggests that considerations other than pure humanitarianism may have shaped the selections. The wording of some media reports reinforces the impression that only those who have proven to be worthy "comprehensive strategic partners" (such as Iran) can be graced with rewards in return for their unswerving friendship.[20]

To tighten the ties that bind, Beijing highlights the need for international cooperation around China. Xi has said that the epidemic is temporary, but cooperation (including the bilateral kind) is everlasting. In a display of its willingness to lead in the setting of regional agendas, Beijing has convened various regional groupings to discuss and establish joint-response mechanisms.

Silk Road, Silken Bonds

The "community of shared future" is intimately associated with the Belt and Road Initiative. The "community" is the envisioned goal; the BRI is the way to knit the community together.[21] This is not to say, however, that the BRI is primarily a physical-infrastructure project. Rather, it is a multidimensional strategy that advances China's notion of itself as an uncontested leading power. Since Xi Jinping launched the BRI in 2013, questions have abounded regarding its economic and financial sustainability. In the wake of the pandemic, will Beijing be able to afford the vast loans and investments in infrastructure projects in developing countries? For the last three years, Beijing has already started to shift the BRI's emphasis toward its "softer" and less costly components. During the current crisis, the focus naturally switched to the Health Silk Road.

In October 2015, the PRC health ministry introduced a plan for "Belt and Road health cooperation" whose professed goals included boosting China's influence in global health matters. Since then, China has carried out a multipronged effort to draw foreign parties into cooperating more closely in areas as diverse as health security, medical research, and the promotion of traditional Chinese medicine. Written understandings now exist between Beijing and such prominent multilateral health organizations as the WHO, UNAIDS, the Global Fund, and the Global Alliance for Vaccines and Immunization. In parallel with declarations of intent, Beijing has been acquiring pharmaceutical companies and starting projects with foreign health centers and businesses. Universities outside China have committed themselves to sharing health-related research and data with Chinese counterparts. This activity under the Belt and Road rubric has given Beijing a flexible network that it can use to promote its interests and spread its views, and all without having to commit enormous sums of money.

Even if the objectives of the Health Silk Road are well defined on paper, the plan is still at an early stage. The covid pandemic has given it an occasion for expansion, both in the developing world and in Western countries where Chinese officials urge cooperation on vaccines and antiviral medications.

As the Beijing-led alternative global-health platform slowly emerges, China is reaping the benefits of its rising influence within existing international institutions, specifically the WHO. The Chinese leadership sought to improve its standing within the WHO in reaction to the organization's harsh criticism of Beijing's handling of the 2003 SARS crisis. Staffers from the PRC are not present in large numbers within the WHO's workforce, however, and the PRC government's financial contributions are low compared to those of other countries.[22] According to French Sinologist Valérie Niquet, Beijing's outsized influence should be understood against the backdrop of China's increased political weight in African countries, especially Ethiopia.[23]

In May 2017, former Ethiopian government official Tedros Adhanom Ghebreyesus was elected to a five-year term as the WHO's director-general, thanks to the support of the PRC and all 55 of the African Union member states. Born in what is now Eritrea, Tedros is a former cadre of the Tigray People's Liberation Front (TPLF), which in the 1970s and 1980s was a self-described Marxist-Leninist movement that engaged in a struggle for control of the Ethiopian government. The TPLF drew support during those decades from the PRC (as well as the PRC's small ally at the time, Albania). In 1991, the civil war ended with the TPLF and its allies victorious, and Tedros later became Ethiopia's health minister (2005–12) and foreign minister (2013–17). Tedros's cabinet posts brought him repeatedly into close engagements with Beijing. While foreign minister, he spoke highly of Ethiopia's relationship with the PRC. As head of the WHO, he has led the way to "stronger and more strategic WHO-China collaborations." In 2017, he praised China's health reforms as "a model for other countries in how to make our world fairer, healthier and safer. We can all learn something from China."[24]

On 14 January 2020, the WHO put out a tweet relaying the official Chinese position that there was "no clear evidence of human-to-human transmission of the novel coronavirus (2019-nCoV) identified in Wuhan, China."[25] Visiting Beijing at the end of that month, Tedros declared his admiration for the Chinese government, which he praised for having "shown its solid political resolve and taken timely and effective measures in dealing with the epidemic." He added that "President Xi's personal guidance and deployment show his great leadership capability."[26]

Through its director and several of its representatives, the WHO has proven a mouthpiece for Beijing, echoing Chinese propaganda by lavishly praising the CCP's efficiency and the advantages supposedly conferred by its system.[27] The WHO has also been a useful pawn supporting Beijing's efforts to exclude Taiwan from international institutions. When asked in a 28 March 2020 remote video interview with Radio Television Hong Kong if the WHO should reconsider Taiwan's exclusion from membership, WHO assistant director-general Bruce Aylward dodged the question, then dismissed another question about Taiwan's coronavirus response, on the ground that he had "already talked about China."[28] A few days later, Tedros refused to answer a Japanese reporter's question about Taiwan, leaving the response to Michael Ryan, the head of the WHO Health Emergencies Programme, who praised the PRC authorities for their early disclosure of information regarding the epidemic.[29]

The WHO ought to be the logical mechanism to turn to for an international investigation into the origins of the pandemic, but its apparent increased politicization at the hands of Beijing does not bode well for a future impartial survey. Yet it remains Xi Jinping's preferred supervisory body for a "comprehensive review of the global response to COVID-19 after it is brought under control," as he declared in a May 18 speech to the World Health Assembly (WHA).

More broadly, the content of Xi's WHA speech is emblematic of China's continual efforts to cast itself as a great, altruistic, responsible power and the leader in particular of the Global South. It repositions China as the leader of global efforts to address the covid crisis, interweaving the familiar discursive themes listed earlier with concrete measures that are meant mainly to woo the developing world. Xi announced the spending of US$2 billion over two years to help with coronavirus response as well as "economic and social development in affected countries, especially developing countries." He vowed that the PRC would build and host a "global humanitarian response depot and hub" to ensure the smooth flow of vital disease-fighting supplies, and promised to found a medical-cooperation mechanism specifically for Africa. To cap his pledges, he said that the PRC would look into solutions for debtor countries and treat any PRC-developed covid-19 vaccine as a "global public good."[30]

In sum, far from recalibrating its strategic goals in light of the pandemic, the CCP leadership remains set on seeing China take center stage in world affairs. Beijing is hoping that over the long run it can use the crisis to more deeply engrain its influence abroad. Yet the regime remains gravely worried about the pandemic's aftermath, not because of the harm that the disease has done to the Chinese people and the world—the regime denies any responsibility for that—but because the damage that the crisis has wrought may threaten to put cracks in the armor of infallibility that the CCP has so tenaciously fabricated. Despite its fears of a postpandemic backlash, therefore, the CCP has chosen *not* to recognize its errors or make amends. Instead, it prefers to carry on its efforts to manipulate outside perceptions.

The way Beijing is waging this campaign says some things about the nature of its power: Even though the CCP regime tries to persuade others of its peaceful benevolence, it can quickly revert to coercion and intimidation when its core interests—to say nothing of its survival in power— are at stake. Beijing's race for pole position is not just happening in the ethereal realm of discourse, however. The current crisis has helped to lay bare the consequences of China's stealthy efforts to increase its influence within international institutions. Unfolding before our very eyes is not merely a battle of narratives but a demonstration of *Realpolitik* by a regime that is a master of it, in which every possible domain, including global health, has become a front along which Beijing seeks to advance its place in the world.

Notes

1. Willy Wo-Lap Lam, "Xi Jinping Warns Against the 'Black Swans' and

'Gray Rhinos' of a Possible Color Revolution," Jamestown Foundation, 20 February 2019, *https://jamestown.org/program/china-brief-early-warning-xi-jinping-warns-against-the-black-swans-and-gray-rhinos-of-a-possible-color-revolution.*

2. Vijay Gokhale, "#COVID19: Reading the Tea Leaves in China," Observer Research Foundation, 19 April 2020, *www.orfonline.org/expert-speak/covid19-reading-tea-leaves-china-64852.*

3. "Resolutely Defeating the COVID-19 Outbreak and Promoting the Building of a Community with a Shared Future for Mankind—Wang Yi," PRC Foreign Ministry, 2 March 2020, *www.fmprc.gov.cn/mfa_eng/wjb_663304/wjbz_663308/2461_663310/t1751673.shtml.*

4. "Mourning for a Medic: Li Wenliang's Death Is a New Crisis for China's Rulers," *Economist,* 7 February 2020.

5. "Commentary: Let the Community with Shared Future Vision Shine Brighter," Xinhua News Agency, 24 March 2020, *www.xinhuanet.com/english/2020-03/24/c_138912849.htm.*

6. Kayla Wong, "Chinese State Media Slams Sweden as 'First Country to Harm the World' with 'Irresponsible' Covid-19 Response," *Mothership,* 15 March 2020, *https://mothership.sg/2020/03/china-global-times-slams-sweden-covid-19.*

7. Zhou Bo, "Why the US and Europe Need to Draw Closer to China and Drop the Hubris," *South China Morning Post* (Hong Kong), 24 April 2020, *www.scmp.com/comment/opinion/article/3081079/why-us-and-europe-need-draw-closer-china-and-drop-hubris.*

8. Chen Qingqing and Liu Caiyu, "Time for US to Learn from China to Deal with the Covid-19 Outbreak," *Global Times,* 17 March 2020, *www.globaltimes.cn/content/1182820.shtml.*

9. "Key Advantages of the Chinese System Overcoming COVID-19," CGTN, 27 April 2020, *https://news.cgtn.com/news/2020-04-27/Key-advantages-of-the-Chinese-system-overcoming-COVID-19-Q2jY4DjrB6/index.html.*

10. "Respect for Science Will Win COVID-19 Fight," *Global Times,* 29 April 2020, *www.globaltimes.cn/content/1187118.shtml.*

11. Laura Rosenberger, "China's Coronavirus Information Offensive," *Foreign Affairs,* 22 April 2020, *www.foreignaffairs.com/articles/china/2020-04-22/chinas-coronavirus-information-offensive.*

12. Hua Ning, "Fighting COVID-19 Requires Solidarity Rather than Slanders," *Juba Monitor* (South Sudan), 9 April 2020.

13. Anna Fifield, "China Wasn't Wild About Mike Pompeo Before the Virus.

It's Really Gunning for Him Now," *Washington Post,* 30 April 2020.

14. "It might be US army who brought the epidemic to Wuhan," he wrote on 12 March 2020. See *https://twitter.com/zlj517/status/1238111898828066823*.

15. "China Acted Responsibly in Global Fight Against Coronavirus: Greek Expert," Xinhua News Agency, 14 March 2020, *www.xinhuanet.com/english/2020-03/14/c_138875830.htm*.

16. Wang Bozun, "China Sacrificed Itself to Win Time for the World to Respond to COVID19: WHO," Global Times, 2 April 2020, *www.globaltimes.cn/content/1184546.shtml*.

17. Bethany Allen-Ebrahimian, "Beijing Demanded Praise in Exchange for Medical Supplies," *Axios,* 6 May 2020, *www.axios.com/beijing-demanded-praise-in-exchange-for-medical-supplies-16f5183e-589a-42e5-bc25-414eb13841b0.html*.

18. Arjun Kharpal, "Canada and France Say Donations of Coronavirus Masks Won't Influence Decisions on Huawei and 5G," CNBC, 10 April 2020, *www.cnbc.com/2020/04/10/coronavirus-canada-france-deny-masks-will-affect-huawei-5g-decisions.html*.

19. Anna Bonfrisco, "Parliamentary Questions: Security Threatened by the 'Health Silk Road' Project," European Parliament, 23 March 2020, *www.europarl.europa.eu/doceo/document/P-9-2020-001768_EN.html*.

20. "Xi Says China Ready to Provide Further Assistance for Iran Against COVID-19 Epidemic," Xinhua News Agency, 14 March 2020, *www.xinhuanet.com/english/2020-03/14/c_138877556.htm*.

21. Nadège Rolland, "Beijing's Vision for a Reshaped International Oder, "*China Brief,* 26 February 2018, *https://jamestown.org/program/beijings-vision-reshaped-international-order*.

22. The PRC's contribution to the WHO was US$86 million in 2019. That is less than a tenth of the total U.S. contribution for the same year. The $10.4 million voluntary contribution that China made in 2017 (the WHO receives both member-state dues and freewill offerings from states as well as nonstate actors such as the Gates Foundation) equaled just 2.5 percent of the U.S. voluntary contribution. François Godement, "L'OMS, la pandémie et l'influence chinoise: un premier bilan," Institut Montaigne, 24 March 2020, *www.institutmontaigne.org/blog/loms-la-pandemie-et-linfluence-chinoise-un-premier-bilan*.

23. Valérie Niquet, "Un défi pour le multilatéralisme: l'instrumentalisation de l'Afrique par la Chine et ses conséquences sur les décisions de l'OMS," Fondation pour la Recherche Stratégique, 14 April 2020, *www.frstrategie.org/publications/notes/*

un-defi-pour-multilateralisme-instrumentalisation-afrique-chine-ses-consequences-sur-decisions-oms-2020.

24. "New Vision and Strengthened Partnership for WHO and China," World Health Organization, 21 August 2017, *www.who.int/news-room/detail/21-08-2017-new-vision-and-strengthened-partnership-for-who-and-china*.

25. See *https://twitter.com/who/status/1217043229427761152?s=21*.

26. "Xi Jinping Meets with Visiting World Health Organization (WHO) Director-General Tedros Adhanom Ghebreyesus," PRC Foreign Ministry, 29 January 2020, *www.fmprc.gov.cn/mfa_eng/zxxx_662805/t1737014.shtml*.

27. Stuart Lau, "WHO Head Stands by His Praise for China and Xi Jinping on Response to Outbreak," *South China Morning Post,* 13 February 2020, *https://tinyurl.com/5fzebnwe*.

28. Aylward's RTHK interview can be seen at *www.youtube.com/watch?v=UlCYFh8U2xM*.

29. A report with footage of the WHO press conference can be seen at *www.youtube.com/watch?v=h43S34daX-U*.

30. "Speech by President Xi Jinping at Opening of 73rd World Health Assembly," Xinhua News Agency, 18 May 2020, *http://xinhuanet.com/english/2020-05/18/c_139067018.htm*.

PART TWO

Blunting Sharp Power's Edge

CHAPTER SEVEN

Transparency Wins in Europe

MARTIN HÁLA

IN 2019, A SMALL BUT RAUCOUS GROUP of overseas Chinese, waving the flag of the People's Republic of China (PRC) and shouting, disrupted a peaceful demonstration of more than a hundred Lithuanians with hands linked in Vilnius's central square in support of Hong Kong's democracy movement. The Chinese ambassador to Lithuania stood to the side and watched. Police were called, two of the Chinese counterprotesters were detained and fined, and Lithuania's government lodged a complaint with the Chinese embassy. Relations deteriorated further under the new Lithuanian government sworn in the following year, which allowed Taiwan to open an official office in Vilnius, urged government officials to abandon Chinese-made cellphones with built-in censorship features, and withdrew from a regional China-led initiative.

In a decidedly lopsided response, China has unleashed the full force of its so-called wolf-warrior diplomacy (taken from the name of a 2017 Chinese action film)—aggressive strong-arm tactics to shout down criticism of China and appear powerful on the international stage. The PRC recalled its ambassador from Vilnius, pressed Lithuania's envoy in Beijing to leave, removed the country from its customs register for a time, and threw up informal barriers not only to Lithuanian exports but even to other countries' products with Lithuanian components—an unprecedented move.

This is just one example of how the PRC has learned to throw its weight around, especially since the 2008 global financial crisis and the 2009 Eurozone crisis. Inspired by the belief that liberal capitalism and the international order were unraveling, the Chinese Communist Party (CCP) began innovating new forms of sharp power. These include "economic diplomacy" and its more recent outgrowth, economic coercion, and the more abrasive tactics and messaging of its wolf-warrior diplomats.

The change in China's international posture caught the outside world mostly off guard and ill prepared. And yet, while the forms of sharp power may be different and bolder today, China is no newcomer to foreign-influence operations. In some ways, the stepped-up international activism is an extension of China's traditional influence-projection toolkit. Mao Zedong used to talk about China's "three magic weapons" for fighting the "enemies of the Revolution": united front work, party-building, and the Red Army.[1] Current CCP general secretary Xi Jinping uses these same terms today. These tools have a long history and are hardwired into the CCP's organizational structure. Numerous foreign-affairs and overseas-trade and -investment agencies support the party's united front work and propaganda efforts abroad.

Xi often speaks of a "grand united front" that underlies his major foreign-policy initiatives,[2] such as the quest for a "human community of shared destiny." The deliberately vague strategic concept could indicate the party's aspiration for a future, CCP-centered "global united front"—a political cooptation of the outside world into a new China-centric system of international relations. It is to that end, perhaps, that China has been strengthening and retooling its sharp-power efforts. Rather than focusing united front work abroad solely on overseas Chinese communities, the CCP now targets foreign governments and foreign businesses active in the Chinese market. It "makes friends" in high places and uses cooptation and corruption to capture powerful foreign elites not only so that they will do China's bidding but also to gain access to (and, ultimately, power through manipulation of) foreign institutions.

These efforts have worked better in some parts of the world than in others, and some of the PRC's early successes turned out to be rather short-lived and even counterproductive. Understanding where and how China's sharp-power efforts have succeeded or failed will help democracies and democratic activists to combat this particular type of authoritarian interference.

The CCP's most striking sharp-power campaign in Europe so far has arguably been the formation of the China–Central and Eastern Europe Cooperation Initiative, better known as 16+1.[3] Formally established at a 2012 Warsaw summit, 16+1 included Albania, Bosnia and Herzegovina, Bulgaria, Croatia, the Czech Republic, Estonia, Hungary, Latvia, Lithuania, Montenegro, North Macedonia, Poland, Romania, Serbia, Slovakia, and Slovenia—all the postcommunist Central and East European (CEE) states except for Kosovo, which China does not officially recognize.

The 16+1 initiative eventually became a cause of concern for the EU. But in the beginning hardly anyone understood what it was supposed to be—including, arguably, some of the CEE leaders who had signed on. Several seemed ill-prepared to meet with their Chinese counterpart, PRC premier Wen Jiabao. For example, the then Czech prime minister Petr Nečas reportedly provoked some consternation among the Chinese delegation by giving Wen Jiabao a bronze statue of Saint George piercing the dragon, considered to be an inappropriate gift given the creature's obvious association with China.[4] Ironically though, this lack of deeper understanding combined with the deliberate vagueness of the initiative may have facilitated its fast and smooth establishment. The 16+1 founding document was replete with lofty statements about win-win cooperation and mutual respect. With nothing specific to object to, the decision to join was easy.

When ill-informed foreign officials join ill-defined PRC-led projects, those officials often incorporate the vague phrases fed to them by their Chinese counterparts, without fully comprehending their meanings, into their own vocabularies to maintain good relations. But as these are CCP-designed expressions and concepts, the CCP has the power to interpret or adjust their meanings at will, according to its preferences at any given moment. The "human community of shared destiny" is a good example of a flexible concept that could mean almost anything. The ungraspable term has increasingly found its way into international documents, including those of UN agencies.[5] What the phrase lacks in specific meaning, it compensates for in feel-good vibes. How could anyone disagree with the notion of a shared future for humankind (whatever that may mean)?

Such slippery language can be found in most Chinese initiatives, including the biggest and boldest, the Belt and Road Initiative (BRI). The not-so-descriptive name has changed several times, adding to the overall fuzziness. What had been the New Silk Road is now the "Belt," and the maritime routes originally called the Twenty-First Century Maritime Silk Road are now the "Road." In Chinese, it is still called "One Belt, One Road," a term that the CCP abandoned in English and other languages in 2016, presumably due to its potentially "hegemonistic" connotation. An uninitiated foreign official could be excused for being somewhat baffled by the convoluted nomenclature.

The elasticity of language is essential to united front work, which is all about "making friends" through means usually not well understood by those targeted. The "friendship" on the CCP side is guided and manipulated by a sprawling bureaucracy in the United Front Work Department and other CCP "systems," which employ tens of thousands of trained "cadres." The unwitting foreigners are not entering into a spontaneous relationship with the Chinese counterparts whom they meet in person, but with a hidden yet formidable top-down bureaucracy that is beyond the ability of most people in open societies to understand because they have encountered nothing remotely comparable to serve as a reference.

The CEE politicians who signed onto 16+1 in 2012, however, presumably could have summoned their own experiences from before 1989 or 1991, respectively. They themselves had, after all, lived in Leninist societies with their own variants of united front work, often called national or patriotic fronts. Apparently, however, their memories had faded in the twenty-three years since the fall of the Berlin Wall. The united front work variants in the old Soviet bloc had also been much less pronounced, less sophisticated, and, crucially, less effective than the current Chinese version.

Moreover, in 2012, few would have considered the PRC a Leninist one-party system comparable to the old Soviet Bloc. For decades, the image of the PRC had been systematically normalized as a recovering dictatorship on its way, through the "reform and opening" process, to rejoining the international community as a "responsible stakeholder."[6] To the United States, these were years of "engagement." To the United Kingdom, it was the "golden era" of its relationship with China. And Germany, some might argue, is still following a change-through-trade policy with China to this day.

The world looked distinctly different in 2012 than it does today, and the CEE leaders who signed up for 16+1 in Warsaw that year did not see the potential risks, only the opportunities. The lingering, seemingly endless aftereffects of the 2008 global financial crisis and subsequent Eurozone debt crisis had many, and not just in Central and Eastern Europe, looking to Beijing for a way out. They did not see a Leninist dictatorship. They saw an economic powerhouse that could help Europe out of its fiscal malaise.

Much has changed since then. After ten years, the initiative has largely failed to deliver on its promises of investment and trade. Over the last decade, the initial enthusiasm has been gradually replaced with "promise fatigue" and creeping skepticism, reinforced by growing concerns about China's true geopolitical goals. Public opinion regarding the initiative and China itself has also soured due to China's wolf-warrior responses to 16+1 countries—especially former member Lithuania—that do not toe the PRC line. Tellingly, it is now only those members with authoritarian tendencies (such as Hungary and Serbia) that still maintain the façade of "friendly cooperation" with the PRC.

Economic Diplomacy or Strategic Corruption?

In 2012, the rationale for 16+1 was to provide a platform for CEE countries to tap into China's economic potential, with few specifics beyond that. The initiative began before the formulation of the BRI, China's flagship "economic diplomacy" project, but was incorporated into it in 2014 as one of its regional "corridors." Yet the BRI model of infrastructure-building— exporting China's excess construction capacity and capital—is not well suited to Central and Eastern Europe, and particularly not the EU members of 16+1.

The EU finances infrastructure projects with its own structural funds disbursed as grants, whereas China finances BRI projects with loans from Chinese policy banks, such as the Export-Import Bank of China. Moreover, EU member states are bound by strict regulations that are often difficult for Chinese companies to comply with or even understand. Poland's A2 Highway project to connect Poland and Germany ahead of the Euro 2012 games illustrated the difficulty of transferring the Chinese infrastructure-building approach to the region. In 2011, Warsaw canceled a deal with the Chinese Overseas Engineering Group (COVEC), the worlds' third-largest construction company, to build a section of the A2 for failing to pay its Polish partners and banned COVEC from bidding on public contracts for three years. This example underscores the difficulties that China faces in free societies with strong regulatory frameworks.

The EU and its individual member states require public tenders and transparent procurement, another benchmark that BRI projects often fail to meet. The one major BRI project in the region to be implemented partially in an EU member state is the Budapest-to-Belgrade high-speed railway designed as a part of a "land-bridge corridor" to connect the Chinese-operated Greek port of Piraeus with Central Europe. The Hungarian segment has been beset by delays and controversy. Both its economic viability and its financing by credit from Chinese banks have been questioned. Feasibility studies and other documentation remain classified, prompting the European Council to launch an official investigation in 2017 that remains in limbo to this day.[7]

It is easier for the PRC to push BRI infrastructure projects in the western Balkan countries outside the EU because their access to EU financing is limited and their regulatory frameworks are looser. Many of these projects have invited controversy similar to BRI projects in other parts of the world.[8] Arguably, the biggest scandal in Central and Eastern Europe has been the Kichevo-Ohrid Highway project in North Macedonia. Construction began in 2014 and was supposed to finish by 2018. Yet it is still not complete as of mid-2022, and its costs have ballooned well above original projections. In 2015, tapes were leaked of government ministers, including then-premier Nikola Gruevski, negotiating multimillion-euro bribes with Sinohydro, the Chinese contractor for the project. The resulting uproar toppled the Gruevski government and eventually led to a criminal case against the prime minister, who absconded to Hungary, where he was granted political asylum in late 2018, apparently by the personal intervention of Prime Minister Viktor Orbán.[9]

Even by the murky standards of Chinese state-owned enterprises (SOEs), Sinohydro is no ordinary company. It is an offshoot of the now-defunct Ministry of Hydroenergy, where many top CCP officials (including former president Hu Jintao) got their start, and is a major BRI contractor globally. As such, Sinohydro has been at the center of multiple controversies and was suspended by the World Bank in 2016 for fraudulent practices in the Philippines, Malaysia, and several African countries.[10] Transparency International's 2005 global corruption report listed one of Sinohydro's BRI projects, the Bakun Dam in Sarawak, Malaysia, as a "monument of corruption" that funneled money to a timber contractor who was a friend of Sarawak's governor. There have been similar cases in Georgia, Venezuela, and elsewhere.[11] The corruption model is almost always the same: an overpriced megaproject financed by a PRC policy bank, whose fat margin is divided between the contractor and local politicians. The 16+1 initiative was China's opening for such opportunities in Europe.

The Gruevski corruption case in North Macedonia suggests a pattern of Chinese "economic diplomacy" providing cover for high-level political corruption throughout the world or at least along the Belt and Road. This kind of political corruption appears to be inherent in the CCP's projection of influence, but it is not always viewed that way. During a recent survey concerning foreign influence in the western Balkans, informed respondents (mostly journalists) could easily identify incidents of Russian and even Turkish meddling, but insisted that the PRC was only interested in business. They did report the Kichevo-Ohrid Highway scandal but tended to explain it away as just another case of the business corruption that is endemic to that part of the world.[12]

Such (mis)perceptions illustrate a vulnerability of open societies in the face of Chinese "economic diplomacy." A corruption case involving a Chinese SOE on one side and a foreign prime minister and his government on the other is hardly a common crime. Many observers may fail to grasp that this kind of "strategic corruption" is an inherent feature of CCP power projection. China may look like a market economy in some respects. But ultimately, the party controls the economy—just like everything in the "East, West, South, North, and the Center," to use a phrase of Chairman Mao's that Xi Jinping inserted into the CCP Constitution. Any company in China, not just SOEs, must do the party's bidding when called upon, a duty now enshrined in binding legislation, including the 2017 National Intelligence Law. A foreign leader compromised by a Chinese enterprise, state-owned or private, will likely become a PRC asset.

Making Friends in High Places

Elite capture is a process whereby a foreign power "captures" local business, political, community and other leaders to influence their attitudes and actions, typically to manipulate the social, economic, and political institutions that they lead or represent. Doing so allows the foreign power to repurpose agencies of democratic governance into tools for achieving its own policy objectives, even if these are at odds with the agency's original purpose.

Foreign governments can capture local elites by various means, outright corruption being just one of many. A more subtle way is by "making friends" through united front work, establishing an asymmetric relationship manipulated by the CCP influence bureaucracy through a mix of incentives in which financial gain, ideological inclinations, naïveté, and other factors may interact to varying degrees. The CCP's International Liaison Department specifically carries out united front work with foreign political elites, but any other PRC institution, including a nominally private business, can step in to assist. Typical targets are foreign national political leaders and leaders in international organizations.

There are many fine examples, but perhaps the most instructive is the story of the now defunct, nominally private Chinese conglomerate CEFC China Energy and its inroads into the Czech and other governments (notably, Uganda's and Chad's) as well as the United Nations. In its heyday, CEFC combined many elements of influence peddling in a concentrated form over a relatively short period of time, with phenomenal success at first and an even more spectacular downfall in the end.

CEFC's business model was an investment-fraud scheme based on easy access to credit from Chinese state-owned banks, particularly the China Development Bank. CEFC also had close ties to hard-liners in the People's Liberation Army and military intelligence. Ostensibly an energy company, CEFC also ran its own eponymous think tank. Under the leadership of its secretary general, Patrick (Chi-ping) Ho, former home secretary in the first post-handover Hong Kong government, the CEFC think tank devoted itself to preaching CCP policies and concepts, including the Belt and Road Initiative, on the global conference circuit and in the United Nations, in particular, where it enjoyed associated status with the Economic and Social Council, which among other things provided CEFC with unfettered access to the UN building in Manhattan and thus key UN players.

In August 2015, then–UN General Assembly (UNGA) president Sam Kutesa of Uganda made CEFC chairman Ye Jianming his "special honorary advisor" for a US$500,000 kickback that was wired to his private account by Patrick Ho, according to a 2017 U.S. federal court indictment.[13] A few months before that, in April 2015, Ye Jianming had become a "special honorary advisor" to Czech president Miloš Zeman, who had in 2013 initiated an ill-advised turn in foreign policy toward China.[14]

CEFC was virtually unknown in the Czech Republic in early 2015, and little known even in China. Zeman made Ye Jianming an advisor in April

2015, several months before the company suddenly entered the country with a series of high-profile acquisitions, including prime real estate in the historic center of Prague—essentially vanity investments and status symbols. With Zeman's support, CEFC was hailed as the flagship of the coming wave of Chinese investment.

All doors were open to the company and its chairman. CEFC established its European subsidiary in Prague, but rather than pursuing business opportunities, it started hiring from among the powerful and well connected. The company put former politicians and high-ranking civil servants directly on its payroll. Many of these figures simultaneously held advisory positions in the government and president's office. At times, it looked as if CEFC was fusing with the Czech state. Miroslav Sklenář, originally head of protocol at Prague Castle, went through the revolving door between the executive office and CEFC three times in two years.

In March 2016, Xi Jinping's only stop in Europe *en route* to the United States was Prague. President Zeman and the Czech government made every effort to accommodate Xi, including restricting protests against his visit. Zeman declared that investment deals signed during the visit would amount to a hundred-billion Czech crowns within the first year (a year on, only about 2 percent of that amount had materialized). In October 2017, CEFC managed to bring the Czech diplomat Štefan Füle, a former European commissioner for enlargement and European neighborhood policy, into its fold.[15] By that time, however, CEFC's free ride in the Czech Republic, and more broadly, was about to end.

In November 2017, Patrick Ho was arrested in New York on corruption and money-laundering charges. In March 2018, Ye Jianming himself was disappeared in China by the CCP disciplinary apparatus and has not been heard from since. CEFC, unable to raise enough credit to offset old debts, quickly collapsed. This cautionary tale of Chinese political corruption made headlines around the world, but had different repercussions in different places.

The news had little impact in Chad and Uganda, whose presidents Patrick Ho, on behalf of CEFC, had bribed along with Ugandan foreign minister Sam Kutesa (previously the UNGA president) in a complicated exchange that included oil rights in Chad and the promise of joint ventures in Uganda. In the United Nations, the scandal was met with thundering silence. CEFC's accreditation with the Economic and Social Council was terminated only in 2019, by which time its think tank was defunct. UN secretary-general Antonio Guterres has yet to order an audit, even though the Patrick Ho–CEFC scandal was just the latest in a series of high-level bribery cases within the organization. In May 2017, Macau tycoon Ng Lap Seng received a four-year prison sentence for bribing John Ashe of Antigua, who preceded Kutesa as UNGA president—another case that involved CEFC. Amazingly, the company had also cultivated Ashe's predecessor, Vuk Jeremiæ of Serbia, and supported his think tank, the Center for International Cooperation and Sustainable Development.

Borrowed Boats in Muddy Waters

Making friends among foreign political elites through united front work, "economic diplomacy," corruption, and other means allows Beijing to repurpose coopted institutions for its own agenda, undermining democratic systems from within. To win over often skeptical foreign audiences, the CCP relies on external propaganda via multiple channels.

Since August 2013, the CCP leadership has been calling for increased "discursive power" and admonishing the Chinese media to "tell the China story well." The propaganda system has been investing heavily in modern electronic media networks such as the China Global Television Network and China Radio International (CRI) to compete with more established television and radio networks broadcasting to the world from democratic countries. Given that Chinese state-controlled media are widely viewed with suspicion by Western audiences accustomed to more media freedom and diversity, however, these efforts are having only limited impact.

A more efficient approach to external propaganda is to "launder" it through local voices that appear more authentic. In CCP jargon, localizing external propaganda through native entities is called "borrowing a boat to reach the sea." The most typical way of "borrowing boats" has been to place *China Daily* inserts in Western newspapers and magazines, including the *New York Times, Wall Street Journal, Washington Post,* and the U.K. *Telegraph.*[16] The same inserts have also appeared in English-language papers in other countries, such as Nepal's *Kathmandu Post.*

There are, however, more sophisticated ways to "borrow a boat." China can buy boats outright—purchasing media outlets either directly or through intermediaries, as was the case with a global network of radio stations (in 2015, more than thirty in fourteen countries) that were secretly majority-owned by CRI, the state broadcaster, and began airing Beijing-friendly reporting.[17] The CCP also sometimes packages its messages for foreign audiences with the cooperation of friends in local foreign media, or even by pressuring businesses with interests in China to do this kind of work in their home countries. Packaging (or "laundering") messages this way is more effective than the inserts, which are widely understood to be foreign propaganda.

In Central and Eastern Europe, such efforts have been documented in most detail in the Czech Republic.[18] When Czech public opinion turned against China after the collapse of CEFC in 2018, pro-Beijing forces took the counteroffensive, attempting to do damage control by manipulating the media and public discourse. These efforts were directed mainly at Project Sinopsis, seen as the driving force behind the backlash against Chinese influence in the country.[19]

For example, Home Credit, the consumer-loans subsidiary of PPF Group, the biggest Czech financial conglomerate, mounted a hidden publicity campaign in 2019 to "rationalize" the debate about China in the Czech Republic.[20] Home Credit, which has considerable investments in China, hired C&B Reputation Management, a Czech PR firm known for "guerrilla marketing" during election campaigns, to place more PRC-friendly content in the Czech media. C&B invoices and timesheets for this work were leaked to the Czech online news site Aktuálné, which published and reported on them. The documents revealed that C&B helped to set up and run an ostensibly independent think tank called Sinoskop, intended to be a counterweight to Project Sinopsis that would influence the public debate in favor of China.

A textbook example of a "borrowed boat" in the Czech Republic came to light in January 2020.[21] In the early 2000s, the famed newspaper *Literární noviny* (Literary News), once associated with the reform movement of the 1960s, fell on hard times financially and in 2009 was acquired by Miroslav Pavel, a former spokesperson for the last two communist-era prime ministers.

The new owner gradually turned the paper into a platform for CCP soft propaganda. In 2017, Pavel established a formal relationship with the

Chinese daily *Guangming Ribao* and its content-sharing platform, Reading China Plus. Under the cooperation agreement, *Literární noviny* has been publishing translated articles compiled by *Guangming Ribao* in Beijing, delivering Chinese state-controlled content straight to Czech audiences. *Literární noviny* has, in consultation with *Guangming Ribao* and the Chinese embassy in Prague, also been preparing special "dossiers" on various topics. Many of these are devoted to Chinese culture, but some cover more-contested issues, such as the covid-19 pandemic or the 2022 Winter Olympics in Beijing.

Using *Literární noviny* as a "borrowed boat" to deliver content from China's state-controlled media is a particularly ingenious way to launder CCP propaganda through local voices. Many Czechs harbor vague memories of the paper's past glory, without awareness of its recent transformation. As direct propaganda is often buried in and among more-neutral "cultural" content, unsuspecting readers might not notice the links to Chinese state-controlled media. Interestingly, *Guangming Ribao,* originally a paper appealing to cultural and intellectual circles in China, has always been known to provide cover for intelligence operations abroad. *Literární noviny* publisher Miroslav Pavel, meanwhile, had himself been recruited by communist Czechoslovakia's secret police (StB) in the 1970s, and many of *Literární noviny*'s authors have similar backgrounds.[22]

Literární noviny's cooperation with *Guangming Ribao* was eventually exposed in January 2020 and discussed in the Czech media, just as was Home Credit's campaign to "rationalize" Czech discourse on China. Exposing authoritarian efforts to distort the information space is the best way to blunt sharp power. Such revelations transform open information systems' vulnerability to PRC media manipulation into resilience. Propaganda and disinformation, once revealed, become counterproductive, inoculating societies against this kind of interference.

Resilience Through Openness

Democratic and Leninist systems each have their respective strengths and weaknesses. And in both systems, the strengths can turn into weaknesses and vice-versa. The openness of democracies, normally an asset, may become a vulnerability when confronted with centrally controlled, laser-focused sharp power. Likewise, the ability to mobilize resources centrally and wield them against an opponent is the greatest advantage of one-party systems. But that advantage, too, can become a liability.

Democracy arguably remains the more attractive system, assuming that most people would prefer to have a say in how their societies are run and organized. To subvert such aspirations, the CCP has relied mostly on cooptation, corruption, propaganda, and, more recently, economic coercion. To be effective, cooptation and propaganda need subliminal cooperation from their intended targets; these weapons will only work if we allow them, whether consciously or unwittingly. United front work thrives on our ignorance and failure to imagine that such a mechanism can succeed.

The basic asymmetry in the battle between open and closed political systems lies in the realm of knowledge and awareness. The CCP has always known that its one-party system is not compatible with "bourgeois" democracy. The West, however, believed until recently in the socioeconomic theory of convergence and that the potential for growth and development through engagement with the outside world would drive China to change. But the comrades in Beijing have always been clear that they do not want to change, that "peaceful evolution" is anathema to them.[23] And because they understand the fundamental incompatibility (or "systemic rivalry," as the EU now phrases it) between the two systems, they also know that gaining a bigger say in the world will require modifying—or conditioning—the competing system, turning its comparative advantages, such as openness, into liabilities, such as complacency.

To do this, the CCP no longer needs to convert anyone to communism or Leninism. The party knows that it will get nowhere singing its own praises or trying to convince outsiders of its system's merits. The PRC regime understands that, in the spirit of the "grand united front" (global cooptation), it will have a better chance at success by allowing other societies in the "human community of shared destiny" to retain their democratic institutions, such as parliaments and elections, while carefully repurposing them through united front work to align with the party's agenda. As exemplified by what has happened in Hong Kong—once the embodiment of coexistence between the two systems—this means coopting, subverting, and hollowing them out from within.

Democratic societies' resilience against this kind of future lies in their ability to wield their own "magic weapon"—their openness, which happens also to be the very thing that makes them most vulnerable. In open societies, we can freely research, analyze, and publicize CCP sharp-power manipulations occurring in our societies. The ensuing public awareness is often enough to thwart CCP efforts and can sometimes even result in undermining the original CCP goals. It is only if we stop being vigilant and remain passive, complacent, and ignorant that our openness will become a liability.

In democratic, pluralistic, and open societies, the CCP style of cooptation—"making friends" through united front work, propaganda, and corruption—faces an uphill battle. It is difficult to achieve the kind of unquestioned "friendship" that the CCP demands in free societies, because there are always people talking back. Leaders can be captured and institutions (sometimes) repurposed, but there will always be a backlash generated by the underlying political plurality. And since the CCP cannot tolerate the slightest dissent, a minor incident can snowball and bring the mighty façade down.

The Czech Republic is again a good example. President Zeman gave Beijing his unconditional friendship in 2013, and the Czech government followed suit until the October 2021 parliamentary elections (seen as a victory over populism). But the Czech Republic is more than the president and parliament. The words and actions of local politicians can also affect relations with the hypersensitive PRC regime. It took little provocation by Prague mayor Zdenek Hrib in early 2019 to send the friendship into a downward spiral and eventual collapse. First, Hrib refused the Chinese ambassador's request to expel Taiwan's representative from a New Year's party. Next, Hrib insisted on removing a clause in the 2016 sister-cities agreement between the Czech and Chinese capitals that avowed Prague's support for the "One China" policy. This immediately prompted Beijing to retaliate, scrapping the treaty entirely and threatening to cancel a visit to China by Prague's orchestra, which likened the move to something that the former Czechoslovak communist regime would have done. But the PRC's measures only provoked more ire and did not stop the mayor from later flying the Tibetan flag from the city hall, a tradition begun during Václav Havel's presidency and stopped only under Hrib's immediate predecessor.[24]

Truly open societies will assert themselves against CCP manipulations, but they must first overcome complacency and ignorance. It is the role of civil society to wake up the people and the politicians by channeling reliable yet easy-to-understand information and analysis into the public discourse, fostering debate, and stimulating resilience through openness and transparency.

The relatively new phenomenon of economic coercion, especially in the metastatic form now seen in Beijing's punitive actions again Lithuania, will require new defensive tactics. The politically motivated, undeclared sanctions against open, export-oriented economies present a threat that only a collective international response—restructuring supply chains, for example—can mitigate. Over the last two decades, we allowed our economic openness to become a vulnerability. We now know that trade and investment are as liable to manipulation as are our political systems, and we must respond accordingly.

Notes

The research for this work was supported by the European Regional Development Fund through the project "Creativity and Adaptability as Conditions of the Success of Europe in an Interrelated World" (No. CZ.02.1.01/0.0/0.0/16_019/0 000734).

1. "Selected Works of Mao Tse-tung: Introducing the Communist," 4 October 1939, *www.marxists.org/reference/archive/mao/selected-works/volume-2/mswv2_20.htm.*

2. Gerry Groot, "The CCP's Grand United Front Abroad," *Sinopsis,* 24 September 2019, *https://sinopsis.cz/en/the-ccps-grand-united-front-abroad.*

3. It was briefly known as 17+1, from when Greece joined in 2019 until Lithuania left in 2021.

4. Personal exchange with a member of his delegation. Similarly, President Zeman reportedly later gifted to visiting Chinese leader Xi Jinping a pair of shoes—the one item explicitly mentioned in basic etiquette guides as the example of a wrong gift in China.

5. "Chinese Landmark Concept Put into UN Resolution for First Time," Xinhua, 11 February 2017, *www.xinhuanet.com/english/2017-02/11/c_136049319.htm.*

6. A phrase the then–U.S. deputy secretary of state Robert Zoellick famously used in 2005.

7. Wade Shepard, "Another Silk Road Fiasco? China's Belgrade to Budapest

High-Speed Rail Line Is Probed by Brussels," *Forbes*, 25 February 2017, *www.forbes. com/sites/wadeshepard/2017/02/25/another-silk-road-fiasco-chinas-belgrade-to-budapest-high-speed-rail-line-is-probed-by-brussels/?sh=4d3e423f3c00.*

8. Bojan Stojkovski et al., "China in the Balkans: Controversy and Cost," *Balkan Insight*, 15 December 2021, *https://balkaninsight.com/2021/12/15/china-in-the-balkans-controversy-and-cost.*

9. Shaun Walker, "Anti-Asylum Orbán Makes Exception for a Friend in Need," *Guardian*, 20 November 2018, *www.theguardian.com/world/2018/nov/20/anti-asylum-orban-makes-exception-for-a-friend-in-need.*

10. World Bank Group, *2016 Integrity Vice Presidency Annual Update: Our Development Resources Must Reach the Intended Beneficiaries*, Annual Update Integrity Vice Presidency (INT), *http://documents.worldbank.org/curated/en/330521476191334505/pdf/INT-FY16-Annual-Update-10062016.pdf.*

11. "The China Deals: Agreements That Have Undermined Venezuelan Democracy," Transparencia Venezuela, August 2020, *https://transparencia. org.ve/project/negocios-chinos/.* Ia Asatiani, "Multiple Violations Don't Stop Sinohydro Tender Success," 23 July 2020, IFact, *https://ifact.ge/en/multiple-violations-dont-stop-sinohydro-tender-success.*

12. Personal communications with participants of the Western Balkans at the Crossroads project; see *www.pssi.cz/projects/11-western-balkans-at-the-crossroads.*

13. See the 18 December 2017 indictment at *www.documentcloud.org/documents/4359469-Patrick-Ho-Indictment.html.*

14. For more on CEFC's activities in the Czech Republic, see Martin Hala, "United Front Work by Other Means: China's 'Economic Diplomacy' in Central and Eastern Europe," *Jamestown China Brief*, 9 May 2019, *https://jamestown. org/program/united-front-work-by-other-means-chinas-economic-diplomacy-in-central-and-eastern-europe/*; and Project Sinopsis's Czech website, *Sinopsis.cz.*

15. "Diplomat Füle dostal vysoký post v čínské CEFC" [Diplomat Füle awarded high post in Chinese CEFC], *Echo24.cz*, 24 October 2017, *https://echo24. cz/a/pA4P6/diplomat-fule-dostal-vysoky-post-v-cinske-cefc.*

16. Louisa Lim and Julia Bergin, "Inside China's Audacious Global Propaganda Campaign," *Guardian*, 7 December 2018, *www.theguardian.com/news/2018/dec/07/china-plan-for-global-media-dominance-propaganda-xi-jinping.*

17. Koh Gui Qing and John Shiffman, "Beijing's Covert Radio Network Airs China-Friendly News Across Washington, and the World," Reuters, 2 November 2015, *www.reuters.com/investigates/special-report/china-radio.*

18. Martin Hala, "Making Foreign Companies Serve China: Outsourcing Propaganda to Local Entities in the Czech Republic," *Jamestown China Brief,* 17 January 2020, *https://jamestown.org/program/making-foreign-companies-serve-china-outsourcing-propaganda-to-local-entities-in-the-czech-republic.*

19. Project Sinopsis was founded in 2016 by the author of this essay.

20. Lukáš Valášek and Jan Horák, "Kellnerův Home Credit platil kampaò na podporu rudé Číny" [Kellner's Home Credit paid a campaign to support Red China], *Aktuálné,* 10 December 2019, *https://zpravy.aktualne.cz/domaci/home-credit-ppf-kampan-cina-pr-agentura-cb/r~5f0774e01a6111ea8d520cc47ab5f122.*

21. Lukáš Valášek and Daniel Konrád, "Literární noviny šíří Čínskou propagandu. A Česko jim dává statisícové dotace" [Literary news spreads Chinese propaganda. And the Czech Republic gives them hundreds of thousands in subsidies], *Aktuálné,* 27 January 2020, *https://zpravy.aktualne.cz/domaci/literarni-noviny-cina-spoluprace/rf68e6648316811eaa24cac1f6b220ee8.*

22. Martin Hála, Filip Jirouš, and Ondřej Klimeš, "Borrowed Boats Capsizing: State Security Ties to CCP Propaganda Laundering Rile Czech Public," *Jamestown China Brief,* 3 December 2021, *https://jamestown.org/program/borrowed-boats-capsizing-state-security-ties-to-ccp-propaganda-laundering-rile-czech-public.*

23. See John S. Van Oudenaren, "Beijing's Peaceful Evolution Paranoia," *Diplomat,* 1 September 2015, *https://thediplomat.com/2015/09/beijings-peaceful-evolution-paranoia.*

24. Robert Tait, "Zdeněk Hřib: The Czech Mayor Who Defied China," *Guardian,* 3 July 2019; Marc Santora, "The Broken Promise of a Panda: How Prague's Relations with Beijing Soured," *New York Times,* 23 November 2019; Rob Schmitz, "Czech-Chinese Ties Strained as Prague Stands Up to Beijing," NPR, 30 October 2019, *www.npr.org/2019/10/30/774054035/czech-chinese-ties-are-affected-as-prague-stands-up-to-beijing.*

CHAPTER EIGHT

Taiwan's Democracy Under Fire

KETTY W. CHEN

T HE REPUBLIC OF CHINA (ROC), or Taiwan as it is more widely known, is currently among Asia's most vibrant democracies. Its Freedom House (FH) score for 2021 (the latest year available) is 94 out of a possible 100, a figure exceeded in the entire Asia-Pacific region only by New Zealand, Australia, and Japan. In FH's "Freedom on the Net" survey, Taiwan ranked fifth of the seventy countries studied last year (the first in which it was included in the report). Only Iceland, Estonia, Canada, and Costa Rica were reckoned to have a freer online environment. The Economist Intelligence Unit (EIU) in its 2021 Democracy Index ranks Taiwan ahead of Japan and South Korea as the leading "full democracy" in Asia. Globally, the EIU ranks Taiwan eighth, up three places from 2020 with an 8.99 on a ten-point scale.[1] The people of Taiwan are proud of their achievement in free self-government, which has been the work of the three and a half decades since democratization began in 1987. According to the latest annual poll of the Taiwanese people by the Taiwan Foundation for Democracy, nearly 80 percent believe that whatever problems their democratic system may have, it remains the best for Taiwan.[2]

Looming over Taiwan's success, however, is the Chinese Communist Party (CCP) and the authoritarian grip it holds on the People's Republic of China (PRC) just a short distance away across the Taiwan Strait. Although the PRC has never governed Taiwan for a single day, it claims that the island is an unalienable part of its territory and has been since the dawn of history. The CCP vows that it will do whatever it takes to annex Asia's most democratic nation. Because Taiwan is of special concern to the PRC, it has long been a prime target of CCP "united front" sharp-power and information operations. The CCP has tested many new methods and tactics on

Taiwan before trying them elsewhere. Taiwan's experiences while battling such intrusions, therefore, may hold useful lessons for other democracies if and when they too find themselves exposed to influence efforts mounted by authoritarian regimes.

The CCP continues to launch influence operations against Taiwan, often using proxies to serve PRC aims. Among the factors working in Taiwan's favor as it resists these efforts is its robust and vibrant civil society, and that civil society's commitment to defending the island nation's democracy. The event that first made PRC influence operations a topic of special interest to Taiwanese civil society and NGOs was the national election of January 2016. In that balloting, the former law professor Tsai Ing-wen of the Democratic Progressive Party (DPP) was elected president with 56 percent of the vote in a three-way contest. The PRC's efforts to penetrate and undermine Taiwan's political institutions, society, election-integrity procedures, and civic organizations formed a major part of Beijing's overall strategy toward Taiwan—a strategy, moreover, whose means had been put in place before Tsai, when her Beijing-friendly predecessor Ma Ying-jeou had held office.

According to a study by the Varieties of Democracy (V-Dem) project based at the University of Gothenburg in Sweden, Taiwan exceeds every other country in the world when it comes to the amount of false information that foreign governments disseminate within its borders via social media. It has held that unenviable number-one position for nine years running. Taiwanese political scientist Wang Yi-ting, a contributor to V-Dem's Digital Society Project (the study's source), noted that while it is hard to pinpoint the origin of false information, the PRC is "known to make extensive use of internal and external propaganda."[3]

Beijing uses its methods of encroachment not only when Taiwan is holding elections, but also during ordinary times. The CCP's efforts, however, have fallen flat. Neither Beijing's "carrots" (various mainland employment, investment, and academic opportunities offered to Taiwanese) nor its "sticks" (economic pressure and coercion wielded against everyone from businesspeople to celebrities to ordinary tourists) have succeeded in making Taiwan's populace feel more favorable toward the PRC regime, or intimidated by it. The strongest evidence of this may have been President Tsai's ability to win a second term by a comfortable margin in January 2020 despite an intense CCP pressure campaign against her.[4]

After seeing its initial (mostly economic) threats and enticements fail,

Beijing turned to manipulating information as a way to affect Taiwan's politics. Early in her term, President Tsai pushed through controversial changes to pension and labor laws that caused her approval rating to drop. Seeing an opportunity, the CCP ramped up disinformation efforts that contributed to DPP losses in the November 2018 local elections. The president's party lost control of most of the municipalities that it had been governing. The highest-profile defeat came in Kaohsiung, Taiwan's second-largest city, where Kuomintang (KMT) populist Han Kuo-yu won the mayor's race. According to Professor Caroline Lin of National Chengchi University, PRC information warfare was of substantial help to the KMT candidate in Kaohsiung. Her study of online "content farms" and Taiwanese social-media platforms found that the former widely distributed false information via the latter. The "fake news" that was spread included fabricated quotes said to be from DPP political rallies as well as a charge that that the DPP mayoral candidate had been wearing a hidden earpiece during a candidates' debate.[5]

The PRC information-warfare campaign that targeted Taiwan in 2018 was a wake-up call for civil society. The Taiwan Foundation for Democracy, the Taiwan Factcheck Center, the Open Culture Foundation, and other NGOs began working systematically to study, track, and raise awareness of Beijing's sharp-power efforts in Taiwan and elsewhere. By the time of the next general election in early 2020, Beijing's political warfare was not only falling flat but backfiring. After four years of intense influence operations and sharp-power efforts, Tsai won reelection with a record number of votes. She topped eight million in a country (current population 23.5 million) whose democratic history had seen no previous contender for the presidency gain more than 7.7 million.

Tsai Ing-wen's party, the DPP, was founded in 1986 as President Chiang Ching-kuo (1978–88) was relaxing the KMT grip on power that dated from the Nationalists' loss of the mainland civil war to Mao Zedong's Communists and "Great Retreat" to Taiwan in the late 1940s. For four decades, the KMT had ruled via a state of exception, having enacted "Temporary Provisions" in 1948 that suspended the Republic of China's 1947 Constitution and instituted martial law under Chiang Ching-kuo's father, Chiang Kai-shek. Throughout the Cold War, the People's Republic of China on the mainland and the Republic of China on Taiwan each claimed to be the sole legitimate government of China. Each also had its own version of single-party rule under the CCP and the KMT, respectively.

In 1971, the ROC found itself expelled from the United Nations so that the PRC could be included. In 1979, developing a policy course that had begun seven years earlier with President Richard M. Nixon's landmark visit to Beijing, the United States severed its official diplomatic relationship with Taipei and placed relations instead on the footing of the Taiwan Relations Act of 1979. Pressed at home by democracy advocates and feeling diplomatically isolated even as actual and potential allies told him that he needed to liberalize, Chiang Ching-kuo began to relax controls and allow more political participation and competition. Martial law was lifted in 1987. In March 1990, a large student protest drive known as the "Wild Lily Movement" called for the president and vice-president to be directly elected and said that all national lawmakers—some of whom had held their seats unchallenged since mainland days in the 1940s—should be required to face the voters in a free election.

The Wild Lily protests went on for six days. President Lee Teng-hui (1988–2000) received fifty student representatives at his formal office, expressed support for their demands, and promised democratization. By the middle of the year, reforms had begun. The Wild Lily Movement marked a turning point in Taiwan's transition to democracy. In 1996, Lee himself would become Taiwan's first popularly elected president.

The DPP spent the 1990s vetting candidates and competing in local elections. In 2000, it captured the presidency with Chen Shui-bian atop the ticket (he won a three-way race with 39.3 percent), though it did not obtain a majority in the Legislative Yuan. The DPP holds strongly to the position that Taiwan is an independent, sovereign state whose official name is the Republic of China, and is not a part of the PRC. The KMT also affirms ROC sovereignty and statehood, but adds the view that there is nonetheless "One China"—albeit a single China subject to "Two Interpretations." Speaking as president of the PRC, Xi Jinping would reject the KMT's model in his 2 January 2019 "Message to Compatriots in Taiwan," insisting instead that only Beijing's favored "one country, two systems" doctrine was admissible as a basis for Taiwan's future.[6]

President Tsai immediately dismissed Xi's attempt to apply to Taiwan the "one country, two systems" formula that Beijing had first devised to deal with Hong Kong after the 1997 handover from Britain, and then had used as cover while stripping away Hong Kong's freedoms and subjugating it to CCP rule. Under the Tsai administration, Taiwan has prioritized its relationship with the United States and other democracies. The KMT, for its part, continues to view strong economic and cultural ties with the PRC—bolstered by a hesitancy to press Taiwan's participation in international organizations—as the key to prosperity. The DPP and the KMT generally take different stances on domestic issues. National and even local elections, however, are coming to hinge not on domestic matters but on questions surrounding Taiwan's relationship with the PRC.

The Election Studies Center of National Chengchi University has for thirty years asked respondents to its island-wide surveys how they identify themselves. The share of people choosing "Taiwanese" more than tripled between 1992 and 2021—going from 17.8 to 62.3 percent. Over that same span, those who describe themselves as both "Taiwanese and Chinese" have fallen in share from 46.4 to 31.7 percent, while those who choose "Chinese" have gone from a quarter of the populace (25.5 percent) to a tiny 2.8 percent.[7] The young are especially likely to call themselves "Taiwanese" without qualification. As these figures suggest, President Xi may dream of a unified Chinese nation that includes Taiwan, but reality is increasingly at odds with that vision.

The PRC's attempts to wage political warfare on Taiwan by turning the island democracy's openness against itself have geostrategic as well as nationalistic motives. Beijing sees Taiwan as a disturbingly near-in base for U.S. influence in the Asia-Pacific region. Under the Taiwan Relations Act, the United States is committed to a "peaceful resolution" of Taiwan's future status, and to providing Taiwan with the weapons that it needs to defend itself. As the PRC has sped up its efforts to replace the United States as the world's superpower, Washington has responded by (among other things) taking stronger and more vocal stands in support of Taiwan's democracy, and by encouraging closer ties between Taiwan and its fellow democracies. The PRC condemns all this as U.S. interference in Chinese "domestic affairs." Beijing also continues to pressure and threaten the very few countries that still maintain formal diplomatic relations with Taiwan. When President Tsai took office in 2016, there were twenty-two countries that had full diplomatic ties with Taipei; now there are fourteen.

Taiwan has forged ahead nonetheless, however, building solid relationships with democratic countries around the world. Since the start of the covid-19 pandemic, Taiwan's friendly relations with Central and Eastern Europe have flourished in a context of mutual aid regarding vaccines and other medical supplies. Since early 2020, under the "Taiwan Can Help" campaign, Taiwan donated 51 million face masks worldwide, sending more than ten million to the United States and seven million to Europe. In addition, Taiwan donated rapid antigen tests, oxygen concentrators, N95 respirators, hazmed suits, and other items of PPE (Personal Protective Equipment). When Taiwan had trouble procuring covid vaccines, other democracies stepped in to help. The United States donated four-million doses, while the Czech Republic, Japan, Poland, and Slovenia sent millions more.

Taiwan's vibrant democracy serves as a constant reminder of what the PRC is not. The reality of democratic Taiwan gives the lie to the CCP's narrative that liberal democracy is a purely Western product that cannot work in a Chinese or Asian culture. (The PRC likes to call itself a democracy, but always adds "with Chinese characteristics"—a portentous phrase that is meant to encode the many ways in which the one-party rule of the CCP differs starkly from any model of liberal, constitutional democracy.) Taiwan's democracy now serves as a model for countries throughout the region: The Taiwanese experience and the vibrancy of Taiwan's civic life show that an Asian country can be not only a democracy, but a prosperous, peaceful, and stable one as well.

Taiwan versus CCP Sharp Power

The terms political warfare, influence operations, and sharp power all refer to a set of methods that the CCP uses on democratic societies in pursuit of its diplomatic objectives. The CCP is always trying to shape the world environment in its own favor while penetrating its target countries' institutions and damaging their social cohesion in order to make them less able to resist CCP pressure and influence.

Amid the current global contest between surging authoritarianism and backsliding democracy, democratic Taiwan stands in the front rank of countries targeted by the CCP's sharp-power methods. The PRC's continual claims that Taiwan is and always has been an unalienable part of its territory reflect a Xi Jinping regime that is becoming increasingly impatient and agitated regarding Taiwan.

The sharp-power campaign aimed at Taiwan can be seen as serving five purposes. The first is to corrode and manipulate democratic institutions, including elections of all kinds (local and national as well as recalls and referendums) so that these institutions lose public trust. The second is to undermine the general confidence and morale of Taiwan's people, leaving them feeling isolated and helpless. (Efforts to make the Taiwanese feel that becoming part of the PRC is inevitable serve this aim.) The third purpose is to intensify divisions and turn Taiwanese against one another. The fourth is to coopt any opinion leaders and influencers (whether politicians, retired military officers, civil servants, journalists, academics, professionals, or businesspeople) who can be induced to mouth Beijing's line and serve its goals. The fifth and final aim is to cow anyone who might criticize and oppose the CCP into silence and retreat.

One of the CCP's favorite ploys is to bypass the central government (and hence the DPP) in order to go straight at "locals" (whether non-DPP municipal governments and politicians or grassroots organizations in fields such as farming, fishing, and tourism) whom Beijing may feel can be more easily swayed toward its ends. Towns and villages across Taiwan have agricultural or fishing associations with their own buildings where local residents gather as part of the process of earning a living, and which can also act as mills for rumor and gossip. The heads of such organizations are prime CCP cooptation targets, since they typically come from respected, deep-rooted families and wield strong influence. The united front strategy tries to link Taiwanese associations with PRC counterparts that are of course arms of the Communist party-state and its propaganda apparatus.

In addition to face-to-face institutions such as these village cooperatives, both traditional and social media have become hunting grounds for CCP sharp power. Disinformation campaigns seek to heighten polarization and undermine support for Taiwan's elected government. Information warfare is nothing new, of course, but the internet age has brought it to a new level and arguably made it more urgently potent than before. Beijing, at any rate, seems to think so: Information operations are its favored means for trying to destabilize Taiwan.

Stepping Up the Information War

From late 2017 on, as tensions in the Taiwan Strait grew, rumors and fake news flooded Taiwanese social media. The PRC's disinformation attacked government institutions, elected officials, civil society, even democratic values themselves. In early 2020 came false reports that Taiwan would soon face a toilet-paper shortage because the raw materials were being diverted into the production of face masks. Digital Minister Audrey Tang, a former "civic hacker" fond of employing "humor over rumor" to correct misinformation, responded with a now-famous meme reminding people that "you only have one pair of buttocks" and explaining (accurately) that toilet paper and face masks are made from different materials with different supply chains.[8]

Amusing examples aside, Beijing's information manipulations have three goals that are not so humorous. The first is to paint the Tsai Ing-wen administration as a collection of inept adventurers, and to tarnish the president's image. Hence the doctored video that circulated online purporting to show Tsai spitting on the national shrine of the ROC war dead in Taipei during a September 2018 ceremony.

The second goal is to exploit and exacerbate contradictions and conflicts within society. In particular, this meant spreading the ideas that the government fails at health measures (such as covid response) and at handling Taiwan's economy. Variations on the "ghost island" meme depict Tsai's Taiwan as a place of chaos and despair that needs a "savior" such as KMT candidate Han Kuo-yu to pull it out of the mire. (Han himself had road-tested a version of this when he ran for mayor of Kaohsiung, painting the city as impoverished and suggesting that selling goods to the PRC was the way out.) The third goal is distraction: Make the Taiwanese authorities chase down rumors until they have little time and energy left for anything else.

The internet is the amplifier for sowing uncertainty and division. When Typhoon Jebi hit Osaka, Japan, in September 2018, for instance, claims spread online that Beijing's consulate there had evacuated stranded Taiwanese tourists from a partly flooded Kansai Airport while Taiwan's representative in the city did nothing. The truth was that Japanese and not PRC authorities had sent the buses, but before clarification could be widely spread, the head of Taiwan's office in Osaka killed himself. The Information Operation Research Group (IORG), a Taiwanese NGO, later found that the fake social-media content originated from IP addresses located in Beijing.[9]

China's state-run media, including the *Global Times*, China Review News, and Twitter and Sina Weibo accounts linked to the CCP also relay disinformation and manipulated content. In Fuzhou, the capital city of Fujian Province on the PRC coast opposite Taiwan, sits Base 311, the home of People's Liberation Army (PLA) Unit 61716. This unit spearheads the PLA's information and psychological operations against Taiwan, and has control of PRC-affiliated media outlets. Unit 61716 belongs to the PLA Strategic Support Force, which Xi Jinping set up in 2015 to serve as the unified outer-space, cyberwar, and electronic-warfare command of the PRC military.

Moreover, the CCP relies on microblogging sites as well as content farms to spread disinformation in Taiwan.[10] Taiwan's PTT Gossip Board, a favorite of college students, is also believed to have been penetrated by pro-CCP entities. Anyone who can "spoof" (counterfeit) an email address ending in "edu.tw" can create an account and start chatting with other users on just about any topic. Facebook is replete with automated, coordinated fan pages that promote the alleged benefits to Taiwanese of unification and PRC citizenship, tell of how much Xi Jinping supposedly "cares" for Taiwan, and sing the praises of the "national rejuvenation" that he is said to be bringing about.[11] YouTube has not escaped, either: It too is a vehicle for manipulated videos and even "deep fakes."

The PRC's information operations originate not only from its territory, but have been seeded on Taiwan itself. Individuals based on the island who have taken part in cross-Strait "new-media forums" have founded outlets in recent years. In 2015, Beijing began hosting annual cross-Strait "summits" for Taiwanese who work in media. These junkets feature speeches by senior CCP propaganda officials such as Wang Yang and Yu Zhengsheng. The first one involved 34 Taiwanese drawn from the fields of television, publishing, new media, film distribution, public relations, and education. By the May 2019 meeting, the number of Taiwanese taking part had risen to seventy. Wang Yang, who along with Xi Jinping is one of the seven members of the CCP Politburo Standing Committee—in other words, a figure from the very highest reaches of the PRC's Communist Party regime—spoke to that group. He not only promoted "peaceful reunification" and the "one country, two systems" formula, but bluntly predicted (in remarks that Xinhua, the PRC's news agency, swiftly took down) that the United States would not and could not defend Taiwan militarily.[12]

The CCP is continually refining its disinformation campaign against Taiwan. One technique is to hire Taiwanese content creators so that everything seems authentically local and idiomatic, and is free of linguistic signs pointing to its true source on the mainland. To meet the challenge, Taipei has been putting more resources into countering disinformation. Premier Su Tseng-chang has ordered government ministries to correct disinformation within two hours of its discovery. The Executive Yuan has set up a webpage and a LINE online-chat group toward this end. In October 2016, President Tsai named Audrey Tang Taiwan's first digital minister, with a portfolio that includes fighting disinformation and improving the public's media literacy.

Along with these efforts, the Taiwanese government has worked to gather concrete evidence of disinformation originating in the PRC or with CCP proxies wherever they are based. Given how easy it is to spoof IP addresses and email addresses or Facebook and Twitter accounts, this is not always easy. The Executive Yuan's National Information Security and Communication Security Taskforce gathers evidence of information manipulation and conducts offensive and defensive cyber drills, using the evidence to revise plans for countering misinformation.

Beijing has at times induced traditional as well as new media to amplify and "legitimize" information in the PRC's favor. In April 2019, the *Nikkei Asian Review* used company filings to show that Taiwanese billionaire Tsai Eng-meng's Want Want Holdings, a large Taiwanese food conglomerate that does business on the mainland, had received as much as US$495 million in PRC subsidies dating back to 2007.[13] Tsai (who is no relation to Tsai Ing-wen) lives in Shanghai and publicly supports reunification. In 2006, he branched out of selling snacks and began to buy television channels and print publications. In 2008, he acquired the venerable Taipei-based *China Times,* which traces its founding to 1950 and so is nearly as old as the ROC on Taiwan itself.

Tsai denies that PRC money has had any impact on his media outlets' editorial stances. In July 2019, however, the *Financial Times* reported that the PRC's Taiwan Affairs Office was telling editors at the *China Times* and a Tsai-owned television channel how to cover cross-Strait relations.[14] In 2019, Taiwan's National Communications Commission (NCC) fined Want Want–owned CtiTV for spreading disinformation.[15] In November, the NCC refused to renew CtiTV's broadcasting license, so Tsai Eng-meng turned it into a livestreamed YouTube channel.

The typical path of a piece of disinformation is to appear first in a CCP or PRC media outlet, and then to spread via Chinese-language social media. Social media is the typical conduit into Taiwan, with the propaganda's originators hoping that traditional Taiwanese media will then pick up the rumor or other fake news if it achieves sufficient prominence.

Civil Society to the Rescue

After the 24 November 2018 local elections, the National Police Agency (NPA) revealed that in the thirty days prior to the voting, it had received 64 reports of disinformation or fake news. The NPA referred forty cases for prosecution and found IP addresses producing fake news and disinformation to be located in countries such as Singapore and the United States. The chief of the Ministry of Justice's Investigative Bureau (MJIB) also testified before the Legislative Yuan in November 2019 that the MJIB, at the time, was investigating more than 33 cases of political candidates receiving PRC funds. Clearly, Beijing cultivates support for its favored candidates while trying to tarnish others, including President Tsai. The ultimate goal is the annexation of Taiwan.

The 2018 local races, as well as the results of the ten-item referendum held the same day, served as a wake-up call for the Tsai administration and civil society. A pair of items that would have furthered sex education and the inclusion of same-sex marriage in the Civil Code, respectively, both failed to pass. According to Puma Shen of the National Taipei University law faculty, the PRC used misinformation to damage Taiwanese politicians—mostly from the DPP—who took the affirmative side on these issues by suggesting that their stances reflected permissive attitudes toward pedophilia and the spread of AIDS.[16]

Amid this CCP sharp-power onslaught, Taiwan's civil society rallied. Digital-democracy NGOs in particular came together to devise strategies and methods for battling information manipulation, for promoting media literacy, for creating automated fact-checking chat bots, and for spreading accurate public information generally. The Taiwan Foundation for Democracy was among the funders that underwrote these efforts to safeguard Taiwan's democratic institutions.

Civil society groups coordinated to spend their time and energy to best effect. Doublethink Lab (DTL) and IORG, for instance, focus on reports meant to inform Taiwan's citizens and the international community about PRC information warfare. Both DTL and IORG have strong online presences and regularly send staffers to attend both online and in-person conferences in the United States and Europe. Beyond reports, each organization also seeks to equip the government with more and better tools for countering information manipulation. To that end, both groups offer policy advice. In 2020, DTL sought to inform the public by publishing a report on "The Chinese Infodemic in Taiwan."[17]

In this report, drawing on its own research as well as data gathered by partners such as the Taiwan FactCheck Center and MyGoPen (phonetic Chinese for "stop lying"), DTL sifted through more than 269,000 Facebook updates posted between January and March 2020 (the early stage of the covid pandemic, in other words) and was able to identify commonly occurring themes and narratives. These tended to promote the notions that Taiwan's government was depicting the virus as more serious than it really was, that the government was also doing a poor job of controlling its spread, and that the Tsai administration's main concern in any case was to exploit covid as yet another tool in its ceaseless "anti-China" campaign.

Working on a similar premise, IORG offers the public a disinformation update every two weeks. By the end of 2021, IORG had noted 68 narratives that were pro-PRC or critical of the United States, Taiwan, and their democratic allies such as Japan. The narratives claimed that Taiwan's government was lying about the numbers of covid infections and deaths, that the DPP administration was refusing for political reasons to buy vaccines from the PRC, that the United States was failing to help Taiwan obtain vaccines, that vaccine shipments from Japan were expiring, and even that the DPP was murdering Taiwanese people with Japanese vaccines. All these falsehoods were meant to make Taiwanese feel demoralized, isolated, divided from one another, and distrustful of their own democratically elected government. The timely DTL and IORG reports on how these phony stories were being spread achieved wide distribution on social media and made news in local traditional media. Since the reports appeared in English as well as Chinese, both organizations and their partners drew frequent invitations to appear on international panels where they could discuss Taiwan's experience.

To supplement data-collection and reporting efforts, organizations such as the Open Culture Foundation and Fake News Cleaner worked to promote information literacy and educate the public about information warfare. Founded in December 2018, Fake News Cleaner announces itself on its website (*fakenewscleaner.tw*) as "a spontaneous group of citizens who care about society." It does in-person outreach, going out into streets, open-air markets, and other venues to discuss with anyone who will listen methods for checking facts and being more internet-savvy. Fake News Cleaner has developed its own information-literacy teaching materials, and claims that since its founding it has held four-hundred face-to-face "physical activities" to spread its message to "almost every city and county" in Taiwan. In a like vein, IORG works with the NGO Taiwan Fang-Ban Association (an alliance of high-school teachers) to deliver lectures at schools and community centers. During 2021, despite the pandemic, IORG and Fang-Ban managed to hold 68 workshops in eight months. They reached 1,800 individuals and surveyed 1,600 to discover what they thought about disinformation and fact-checking.

The IORG and Fang-Ban surveys found that most respondents knew about the existence of disinformation, but did not think that they could be tricked by information-manipulation techniques. After attending Fang-Ban workshops, 70 percent of participants said that they would use the tools the workshop had given them in order to verify factual claims they encountered. More than half rated themselves keenly aware of information-manipulation methods, and most also avowed that they would actively combat information warfare.[18]

While such responses are encouraging, the NGOs also point out that most Taiwanese go through school without receiving any media-literacy training. The recent introduction of the "108 Curriculum," however, has upgraded the importance of "civic literacy" as a topic of study.[19] Detecting a strong demand among middle- and high-school teachers for lesson plans in this area, IORG and Fang-Ban organized fifteen teacher workshops to discuss ways of rousing students' interest in information literacy and giving them lifelong means of maintaining their information integrity.

Last but not least when it comes to the fight against Beijing's information operations are the organized fact-checking groups. The volunteers of the Taiwan FactCheck Center, MyGoPen, and CoFacts all work tirelessly and donate their technical and other expertise to correct disinformation, clear up confusion, and validate factual claims. MyGoPen and CoFacts have developed chat bots that individuals can add to their LINE chat apps.

MyGoPen seeks out disinformation and provides clarifications via its LINE group. CoFacts allows users to submit questions on the information or links that they receive through LINE, and then provides users with a clarification or explanation concerning the information submitted. Questionable information can be copied and pasted into a fact-checking chat bot, which will then rate the claim as true, partly true, or false, and link to sources that explain why. The information submitted for evaluation is saved to a database for further analysis and possible clarification. The ability to identify "partial truths" is a key feature of any fact-checking program since Beijing's most recent disinformation campaign relies not only on "fake news" but also on manipulated facts or half-truths meant to mislead and confuse Taiwan's citizens.

In the poll, mentioned early in this essay, that the Taiwan Foundation for Democracy took last year, more than 90 percent of respondents agreed that disinformation was hurting the development of Taiwan's democracy and its quality. According to Professor Eric Yu, who helped to run the survey, this was the highest level of agreement elicited by any item in the poll. As noted above, the CCP's political warfare tries to create confusion, division, and a sense of despairing isolation among the people of Taiwan. Heightened citizen awareness—the fruit of lessons learned the hard way as the People's Republic of China beats on the information portals of the Chinese-speaking democratic citadel just off its shores—is key to guarding against authoritarian influence operations. Taiwan's government and its civil society have made defense against Beijing's political warfare a priority. Taiwan will not give up the democracy that its people have fought so long and hard to establish. Their determination is and must remain the mainstay of Taiwan's effectiveness in battling Chinese Communist Party sharp power.

Notes

1. "Democracy Index 2021: The China Challenge," Economist Intelligence Unit, *www.eiu.com/n/campaigns/democracy-index-2021*.
2. "2021 TFD Survey on Taiwanese View of Democratic Value and Governance," Taiwan Foundation for Democracy (press release), 29 December 2021, *www.tfd.org.tw/export/sites/tfd/files/news/pressRelease/ENG_press_release.pdf*.

3. Yang Mien-chieh and Jonathan Chin, "Taiwan Most Targeted for False Information: Study," *Taipei Times,* 20 March 2022, *www.taipeitimes.com/ News/taiwan/archives/2022/03/20/2003775114.*

4. Kharis Templeman, "How Taiwan Stands Up to China," *Journal of Democracy* 31 (July 2020): 85–99.

5. Chao-Chen Lin, "The Models of Fake News and Media Convergence: An Exploration on the 2018 Taiwan Election," *Journalism Research Journal 142 (Winter 2020): 111–53.*

6. In his 2 January 2019 message, Xi emphasized "One China" and left no room for "different tables." Xi added that the only way Taiwan is to be "reunified" with the PRC is under the "one country, two systems" framework. He stressed as well that the PRC has not relinquished the option of using force to "take back" Taiwan.

7. See the chart "Changes in the Taiwanese/Chinese Identity of Taiwanese as Tracked in Surveys by the Election Study Center, NCCU (1992–2021)," *https:// esc.nccu.edu.tw/upload/44/doc/6961/People202112.jpg.*

8. Anne Quito, "Taiwan Is Using Humor as a Tool Against Coronavirus Hoaxes," *Quartz,* 5 June 2020, *https://qz.com/1863931/taiwan-is-using- humor-to-quash-coronavirus-fake-news.* See also Stephen Fung, "Taiwan Tackled COVID-19, Toilet Paper and Triumphed," *APP SHOW* (podcast), 5 May 2020, *https://getconnectedmedia.com/app-show-video-podcast-taiwan- tackled-covid-19-toilet-paper-and-triumphed.*

9. For IORG's claim, see *https://iorg.tw/r/b1.* The organization also presented its findings at an October 2020 press event, *www.inside.com.tw/ article/21268-iorg-china-information-cognitive-war-taiwan-ait.*

10. Or pro-PRC "content mills" such as *Cocoo1, CocooX, Reado1.com, kknews.cc,* and others.

11. According to the IORG annual report, certain Facebook fanpages would cross-post the link to the same disinformation within a minute or less of each other. In IORG's parlance, this is called "clustered posting." IORG's final research report is at *https://iorg.tw/r/2021.*

12. Dave Brown, "Why Did Beijing Suppress Wang Yang's Remarks on Taiwan?" *Diplomat,* 30 May 2019, *https://thediplomat.com/2019/05/why- did-beijing-suppress-wang-yangs-remarks-on-taiwan.* See also J. Michael Cole, "More Than 70 Participants from Taiwanese Media Industry Attend 4th Cross-Strait Media Summit in Beijing," *Taiwan Sentinel,* 11 May 2019, *https://sentinel.tw/more-than-70-participants-from-taiwanese-media- industry-attend-4th-cross-strait-media-summit-in-beijing.*

13. Kenji Kawase, "Chinese Subsidies for Foxconn and Want Want Spark Outcry in Taiwan," *Nikkei Asian Review,* 30 April 2019. See also J. Michael Cole, "An Analysis of Possible Chinese Influence Operations Against Taiwan: The Want-Want Case," *Prospect Foundation Newsletter,* 6 May 2019, and Templeman, "How Taiwan Stands Up to China," 88.

14. Katherine Hille, "Taiwan Primaries Highlight Fears over China's Political Influence," *Financial Times,* 16 July 2019, *www.ft.com/content/036b609a-a768-11e9-984c-fac8325aaa04.*

15. Shelley Shan, "CtiTV Penalized Another NT$1m for Pomelo Story," *Taipei Times,* 11 April 2019, *www.taipeitimes.com/News/taiwan/archives/2019/04/11/2003713194.*

16. Puma Shen, "How China Initiates Information Operations Against Taiwan," *Taiwan Strategists* 12 (December 2021): 19–34, *www.pf.org.tw/article-pfch-2122-7675.*

17. Poyu Tseng and Puma Shen, "The Chinese Infodemic in Taiwan: A Preliminary Study on the Dissemination Model of Disinformation, Taking COVID-19 as an Example," Doublethink Lab, 26 July 2020, *https://medium.com/doublethinklab/the-chinese-infodemic-in-taiwan-25e9ac3d941e.*

18. For a compendium page providing links to all the activities that IORG carried out in various locales in 2021, see *https://iorg.tw/e.*

19. Yvonne Cho, "Taiwan's New '108 Curriculum' Education System," *Taiwan Times,* 17 April 2021, *https://thetaiwantimes.com/taiwans-new-108-curriculum-education-system.*

CHAPTER NINE

How Australia's Civil Society
Led the Way

JOHN FITZGERALD

I N 2013, THE YEAR THAT XI JINPING BECAME PRESIDENT of the People's Republic of China (PRC), Australia's relations with China were at their peak. Trade and investment had never been higher, growing numbers of PRC tourists and students were visiting Australia, and China was basking in strong approval ratings from the Australian public. President Xi paid his own visit in November 2014 to hail the "goodwill" between the two countries.

Just three years later, however, much of that goodwill had evaporated. The PRC was on its way to cutting off all ministerial-level contacts with Australia and imposing punitive tariffs on a wide range of Australian imports including beef and wine. By 2021, Beijing had suspended its annual bilateral Comprehensive Strategic Dialogue with Canberra.

Why the deep freeze? One reason is Australian civil society—including not a few Chinese-Australian groups and individuals—had finally succeeded in alerting authorities to the PRC's extensive sharp-power operations in Australia, and had strengthened the government's resolve to deal with them. The government's concern over foreign interference converged with the pushback against PRC "sharp power" that civil society had already begun. The upshot was the exposure of a degree of PRC political interference in Australian politics and public life that strengthened Canberra's resolve in dealing with Beijing, and led China's government to punish Australia as a warning to others that might be tempted to follow its example.

It has been alleged that local media and civil society generally were duped by security agencies that used them to fabricate a "China panic" in Australia.[1] This gets things backward. In fact, civil society was ten years ahead of the government and its agencies in exposing PRC surveillance and interference among local diaspora communities and in working to defend the rights of those belonging to these communities as equal citizens of Australia. The only security agencies that were on the case early were Beijing's—Canberra was preoccupied with terrorism and other challenges. By 2016 and 2017, it was civil society that was confirming—and in some cases revealing—what was happening on the ground. The official custodians of Australia's national security were getting their information from civil society, not the other way around.

Civil society, moreover, took its charge not from the angle of geopolitics and international rivalries, but rather with a concern for freedom, rights, and equal treatment for all Australian citizens. Australians of Chinese heritage, in particular, spoke out to defend their freedoms of speech, association, and religion against Beijing's attempts to control local media, interfere in community groups, and intimidate people of religious faith. Chinese-Australian journalists, academics, and civil society organizers refused to tolerate on Australian soil the surveillance and intimidation that they had been subjected to in China.2 Other journalists and analysts learned what was happening among local Chinese communities through friends who were willing to share their stories but unwilling to place their families at risk by speaking out themselves. These shared concerns for civil liberties became geopolitical because the CCP sees the exercise of civil liberties by Chinese-Australians as an existential threat to the party's authoritarian grip on China.

Confronting the CCP Playbook

The Australian case of civil society pushback against foreign-government interference is typical in some ways but atypical in others. Overall, CCP conduct in Australia conforms to the standard "united front" template that New Zealand political scientist Anne-Marie Brady has laid out in classifying the party's foreign operations.3 Former officials of the target country are cultivated to act as go-betweens with current officeholders, respected domestic voices and institutions are urged to promote the PRC's foreign policy, city-to-city and state-to-province ties are fostered, the good things said to be expected from "China's global rise" are extolled, and interest groups are lined up to back the Belt and Road Initiative (BRI) or PRC claims in the East and South China seas. Of special interest to the CCP are communities belonging to the ethnic-Chinese diaspora. Chinese-language media outlets and community groups with their local-government contacts never escape Beijing's attention. On the information front, efforts focus on silencing Beijing's critics, inserting its propaganda into the media and the classroom, and collaborating on cutting-edge research that will serve PRC plans and priorities. In confronting these kinds of sharp-power activities, Australia was hardly alone.[4]

Familiar types of PRC interference drew accustomed responses. Reporters in Sydney and Melbourne, for instance, had covered public corruption (and coped with defamation suits) before. These journalists were used to finding aspiring politicians, political-party officials, and retired public servants taking political donations or even personal gifts to place favorites in office or lobby on behalf of developers or industry groups. To detect such individuals doing favors for Beijing was not a huge stretch. Once the press got onto the story, its seasoned scribes were not easily deterred.[5]

What was new was the willingness of political lobbyists to play the race card to disarm their critics.[6] Few of these lobbyists would acknowledge that it was in fact Chinese-Australian activists who were exposing PRC sharp-power operations and Chinese-Australian journalists who were laying the "foundation of investigative reporting on the party's concealed links to Australian politics."[7]

In the academy, pushback was strong among faculty with personal experience of higher education in China. They had little desire to see the kind of surveillance and repression found on China's campuses replicated on Australian ones. Some of these scholars faced intimidation themselves. Civil society organizations such as the Australian Academy of the Humanities (of which I have served as president) and Human Rights Watch did important work highlighting vulnerabilities on Australian university campuses.[8]

In sum, little CCP conduct in Australia fell outside the party's united front playbook, and local civil society responses were predictably well matched. A distinctive feature of Australia's national response was the convergence of civil society's activism with the federal government's growing concern over the risks to national security and cohesion presented by Beijing's efforts to mobilize "astroturfed" networks mimicking grassroots community organizations in support of China's geostrategic ambitions. Independent civil society actors had an impact on bilateral relations out of proportion to their number once the CCP tried to match them with its astroturfing tactics.

By inadvertently prompting the federal government to respond, Beijing's actions had the unintended consequence of linking Australian civil society's activism to Canberra's management of formal state-to-state relations. To understand how civil society and the federals teamed up to stop China's sharp-power operations in Australia, it is useful to think of how state-to-state relations move on several tracks at once.

Tracking Relations

Students of international relations speak of "Track 1" dealings, meaning formal relations between sovereign states, and "Track 2" matters, which involve nongovernmental actors including those from organized society, the media, the business world, the academy, religious bodies, and so on. (Some writers see more than just two tracks, but Track 1 is always the formal one.) When challenged, Track 2 actors often turn to the nation-state to press their advantage or guard their interests—in other words, they veer toward Track 1. Governments receive demands or requests from businesses, ethnic diasporas, or rights campaigners—to name a few of the types of groups that may lobby—and then decide what to do. The response (or nonresponse) from the government of the day will always depend on shifting factors such as which party is in office, how the national economy is doing, how officials read the strategic environment, what allies and multinational organizations will think, and the like.

From the 1980s through the early 2010s, the foreign-policy "stakeholder" that Canberra listened to the most as it dealt with Beijing was the Australian business community. In 1987, the federal government merged its foreign and trade ministries to form a new Department of Foreign Affairs and Trade. The aim was to integrate Australia more closely into the global economy in general and, in particular, to take advantage of the PRC's economic reforms and opening: Trade was to guide foreign policy. For three decades until Xi Jinping's rise, commercial interests dominated Australia's relations with China while civil society and rights activists enjoyed little traction.

Xi had not been in power long when it began to become clear that commerce could no longer be separated from China's geopolitical ambitions. Early in his tenure, Beijing began pressing the trade lever as a means of nudging Canberra away from the U.S. alliance that has been at the heart of Australia's foreign and security policy since World War II. The federal government began worrying about PRC investments in critical national infrastructure. In August 2016, citing national security, Canberra blocked an attempt by China's State Grid Corporation and a Hong Kong–based holding company to buy a majority stake in Ausgrid, the network that supplies almost two-million homes and businesses in New South Wales (NSW) with electricity.[9]

The integration of trade, investment, and security policy needed time to work its way through the system. The federal decision to stop the PRC's State Grid from buying up local power infrastructure was announced in the same week that an authoritative bilateral report calling for closer economic engagement was presented to President Xi and Australia's prime minister at the time, Malcolm Turnbull.[10] The odd juxtaposition of an upbeat report on investment prospects and the government's veto of Chinese investment in a sensitive area was not lost on media observers. Would the business sector's vision of economic integration between the two countries, one asked, "make Australia more vulnerable to China's strategic leverage and [was it] the inevitable consequence of closer economic ties"?[11]

Such questions became still more pointed in following months as the Australian media revealed how widely and deeply PRC influence operations were reaching into Australia's core political and civic institutions. By 2016–17, it was becoming clear that Beijing had a long-term strategy to influence Australian institutions across a broad front—political parties, media firms, community groups, big businesses, and schools—to advance PRC ambitions.

In his memoirs, Turnbull notes that during Xi's early years in power, China shifted appreciably. A member of the Liberals (Australia's center-right party), Turnbull served as prime minister from 2015 to 2018. "Under Xi," he writes, the PRC "became more assertive, more confident and more prepared to not just reach out to the world, as Deng [Xiaoping] had done, or to command respect as a responsible international actor, as Hu Jintao and Jiang Zemin had done, but to demand compliance."[12] Tony Abbott, the Liberal prime minister from 2013 to 2015, has said that in their dealings with Australia, Chinese officials began to use trade as a strategic weapon to be turned "on and off like a tap" for geopolitical purposes.[13]

Once Xi began fusing commercial relations with geopolitical demands inimical to Australia's national interests, the government-to-government China-relations track could no longer run parallel with the business track. As the two tracks diverged, business leaders continued to press publicly for access and influence, but were disappointed. State and national business councils asked Canberra to sign onto the BRI, but to no avail. The gap between business interests and reasons of state was widening.

At the same time, the federal government drew closer to the civil society or people-to-people track in relations with China. The term "people-to-people" covers everything from educational, cultural, and sporting institutions to nonprofit and media organizations, diaspora associations, and religious congregations active on the margins of bilateral relations. In some respects, the new alignment was more intrusive, particularly for universities which came under closer federal scrutiny. In other respects, it was more inclusive. Canberra began engaging more with representatives of Chinese-Australian communities, and these rose in prominence as important stakeholders in relations between Australia and the PRC. For four decades, the highest-level civic body advising the government on people-to-people ties with China had been the business-dominated Australia-China Council. In 2019, Canberra did away with it in favor of a new National Foundation for Australia-China Relations under an advisory board on which Chinese-Australians hold five of the fourteen seats. (Full disclosure: I sat on the earlier Australia-China Council and now sit on the advisory board of the new foundation.) Further, while the old Council had lacked an explicit mandate to concern itself with diaspora diplomacy, the new Foundation made the situation of the Chinese-Australian community a priority.

On the formal track, tensions rose over the PRC's November 2013 declaration of a new East China Sea Air Defense Identification Zone (ADIZ). This covered a swath of ocean from the northern tip of Taiwan to a latitude not far from South Korea, and which included the Senkaku (or Diaoyu) Islands (where China disputes Japanese sovereignty) as well as a periodically submerged rock that both South Korea and China claim and on which the former built an oceanographic research station in 2003. The Australian foreign minister's official conveyance of concern over the ADIZ drew a stiff public rebuke from her PRC counterpart. One senior official in Canberra said that it was the rudest diplomatic conduct Australia had met with in thirty years.[14] Prime Minister Abbott strongly supported his foreign minister, and a chill set in between two nations whose interests and views went different ways on matters such as regional security, respect for the international rule of law, and the preservation of the U.S.-led post-1945 order.

That chill turned to a freeze in July 2016, when Canberra spoke in favor of a ruling by the intergovernmental Permanent Court of Arbitration at The Hague that dismissed China's claims to the oil-rich South China Sea. In the case, which the Philippines had brought against the PRC under the Law of the Sea Treaty that both countries had ratified in the late twentieth century, the tribunal rejected Beijing's claimed "nine-dash line" and said that China had no right to control resources found within it. The ruling further found that China's claims encroached on the treaty-defined exclusive economic zone of the Philippines. The PRC had refused to take part in the arbitration, and immediately denounced the ruling.

To say that Canberra's public expression of support for these findings—the support took the form of a joint statement issued with the United States and Japan—was not welcomed in Beijing would be an understatement. Charges were heard in the PRC that Australia was growing increasingly "anti-China" and even racist. The CCP-owned *Global Times* sneered at Australia as a former "offshore prison" of Britain and said that China "must take revenge" for the insult of Canberra's daring to back the Philippines.[15] Relations since have not improved.

These maritime disputes, while tense, might have remained manageable had Beijing not chosen to push its claims by interfering in Australian domestic politics. Civil society had been highlighting and warning of Beijing's united front tactics for years; the maritime dispute made Canberra sit up and take notice too. As Frances Adamson, who served as foreign and trade secretary from 2016 to 2021, put it:

> We've seen China seeking to assert itself in this region, in the Indo-Pacific and globally, in ways that suit its interests but don't suit the interests of countries like Australia. . . . But when influence builds into interference, that is something we don't want to see, our government won't tolerate [it] and I think most Australians are broadly supportive of that.[16]

Chinese-Australians at the Fore

In 2016 and 2017, a series of explosive headlines fused independent civil society concerns with emerging government concerns to limit foreign interference in local party politics, build community cohesion, and improve information and intelligence-gathering about PRC sharp-power operations in Australia. For activists, this was novel. Along with a number of journalists and analysts, they had been trying for years to shield local communities from PRC surveillance and harassment, and to safeguard the integrity of elections and other civic institutions. For years, their pleas had been ignored. Now they were being taken seriously.

In 2005, a junior PRC diplomat posted in Sydney, Chen Yonglin, sought Australian asylum. He spoke publicly of an extensive network of CCP agents in Australia who were monitoring Chinese-Australian activists and religious believers through the PRC's Sydney consulate. Some local academics had firsthand experience of this kind of surveillance and intimidation, but most Australians were shocked to hear that around a thousand agents were actively reporting to Beijing, Stasi-style, on members of the Chinese-Australian community. The scale of PRC sharp-power activities in Australia had received its first public confirmation.

As I remarked to a Senate inquiry in June 2005, Chen Yonglin's brave testimony revealed that China's crackdown on religious believers and democratic activists was not merely domestic, but was being extended internationally and reaching deeply and widely into Australia. Chinese-Australians needed help. In talking with them, I had learned that they felt unprotected, and as if their equal right, under Australian law, to be shielded from surveillance by a foreign power meant nothing. The PRC's official representatives in Australia, I added, needed to be told that Australian sovereignty and citizenship could never be compromised and that PRC interference had to stop.

Sadly, Chen Yonglin's pleas went unheeded before resurfacing a decade later, like a message in a bottle, to warn of things to come. By the time Xi Jinping finished claiming the top offices in 2013, CCP interference in Australia extended well beyond surveillance and harassment of local democrats and religious believers to the exercise of direct control over Chinese-language media (print, radio, and online), indirect management of local community groups, influence on university executives, attempts to shape the foreign-policy positions of mainstream political parties, and the establishment of formal united front agencies across Australia including branches of a council to promote China's "peaceful reunification" with links to the Sydney consulate and the CCP in Beijing.

Starting around 2014, community activists, investigative journalists, and independent analysts worked to bring the details of PRC interference to light. Clive Hamilton's 2018 book *Silent Invasion* brought many of their findings to a wider audience, adding new evidence of what the PRC had been up to in the world of Australian higher education.[17] Most of the research by Hamilton and others drew on publicly available sources: Civil society, not government, was leading the way in exposing the problems that Chen Yonglin had first identified.

Having been involved in these events, I can affirm that topmost in civil society's mind was not diplomacy but the welfare of Chinese-Australians who were being bullied and spied on, the integrity of civic institutions vital to democracy, and the preservation of the values and principles that undergird the Australian way of life. It was these burning matters, and not legal analyses of China's maritime claims or erudite reflections on the post-1945 international order, that drove us.

Sharp Power Lights Up

Beijing's reaction to the 2016 South China Sea decision was like a light turning on. The influence operations that community activists and investigative journalists had been talking about suddenly went live like the integrated network they were. As soon as the ruling appeared, scores of recently formed "community groups" backing PRC claims began making public declarations and marching through the streets of Australian cities. Prominent business figures with close China ties spoke about the dangers of offending Beijing. Lawmakers told Chinese-language media that Australia had no standing to talk about the South China Sea. Some of these comments may have been spontaneous, but to activists on the ground it seemed as if Beijing was leveraging its old ties to business and political elites and selected Chinese-Australian community groups and media outlets with strategic singlemindedness.

Supporting evidence soon arrived. In August 2016, Chris Uhlman of the Australian Broadcasting Corporation (ABC) reported that from 2013 through 2015, the largest share of foreign-sourced donations to Australian political parties (a share worth more than AU$5.5 million all told) had come from PRC-linked entities.[18] That same month, the *Australian Financial Review* reported that the Labor Party's key fundraiser in NSW, Senator Sam Dastyari, had "pledged to respect China's position on the South China Sea at an election campaign press conference he held with a Chinese political donor who had previously paid his legal bills. He had also urged Australia to drop its opposition to China's air defence zone in the contested region."[19] Senator Dastyari's comments ran counter to his own party's position and led to his eventual downfall. He resigned his seat in early 2018.

The role of party fundraising in this episode came to light when it emerged that the billionaire PRC national Huang Xiangmo (a Sydney resident) had threatened to withhold a large donation to the NSW Labor Party unless it stopped opposing Beijing's South China Sea claims. Senator Dastyari later admitted to a commission of inquiry that he wondered, looking back, if this "very big donor" had been a PRC "agent of influence."[20]

Huang was also instrumental in helping Ernest Wong to climb from Sydney-area local-government posts into the NSW Legislative Council, as the upper house of the state legislature is called. Wong, who would go on to repeat Beijing's South China Sea talking points, was another capable fundraiser for the Labor Party. In 2013, Wong succeeded a former Labor Party figure in the NSW senate under rules that allow occasional vacancies to be filled by nomination between elections. As a member of the upper house three years later, Wong backed the PRC in the maritime dispute and claimed that Canberra's support for the Philippine position had offended Chinese-Australians. "Their hearts," he said, "belong to their ancestral land." This was textbook united front: A deep-pocketed operative aided the rise of a politician who faithfully repeated Beijing's line. Also in keeping with united front guidelines had been the invocation of allegedly aggrieved Chinese-Australians.

On the media side, Australian stations owned by Beijing's China Radio International (CRI) ran programs supporting Beijing's claims while ignoring other views. The story online and in print was much the same. Outlets owned by CRI, or that had contractual relations with China News Service, an official PRC news agency, were typically involved. Another means by which Beijing had sought to spread its line was the annual media-personnel training given to Chinese-Australian journalists under united front auspices. During expenses-paid trips to the PRC, Chinese-language journalists from Australia and more than thirty other countries have received extensive exposure to the CCP's view of things.

Mainstream media were little different. On 26 May 2016, not long before the South China Sea ruling, PRC and Australian media outlets met in Sydney to sign six agreements. Liu Qibao, the head of the CCP's Central Propaganda Department, flew in to watch as representatives from Xinhua, CRI, *China Daily,* the *People's Daily* online, and Qingdao Publishing Group sat down with counterparts from Fairfax Media, Sky News Australia, Global China-Australia Media Group, Weldon International, and former foreign minister Bob Carr's Australia-China Relations Institute at the University of Technology Sydney.[21] The next day, the *Sydney Morning Herald,* the *Melbourne Age,* and the *Australian Financial Review* (all Fairfax publications) carried an eight-page supplement with a full-page article titled "Manila Has No Leg to Stand On." The ruling had not yet appeared, but Beijing's line on it was already receiving friendly mass coverage.

Among the Beijing-friendly media organs was the taxpayer-funded ABC. In 2014, it had shut down its Chinese-language news and current-affairs programs before securing access to the China market for ABC programming. On the ABC's own *Media Watch* television show, host Paul Barry reported that the public broadcaster nonetheless did carry Chinese-language coverage of Prime Minister Turnbull's April 2016 visit to China, in the process censoring some things he said during his trip that had to do with Canberra's concerns about the PRC's South China Sea claims. In the relevant English-language ABC report, Turnbull is said to have "urged a peaceful resolution of territorial disputes with the five other nations that make overlapping claims." The Chinese-language ABC version, however, leaves out any mention of other nations with claims that overlap the PRC's in these waters.[22]

In 2016, Australia clearly had a problem. Beijing had been able to mobilize influence and interference networks—long cultivated but left mostly latent—with surprising speed, and with the goal of making Australia acquiesce as the PRC occupied and militarized the South China Sea. These highly strategic interventions in Australian public life transformed long-standing civic concerns about foreign interference in community and public affairs into an urgent question of national security.

Consistent with wider community concerns, intelligence agencies had been focusing mostly on terrorism. Few paid attention to PRC interference activities other than a small group defending civic rights and freedoms. To the extent that agencies such as the Australian Security Intelligence Organisation (ASIO) were involved, their role was to monitor attempts by all foreign governments to compromise senior government officials. This general net did catch evidence of PRC activities: In December 2017, when Prime Minister Turnbull introduced a proposed law to counter foreign interference, he noted ASIO's "breakthroughs" on the subject starting in 2016. Beijing's covert activation of influence networks gave earlier agency work political traction and alerted the general public to flagrant instances of covert foreign interference. Federal authorities were compelled to act.

For the federal government, China's united front operations presented a particular challenge. How was the Australian government to balance its commitment to multiculturalism with its responsibility for national security? Who spoke for Chinese-Australian communities? How were elected representatives to distinguish genuine grassroots groups from others that Beijing had fabricated? How, likewise, to distinguish between elected representatives sincerely voicing their constituents' concerns and others who might only be mouthing what they were, in one way or another, being paid to say? When a geopolitically ambitious China put pressure on Australia's social and political fabric, in other words, how resilient would that fabric prove to be? Beijing's use of sharp power made that question salient indeed.

From mid-2016 to early 2017, the Turnbull government attempted to answer these questions through a confidential review of China's interference operations. The review revealed "unprecedented" threats of covert, coercive, and corrupting behavior, and triggered laws banning foreign interference and upgrading intelligence powers, new regulations on political donations and critical infrastructure investments, and several executive interventions to protect national infrastructure and social cohesion. Prime Minister Turnbull told Parliament of the important role that civil society (and especially journalists) had played in revealing that "the Chinese Communist Party has been working to covertly interfere with our media, our universities and even the decisions of elected representatives right here in this building."[23] The alarm had been sounded first not by government security agencies, but by Australian civil society.

Once the government took up the problem, civil society moved from exposés to solutions. Here, universities (still largely in denial) proved less helpful than think tanks that had come to grasp the security dimensions of what had formerly been a human-rights problem. Elaine Pearson wrote a full Human Rights Watch report on Beijing's interference in Australian student life, for instance, only to have the director of international-student recruitment at the University of New South Wales, where she teaches law as an adjunct professor, repudiate the document. At the Australian National University (ANU) in Canberra, Chinese-Australian student Alex Joske wrote of his personal experience with PRC intimidation on campus but found the ANU student union unsympathetic to his concerns. He found support elsewhere in the capital at the Australian Strategic Policy Institute (ASPI), which commissioned him to report on ties between Australian universities and researchers working for the People's Liberation Army. The result was the acclaimed China Defence Universities Tracker (*unitracker.aspi.org.au*), which helps universities around the world to identify high-risk PRC partners. Mindful that public concerns about PRC influence, however valid, could fuel racism, ASPI commissioned me to write a paper—aptly titled "Mind Your Tongue"—suggesting to officials and the media how they could discuss this sensitive topic without casting Chinese-Australians in an unfairly negative light.[24]

The PRC's "Own Goal"

Beijing's 2016 decision to activate its influence network in Australia had the effect of putting state-to-state relations and civil society on the same track. Civil society groups and activists who had long been informally worried about PRC surveillance and interference in Chinese-Australian communities, on campuses, and in the halls of journalism and politics suddenly saw their concerns take on immediate national-security relevance as Beijing turned up the heat over the South China Sea matter. To learn the true depth and extent of China's surveillance and united front operations in Australia, the government turned to these groups and activists: They were the real experts.

Their findings confirmed warnings that had begun to emerge from federal intelligence agencies. The upshot was federal legislative action to limit foreign-government interference, enhance intelligence powers, protect critical infrastructure, and manage the interactions between Australia's subnational governments and other countries. Action is proceeding at the state level as well: In February 2022, the Independent Commission Against Corruption of NSW uncovered evidence that a former NSW legislator had received and sought to hide an illicit political donation from united front figure Huang Xiangmo.[25] The claim has yet to be tried in court.

As these reactions indicate, the PRC has kicked the ball squarely into its own net. Before 2016, Australian civil society paid little heed to dealings between Canberra and Beijing. The focus was on defending basic rights and freedoms and protecting the integrity of civic institutions. Civil society was pushing back unofficially against PRC sharp-power operations long before the Australian government roused itself on the matter. Yet when Beijing, enraged by Canberra's refusal to keep quiet about the South China Sea, threw its sharp-power activities into high gear starting in 2016, that changed. It turned out that when you are dealing with Xi Jinping's China, domestic issues of freedom, rights, equal treatment, and institutional integrity are also matters of national security.

What lessons should civil society draw? One is that governments matter. International law treats national governments as sovereign actors entitled to protect their respective territories, communities, and ways of life through the application of lawful authority. Civil society actors enjoy no comparable recognition and by themselves wield little power or influence. In Australia, they played a seminal informational and publicity role by exposing foreign interference in domestic affairs, but in the end it is government that makes decisions, and it took the government to curb China's sharp-power operations in Australia.

A further lesson is to expect resistance from sections of civil society that might normally be expected to fight for human dignity and freedom. Many universities rely heavily on the high fees that international students pay, and worry a lot about global rankings. When administrators at these schools were confronted with evidence of Chinese-government surveillance and intimidation involving their student bodies and faculties, they brushed it aside. Some faculty members responded seriously, but others turned a blind eye to civil society's role in exposing PRC sharp power and retreated instead into conspiracy theories about Australia's security agencies and U.S. machinations.

From a civil society perspective, to the extent that there was anything like U.S. involvement, it worked against and not for greater awareness of PRC sharp power. Kevin Rudd of the Labor Party, who had been Australia's prime minister from 2007 to 2010 and then again for a few months in 2013, had become the head of the New York–based Asia Society Policy Institute. In May 2018, at the height of civil society and government pushback against China's interference operations, Rudd attacked Prime Minister Turnbull in Mandarin on PRC social media as well as in English on Australian television. Rudd called Turnbull "paranoid" and said that he had "derailed" China-Australia relations for political gain.[26] Rudd has more than six-hundred thousand followers on Sina Weibo. His comments undermined a serving prime minister working to uphold the integrity of institutions and the autonomy of civil society, and elevated the standing of Rudd's powerful U.S.-based organization over that of Australian civil society activists.

Taken together, these experiences point to a further lesson: A new Cold War is likely to repeat the pattern of the old at home, as well as abroad, with domestic ideological conflicts and political posturing forming a constant challenge to civil society activists working to defend human dignity, rights, and freedom.

Notes

1. These allegations are made by Da vid Brophy, *China Panic: Australia's Alternative to Paranoia and Pandering* (Melbourne: La Trobe University Press, 2021).

2. John Garnaut, "How China Interferes in Australia," Foreign Affairs, 9 March 2018, *www.foreignaffairs.com/articles/china/2018-03-09/how-china-interferes-australia*.

3. Anne-Marie Brady, "Encircling the City from the Countryside: A Template of CCP United Front Work at Subnational Level," in John Fitzgerald, ed., *Taking the Low Road: China's Influence in Australian States and Territories* (Canberra: ASPI, 2022), 183–95. For more details on China's sharp-power operations in Australia, see Clive Hamilton, *Silent Invasion: China's Influence in Australia* (Melbourne: Hardie Grant, 2018) and John Fitzgerald, "Overstepping Down Under," *Journal of Democracy* 29 (April 2018): 59–67.

4. Clive Hamilton and Mareike Ohlberg, *Hidden Hand: Exposing How the Chinese Communist Party Is Reshaping the World* (Melbourne: Hardie Grant, 2020).

5. Kelsey Munro, "A Free Press Is a Magic Weapon Against China's Influence Peddling," *The Interpreter* (Lowy Institute) 18 December 2017.

6. See former Labor foreign minister Bob Carr's article in the CCP-owned China Daily accusing journalists and independent analysts of racism for drawing attention to China's sharp-power operations: "Australians with Chinese Origins Need to Come Together," *China Daily,* 30 April 2019.

7. Garnaut, "How China Interferes in Australia."

8. John Fitzgerald, "Academic Freedom and the Contemporary University: Lessons from China," *Humanities Australia,* 2017, *www.humanities.org.au/ wp-content/uploads/2017/09/AAH-Academy-Lect-Fitzgerald-2016.pdf*; "'They Don't Understand the Fear We Have': How China's Long Reach of Repression Undermines Academic Freedom at Australia's Universities," Human Rights Watch, 30 June 2021, *www.hrw.org/report/2021/06/30/they-dont-understand-fear-we-have/ how-chinas-long-reach-repression-undermines.*

9. James Massola et al., "Treasurer Scott Morrison Blocks Sale of Ausgrid to Foreign Bidders," *Sydney Morning Herald,* 11 August 2016.

10. Peter Drysdale and Zhang Xiaoqiang, *Partnership for Change: Australia-China Joint Economic Report* (Canberra: EABER and China Center for International Economic Exchange, 2016).

11. Paul Kelly, "Friend or Foe? Our China Dilemma Is Our Biggest Test," *The Australian,* 17 August 2016.

12. Malcolm Turnbull, *A Bigger Picture,* Hardie Grant, Melbourne, 2020.

13. Patrick Daly, "Abbott Warns UK on China Dependency," *Canberra Times,* 28 July 2021.

14. David Wroe, "China's Rebuke of Julie Bishop 'Rudest' Conduct Seen in 30 Years, Says Senior Foreign Affairs Official," *Sydney Morning Herald,* 27 February 2014.

15. Gavin Fernando, "A Prominent Chinese Media Outlet Has Launched a Scathing Attack on Australia," *news.com.au,* 2 August 2016.

16. Cited in Cameron Stewart, "Chinese Bullying Won't Be Tolerated," *The Australian,* 12 September 2020.

17. Hamilton, *Silent Invasion.*

18. Chris Uhlman, "Australian Businesses with Close Ties to China Donated $5.5 Million to Political Parties, Investigation Shows," ABC News, 22 August 2016. *www.abc.net.au/news/2016-08-21/ australian-groups-strong-ties-china-political-donations/7768012.*

19. Primrose Riordan, "Sam Dastyari Pledges to Support China on South

China Sea Beside Labor Donor," *Australian Financial Review,* 31 August 2016.

20. Tom Rabe, Kate McClymont, Alexandra Smith, "Dastyari, ICAC and the Chinese 'Agent of Influence,'" *Sydney Morning Herald,* 29 August 2019.

21. Wang Hui, "China Media Signs Deal with Fairfax Media," *China Daily,* 27 May 2016.

22. Paul Barry, "ABC and the Great Firewall of China," Media Watch, 9 May 2016, *www.abc.net.au/mediawatch/transcripts/s4458872.htm.*

23. Christopher Knaus and Tom Phillips, "Turnbull Says Australia Will 'Stand Up' to China as Foreign Influence Row Heats Up," *Guardian,* 8 December 2017.

24. John Fitzgerald, "Mind Your Tongue: Language, Diplomacy and Community Cohesion in Australia–China Relations," ASPI, 2 October 2019, *www.aspistrategist.org.au/mind-your-tongue-language-diplomacy-and-community-in-australia-china-relations.*

25. Australian Associated Press, "ICAC Finds Former NSW Labor MP Engaged in Corrupt Conduct over $100,000 Donation," *Guardian,* 28 February 2022.

26. Vicky Xiuzhong Xu, "Why Is Kevin Rudd Using Chinese Social Media to Criticise Malcolm Turnbull in Mandarin?" ABC News, 5 May 2018, *www.abc.net.au/news/2018-05-05/why-is-rudd-using-weibo-to-slam-turnbulls-china-policies/9726756.*

CHAPTER TEN

Countering Beijing's Media Manipulation

SARAH COOK

THE PEOPLE'S REPUBLIC OF CHINA (PRC) has long sought to influence public debates and media coverage about China in other countries.[1] During the past decade, the Chinese Communist Party (CCP) regime has dramatically expanded its efforts to shape media content in every region of the world. This influence campaign seeks to present China's authoritarian regime as benign, to promote China as a model for governance and information management in developing countries, and to encourage openness to Chinese financing and investment. The campaign simultaneously aims to suppress criticism of the country's domestic policies and the activities of PRC-linked entities abroad, and to win foreign policymakers' vocal support for the regime's positions on matters such as Hong Kong, Taiwan, Tibet, the Xinjiang Uyghur Autonomous Region, and the Falun Gong spiritual group. In addition, the regime is increasingly trying to sway international public opinion on topics less directly linked to China, including U.S. response to the covid-19 pandemic, the effectiveness of Western-made vaccines, Europe's relations with its neighbors, and Philippine presidential candidates.

The CCP's tactics range from traditional public diplomacy to more covert and coercive moves. Somewhere in the middle fall "sharp power" activities that take advantage of the public sphere in open societies and undermine democratic norms, erode national sovereignty, weaken independent media, and violate local laws. No country is immune: The targets include poor, fragile states as well as wealthy democratic powers.

The PRC seeks to manipulate foreign information environments in four key ways—through propaganda, spreading disinformation, censoring critical coverage, and acquiring or building the infrastructure used to disseminate news and share information. Today, hundreds of millions of news consumers around the world are routinely—and often unwittingly—viewing, reading, or listening to information created or shaped by the CCP. Yet while the party's reach has grown and its practices have adapted to local media environments, awareness of its capabilities and impact has not kept pace.

The January 2020 Freedom House report "Beijing's Global Megaphone" found that the constant evolution and expansion of the PRC's media toolbox has accelerated since 2017. The pace of change seems to have increased even more in recent months, as the CCP works to undo the damage to its international reputation from its initial cover-up of covid and to take advantage of the economic troubles and political divisions that have emerged within and among democracies during the pandemic.

Although Beijing's foreign-influence campaign has yielded some gains, it has also encountered obstacles—for example, journalistic integrity, public skepticism about state-run media in target countries,[2] and the outspoken refusal of prominent international institutions and individuals to remain silent about egregious CCP violations, be they mass detentions of Uyghurs or the November 2021 disappearance of tennis star Peng Shuai.

In many countries, governmental and nongovernmental actors alike have come to recognize the threat to democratic freedoms and structures posed by CCP media influence. In the last three years, a wave of resistance has come from the media itself as well as from policymakers, the technology sector, and civil society. Because Beijing is continually refining its strategy and expanding its efforts to new countries, platforms, and issue areas, however, a more coordinated and comprehensive response is needed.

To combat the CCP's media-influence campaign, we must first understand how it operates, how it is evolving, and its effects and limitations. Governmental and nongovernmental actors have been working to counter Beijing's media infiltration and to protect democratic institutions from it. If such efforts are to succeed, they must be upgraded to address China's expanding and evolving strategies.

Propaganda

The Chinese government and state media are spending hundreds of millions of dollars annually to spread their messages to global audiences. Some of these efforts fall within the scope of public diplomacy or soft-power strategies that other governments, including democracies, use. But there are also clear patterns which suggest that Beijing uses covert means to spread its narrative. Chinese state-media content is often disseminated in opaque ways and sometimes relies on either coopted private media or coproductions with private outlets, further obscuring the political and economic motivations behind certain reporting. Such tactics have been used for decades by overseas Chinese-language media to spread CCP messaging, subvert local outlets, amplify pro-Beijing voices, and suppress critical coverage. They are now being applied to mainstream media in other languages.

Key CCP propaganda tactics include a wide variety of means. To raise their profile and extend their influence abroad, official state media publish, under their own names, in foreign media outlets and on social-media platforms such as Twitter and Facebook that are blocked in China. Yet the taglines and profiles used by these Chinese media entities typically omit any reference to their state-run status, while past advertisements have been designed to gain followers among internet users outside of North America and Western Europe.[3] A newer phenomenon is the emergence of Chinese social-media influencers, often sponsored by China Radio International, who post videos on multiple platforms in dozens of languages.[4]

The CCP places its views in foreign mainstream media via op-eds by Chinese diplomats and officials, whose ties to the Chinese state are clear, or through paid "advertorials" and content-sharing agreements that at least partly obscure the content's origins and party-state funding. These methods enable content created by Chinese state media or official sources to circulate widely, reaching foreign audiences through their preferred outlets. For example, since 2018, China's official Xinhua News Agency has signed content-exchange agreements with local news services in both democratic and authoritarian countries, including Australia, Bangladesh, Belarus, Egypt, India, Italy, Laos, Nigeria, Thailand, and Vietnam. Average news consumers in these countries are unlikely to notice Xinhua in an article's byline and might not be aware of the agency's subservience to the CCP in any case.

The PRC also recruits foreign outlets and journalists to produce their own pro-China content. Chinese embassies, provincial governments, and CCP-linked organizations reach out to editors and media owners (at times using implicit or explicit coercion), provide trainings and all-expenses-paid trips to China, sign memoranda of understanding with journalists' unions, and sponsor coproductions and other partnerships that provide political or economic benefits to local media, often in exchange for more positive and less critical coverage of China and its government.[5]

Over the past decade, the PRC has sponsored thousands of choreographed trips to China for journalists, editors, and managers from news outlets around the world. During such trips, the movements of these media guests are monitored and they are typically shown only a limited set of official perspectives on China's development, institutions, and culture. On their return, journalists may be expected to publish glowing articles about China in their home media. Follow-on meetings and conferences targeting senior foreign journalists and editors—organized by Chinese embassies or local-proxy NGOs and research institutions—reinforce the relationships and themes established during the China trips.[6]

Finally, Chinese state entities, private companies with close government ties, and pro-Beijing Chinese and local businesspeople have been buying into existing local media or establishing new outlets in foreign markets. Even when acquisitions do not give such buyers a controlling stake, the access that they obtain enables potential editorial interference. While some outlets have resisted infringements on their independence, others have not. In well-documented cases in the Czech Republic, South Africa, and Taiwan, media outlets have shifted their editorial lines after CCP-linked companies or individuals bought into them.

As these and other forms of CCP influence unfold in various countries, additional dynamics and trends are emerging. First, there is an increasingly clear intersection between broader CCP political influence in a given setting and attempts to shape the media narrative there. Specifically, as particular local leaders, especially high-ranking officials, seek Beijing's favor for political and economic reasons, they echo pro-China talking points and take actions—sometimes at the request of Chinese officials—that reinforce preferred CCP narratives and gain significant local-media attention. For instance, at the beginning of the covid pandemic, top government officials in Europe, including the president of Serbia and the foreign minister of Italy, greeted planeloads of medical supplies arriving in their countries from China and made effusive public statements of gratitude for the assistance. This political theater generated notable media attention and reinforced false public perceptions that China had provided more assistance than had the European Union.

Second, Chinese state media and other propaganda organs continue to diversify their foreign-language output. Initially, major state media such as China Global Television Network (CGTN), the international arm of state broadcaster China Central Television, expanded from providing English and Chinese programming to also broadcasting in Spanish, French, Russian, and Arabic. Today, the state-media footprint is evident in a much wider array of languages and markets: For instance, Thai-vernacular media are replete with content produced by Chinese state media. Much of the China-related news coverage offered by one of Italy's major news agencies is drawn from Xinhua. And Macau-based businessman Kevin Ho's company purchased a 30 percent stake in Portugal's Global Media Group in 2017. Ho has since become a delegate to the National People's Congress, China's largely rubber-stamp parliament, and the media group is seeking new partnerships in other Portuguese-language markets, including Brazil and Mozambique.[7]

Third, in addition to positive messaging about China and its regime, more negative and belligerent narratives targeting perceived CCP competitors and adversaries have emerged. This was first evident when protests against a proposed extradition bill flared in Hong Kong in mid-2019. On the Twitter and Facebook feeds of Chinese state media—sprinkled among glowing posts about pandas, bullet trains, and the Belt and Road Initiative—were videos likening Hong Kong protesters to the Islamic State militant group and the presence of student activists to the use of child soldiers.[8] As U.S.-China relations have soured over the past year, particularly following the coronavirus outbreak, anti-American narratives—including debunked claims that covid originated at a military base in the United States and denigration of the Biden administration's December 2021 Summit for Democracy—have been aggressively promoted.

Disinformation

In 2016, when Russian agents used disinformation tactics to influence the U.S. election, there was sparse evidence that Beijing engaged in similar strategies to manipulate discourse on global social-media platforms. This has clearly changed, as numerous disinformation campaigns and content-manipulation efforts have been attributed to China-based actors.

According to the Oxford Internet Institute, it was in 2019 that the Chinese government displayed "new-found interest in aggressively using Facebook, Twitter, and YouTube."[9]

Over the past two years, those social-media platforms have announced large-scale takedowns of inauthentic China-linked accounts, and independent investigations by journalists, think tanks, and NGOs have revealed repeated and persistent campaigns to spread covid-related conspiracy theories as well as false and demonizing information about Hong Kong pro-democracy protesters, CCP critics and Chinese civil society activists inside and outside of China, and Taiwanese politicians and electoral candidates from the Democratic Progressive Party. The tools employed include content farms that push out information simultaneously across multiple platforms; hijacked or purchased Facebook groups, pages, and accounts; text-messaging campaigns; coordinated trolling activities meant to manipulate search results; and automated "bot" networks organized to influence Twitter hashtags. In many cases, direct attribution to Chinese party-state actors has been challenging, but evidence of such ties has been found in several instances. And in all cases, the campaigns and networks appeared to support well-documented political and content preferences of the CCP.[10]

As with propaganda efforts, disinformation activity appears to be expanding, both in scale and audience.[11] Moreover, some of the campaigns—in the United States, Taiwan, Argentina, and elsewhere—appeared designed to sow divisions within democratic societies and alliances, rather than simply to promote pro-Beijing viewpoints.[12]

Censorship

A decade ago, the CCP's efforts to censor external media appeared to focus mainly on international outlets operating within China and on Chinese-language outlets abroad, including those in Hong Kong and Taiwan.[13] Campaigns to influence the mainstream media in Africa, Europe, Latin America, Southeast Asia, and elsewhere were generally limited to propaganda—the promotion of Chinese state-media content and narratives—and did not aim to suppress critical local coverage. This too appears to be changing, particularly as PRC-linked entities increase their investments abroad and grow more sensitive to local debates about China's role in those countries. Chinese officials have begun to use economic leverage to silence negative reporting or commentary in local-language media with greater frequency.

The CCP's methods for securing silence can be grouped into four main categories: direct action by Chinese-government representatives; positive and negative incentives for self-censorship among media owners; indirect pressure through proxies such as advertisers and local governments; and physical, cyber, or verbal attacks. In Sweden and Russia, for example, Chinese embassy officials insulted and threatened journalists and news outlets in response to critical reporting about the CCP regime's persecution of abducted bookseller Gui Minhai and the state of the Chinese economy. Although the journalists did not appear to adjust their coverage as a result, the pressure demonstrated the possible costs that similar future coverage could entail. In Nigeria, the editors of an outlet whose journalists sought to cover stories that could have been unfavorable to China reportedly submitted to input from PRC embassy officials and pushed a more positive angle. In South Africa, five years after two companies with ties to the Chinese government and state media purchased a 20 percent stake in the country's second-largest media group, a writer who covered China's repression of Uyghurs in Xinjiang saw his column abruptly dropped.[14] And in May 2019, Nepal's state news agency, which has a content-sharing agreement with Xinhua, launched an investigation into three reporters who had circulated a news item about the Dalai Lama, the exiled Tibetan spiritual leader whose very name and image are strictly censored inside China.[15]

It is not by chance that Beijing's multibillion-dollar effort to expand the reach of state-run media has been coupled with increasing attempts to silence critical voices and reporting in other countries. For the party's narrative to be convincing to audiences inside China and beyond, reporting about the darker sides of CCP rule at home and of PRC activities abroad must be controlled and suppressed. Indeed, in several instances, the expansion of Chinese state media in a given setting—in media markets as diverse as Cambodia, France, Hong Kong, and Papua New Guinea—has coincided with or directly resulted in the displacement of information sources that are more editorially independent or critical of the Chinese government. For example, when top leader Xi Jinping visited Papua New Guinea in November 2018, local and international journalists were barred from covering his meeting with eight regional leaders and told instead to use reporting by Xinhua or video from China Central Television as the basis for their coverage.[16]

Over the past decade, Chinese companies have become increasingly active in building information infrastructure and content-dissemination systems abroad. Although privately owned, technology giants such as Huawei and Tencent retain close ties with the PRC government and security services, routinely providing censorship and surveillance assistance to the party-state. The international expansion of such companies has received the explicit blessing of the CCP.

As these and other China-based firms gain more influence and control over the avenues of content transmission and dissemination, they open the door to a whole new level of influence. CCP-friendly gatekeepers are now positioned to manage information flows in other countries. Intelligence analyst Peter Mattis has argued that the CCP's approach in the last ten years has been at least as much about controlling the medium as about controlling the message: "This way . . . they can have essentially a monopoly on the information environment—that makes it easier for their narratives to be received and accepted."[17]

There is already evidence of Chinese companies using their control over dissemination channels to create advantages for Chinese state media or to suppress information deemed undesirable by Beijing. In the digital-television sector, the Chinese company StarTimes has become a dominant player in Africa. Although it offers television service to millions of people who previously lacked access, its efforts are aiding Chinese state media. The most affordable and therefore most popular packages feature a combination of local stations and Chinese state-run outlets. Packages that include more independent global-news sources such as the BBC and CNN are significantly more expensive. Beyond Africa, China-based companies are facilitating digital-television expansion in countries such as Cambodia, Pakistan, and Timor-Leste, again seemingly to the advantage of Chinese state-television stations.

In the social-media sphere, China-based companies' growing role in content-dissemination systems creates opportunities for the CCP to influence not only foreigners' views about China, but also the news that they receive about their own countries and political leaders, with possible implications for policymaking and election outcomes.[18] This was already the case among Chinese diaspora communities, where WeChat, Tencent's popular messaging application, has been found to censor the posts of Chinese activists and independent media while allowing pro-Beijing media and narratives to spread widely. The app's design has also been criticized for its tendency to deemphasize the source and credibility of information, aiding the spread of misinformation and making the fight against fake news even more difficult than it is on other social-media platforms.[19] The growing use of WeChat among non-Chinese speakers in settings ranging from Malaysia and Mongolia to Australia and Canada also creates a strong foundation for future CCP disinformation campaigns and election meddling.

An August 2020 Reuters report revealed that, from 2018 to mid-2020, the Chinese tech firm ByteDance censored articles critical of the Chinese government on its Baca Berita (BaBe) news-aggregator app, which is used by millions in Indonesia. ByteDance did so per instructions from a team at the company's Beijing headquarters. The restricted content reportedly included references to "Tiananmen" and "Mao Zedong," as well as to China-Indonesia tensions over the South China Sea and a local ban on the video-sharing app TikTok, which is also owned by ByteDance.[20] Conflicting reports from the company and sources cited in the article claimed that the moderation rules became less restrictive in either 2019 or mid-2020.

The Campaign's Impact

As the Chinese party-state pours resources into its foreign-propaganda and censorship efforts, it is important to ask how effective they have been in different parts of the world at shaping public perceptions or achieving other CCP goals, such as suppressing criticism. The answer to this question is mixed. Some of Beijing's initiatives have run into significant stumbling blocks, particularly in regard to the onset of the pandemic and the mass detention of Uyghurs and other Turkic minorities in Xinjiang, offsetting previous gains. Other projects have been remarkably effective or laid the groundwork for long-term advances.

In terms of China's image around the world, Pew Research Center public-opinion surveys and academic studies indicate that in the early years of state-media expansion, views on China and Xi Jinping improved—particularly in parts of the global South, including several African countries, as well as in Argentina, Brazil, India, and Lebanon.[21] Since 2015, however, the share of respondents expressing a favorable view of China in Pew surveys has declined—sometimes precipitously—in influential developing countries such as Argentina, Brazil, India, Indonesia, Kenya, and the Philippines.[22] Although it is difficult to isolate the precise cause, the dip has coincided with Beijing's taking increasingly aggressive actions in the South China Sea, enacting a program of mass detention in Xinjiang (and its exposure by international media and researchers), and making dramatic moves to curtail freedom and autonomy in Hong Kong. After news reports relayed how an initial cover-up by CCP officials had exacerbated the global spread of the novel coronavirus, public views of China and Xi Jinping reached historic lows in many countries, especially those with advanced economies.[23]

Indeed, the regime's ability to shift public perceptions in its favor has encountered serious challenges. A YouGov–Cambridge Globalism Project survey of 26,000 people in 25 countries, published in October 2020, found that the overwhelming majority of participants in every country but China believed that the coronavirus was first detected in China—including more than 85 percent of respondents in Nigeria, South Africa, and Spain, and 83 percent in Saudi Arabia.[24] This is despite the persistent efforts of state media and PRC diplomats on Twitter to deflect blame and relocate the virus's origin to the United States, Italy, or elsewhere. More broadly, surveys and focus groups conducted in Kenya and South Africa, as well as interviews with media professionals in the countries of the Mekong River region, suggest that journalists in many developing countries are skeptical of Chinese state media.[25]

But measurements of public or journalistic opinion do not tell the full story. Of equal or greater significance are the more subtle ways in which Beijing has successfully insinuated its content, economic leverage, and influence into foreign media markets, and the extent to which this has begun to bear fruit. Content-sharing agreements signed by Xinhua and other such partnerships established over the course of many years have resulted in vast amounts of Chinese state-media content flooding the news in countries such as Italy and Thailand. In some countries, coverage of the potential risks of China's foreign investments and lending has been stifled, and outlets critical of Beijing have suffered from or been threatened with financial difficulties. Ongoing efforts to coopt or marginalize independent Chinese-diaspora news outlets and to censor critical views on Chinese-owned social-media platforms such as WeChat have reduced overseas Chinese audiences' access to unbiased information—not only about events within China, but also about their home country's relationship with Beijing and other topics relevant to their day-to-day lives.

CCP Strengths and Democratic Vulnerabilities

Beijing's growing influence on foreign media can in part be explained by China's emergence as a global power over the past two decades. In 2000, China was the world's sixth-largest economy, and it accounted for only 22 million internet users. It is now the world's second-largest economy and boasts the most internet users by far—more than 900 million as of March 2020, according to government figures.

Added to the general increase in China's global presence are the vast human and financial resources that the CCP, state media, and Chinese tech entrepreneurs invest in expanding their reach among foreign audiences, credibly estimated to cost hundreds of millions of dollars annually. Beyond the media sector, Chinese-government–led engagement with foreign states—including through the Belt and Road Initiative, a sprawling trade and infrastructure-development program launched in 2013—has created new incentives for local politicians to curry favor with Beijing. When investment flows to industries or locales of political significance or serves the business interests of local-media owners, news coverage is more likely to reflect Beijing's implicit or explicit preferences—whether in terms of uncritical promotions of China-linked projects or a reluctance to publish investigations or commentary that call such projects into question. China's massive internet-user population is also a powerful inducement for foreign-media entities seeking consumers for their entertainment and other products to tread carefully with the Chinese authorities.

Although numerous important CCP assets support the regime's media-influence efforts, their success is aided by existing weaknesses within democratic and semidemocratic countries that should not be ignored. These include the financial vulnerability of local media; high levels of political polarization and mistrust in the media; an imbalance of expertise between Chinese actors, on the one hand, and local politicians, journalists, think tanks, and civil society, on the other, to the benefit of Beijing; longstanding inroads in the Chinese-language media sector; the increasingly widespread use of social media or news-aggregator apps owned by PRC-based companies; and a high degree of anti-U.S. or anti-Western sentiment in many parts of the world.

A Shifting Tide?

Despite the strengths brought to bear by the CCP and the opportunities provided by certain democratic weaknesses, a review of recent global developments points to a growing accumulation of advocacy, expertise, policymaking, legislation, and activities aimed at countering Beijing's media influence and protecting democratic institutions. These actions span the governmental, civil society, and private sectors.

Exposing and analyzing disinformation campaigns and tactics are among the key efforts to address Chinese influence on foreign media. Over the last two years, think tanks, investigative journalists, technology firms, and cybersecurity companies have been examining datasets related to China-linked disinformation campaigns. These studies have generated a body of literature on the topic and provided guidance for improvements in prevention, monitoring, and remediation.

In the technology sector, international social-media companies such as Twitter, Facebook, and YouTube, in coordination with researchers and civil society, have built upon the accumulated knowledge and put in place new measures to track inauthentic activity linked to China, expose emerging disinformation campaigns, take down problematic accounts, and implement labeling that clearly designates Chinese state-funded or state-affiliated accounts. In the media sector, several prominent U.S. and U.K. news outlets have discontinued paid advertorial supplements from Chinese state media. Although the outlets have not made public statements explaining the policy change, it coincides with reports spotlighting problematic content about covid in CCP-linked advertorials; increased transparency about the revenue generated from the advertorials; and the expulsion from China of the outlets' own correspondents.[26] Journalists, editors, and broadcasters in countries as diverse as Argentina, Ghana, Sri Lanka, and Thailand have been taking steps to thwart problematic CCP media influence—for example, publishing op-eds by activists in response to those of Chinese ambassadors, writing detailed accounts of how Chinese state-media content reaches local audiences, rejecting offers of misleading paid content from Chinese agents, and urging regulators to reconsider granting a digital-TV bid to StarTimes.

In Hong Kong and Taiwan, English- and Chinese-language digital media start-ups have become increasingly influential, providing a counterbalance to self-censorship among traditional media. Many such outlets are nonprofits or were founded by prominent print and television journalists who were concerned about encroaching self-censorship on China-related issues; this may make them less vulnerable to ownership changes that could curtail their editorial independence. Still, their experiments with funding models have had mixed results, and Hong Kong–based outlets have faced new threats (including prosecution and closure) since Beijing's imposition of the repressive National Security Law in the territory in June 2020.

Civil society actors across several countries and regions have launched new initiatives to monitor Chinese state media and other forms of CCP influence. These include projects to support investigative journalism related to China, documentation of media narratives and social-media activity by Chinese state outlets and diplomats, in-depth case studies of influence networks in various settings, and well-informed policy briefs offering concrete legislative, regulatory, and other solutions to decisionmakers.

Some of the most effective responses to problematic CCP media influence have been the result of cross-sector collaboration. For instance, a joint project by a data-analysis firm and an investigative journalist produced a report on a Twitter-bot manipulation campaign in Italy; the United Kingdom's media regulator, the Office of Communications, prompted by submissions from a British citizen and a European civil society group, investigated CGTN and found it guilty of violating broadcasting rules; and the aggressive attention and efforts of Taiwanese-government entities, international technology firms, and local civil society initiatives appear to have helped reduce the influence of Chinese-state–linked disinformation campaigns on Taiwan's January 2020 general elections from the level seen during the November 2018 mayoral elections.[27]

These actions have had some success in curtailing problematic media investments, thwarting disinformation campaigns, increasing transparency, and shifting incentives in a direction less favorable to Beijing.

Nevertheless, there remains enormous untapped potential for media-development projects, journalism training and education, and broadcasting regulations aimed at protecting and enhancing media independence. These tools can and should be deployed more systematically to address the challenges posed by China's foreign-media influence. Indeed, many of the actions that would inoculate foreign media against CCP manipulation would also serve to protect them from other forms of malign influence—whether foreign or domestic—and would generally improve a country's journalistic capacity and autonomy.

Facing the Future

The global media landscape has undergone a quiet but notable change over the past decade. China and its ruling Communist Party have become integral players in media markets around the world, demonstrating repeatedly that no market is too small to warrant attention. This phenomenon continues to expand. Every democracy or semidemocracy faces a host of domestic concerns, challenges, and regulatory debates surrounding press and internet freedom. But today it is imperative that all actors engaged in the media space—be they journalists, regulators, technology firms, or press-freedom groups—acknowledge the influence exerted by China's authoritarian regime on the news and information circulating in their print publications, radio broadcasts, television programs, and social-media feeds. They need to be aware of the CCP's tactics, alert to the pitfalls inherent in media engagement and partnerships with Chinese state-run outlets, and prepared for the economic and political pressure they may face to adjust content or otherwise submit to pro-Beijing propaganda, disinformation, censorship, or self-censorship.

Hundreds of incidents that have occurred around the world over the past decade demonstrate that once the CCP—or a company, media outlet, or owner with close ties to the party—gains a foothold within an information-dissemination channel, manipulation efforts inevitably follow. This may not occur immediately, but can evolve over time or be activated as soon as a test case with sufficient significance to Beijing emerges. At that point, CCP leaders, Chinese diplomats, and other state-linked actors will not hesitate to use previously acquired economic and political leverage to impose their will.

The linguistic and topical reach of the CCP's media influence is expanding more deeply into the internal affairs of other societies—targeting, for example, Chinese-diaspora communities, investment deals, and electoral contests. As this expansion continues, the areas of daily life and policymaking within foreign democracies in which Beijing has a stake will grow commensurately, as will the CCP's desire to push public debate in its desired direction.

The modern media landscape is vast and complex. The number of nongovernmental actors and industries alone that must respond to Chinese pressure is enormous. These include the media industry, particularly editors and owners, because they are often more susceptible to economic coercion or political pressure to kill stories than are frontline reporters; technology firms, which are still grappling with the problem of how to manage state-media accounts that have tens of millions of followers as well as emerging troll and bot networks that spread disinformation; scholars and researchers, who monitor, track, and expose media-influence activities and disinformation campaigns; and press-freedom groups, human-rights advocates, and journalists' unions, which are essential channels for influencing policy, training reporters, and raising awareness among media, governments, and the general public.

From this perspective, despite the recent increase in scattered activities to counter CCP media influence, one of the greatest needs is for the "CCP factor" to be integrated into all nongovernmental work related to protecting media and internet freedom. This could be accomplished as part of a broader initiative to address foreign authoritarian influence in the media sector and to enhance local resilience in the face of such pressures. But China is by far the largest and most well-resourced actor in this space globally, and some of its tactics and avenues for insinuating content are unique to Beijing. An effective response therefore requires focused awareness-raising efforts. The CCP takes a whole-of-society approach to authoritarian control, and a whole-of-society approach—as appropriate in a democratic polity—is necessary in response. Absent such action, within a decade, one of the world's most repressive and intrusive regimes could have an even firmer foothold in the local media ecosystems of democracies across the globe, to the grave peril of free expression, public debate, and electoral integrity.

Notes

1. Sarah Cook, "The Long Shadow of Chinese Censorship," Center for International Media Assistance, 22 October 2013, *www.cima.ned.org/wp-content/uploads/2015/02/CIMA-China_Sarah%20 Cook.pdf*; Herman Wasserman and Dani Madrid-Morales, "The Limits of Chinese Interference in Africa's Media Landscape," Asia Dialogue, 16 October 2018, *https://theasiadialogue.com/2018/10/16/the-limits-of-chinese-interference-in-africas-media-landscape*.

2. Herman Wasserman and Dani Madrid-Morales, "How Influential Are Chinese Media in Africa? An Audience Analysis in Kenya and South Africa," *International Journal of Communication* 12 (2018): 2212–31.

3. This conclusion is based on analysis of Facebook ads issued from CGTN accounts in multiple languages, conducted in November 2018 and December 2019.

4. Clint Watts, "'The One Like One Share Initiative'—How China Deploys Social Media Influencers to Spread Its Message," 21 September 2021, *https:// clintwatts.substack.com/p/the-one-like-one-share-initiative*.

5. Louisa Lim and Julia Bergin, "The China Story: Reshaping the World's Media," IFJ Research Report on China and Its Impact on Media 2020, June 2020.

6. Nadège Rolland, "Commanding Ideas: Think Tanks as Platforms for Authoritarian Influence," Sharp Power and Democratic Resilience Series, International Forum for Democratic Studies, December 2020.

7. Jasmine Chia, "Thai Media Is Outsourcing Much of Its Coronavirus Coverage to Beijing and That's Just the Start," *Thai Inquirer,* 31 January 2020. "ANSA-Xinhua Collaboration Accord Signed," ANSA, 22 March 2019; Gabriele Carrer, "Beijing Speaking: How the Italian Public Broadcasting TV Fell in Love with China," *Formiche,* 8 April 2020; "Kevin Ho's Macau Firm Buys 30% Stake of Portuguese Media Group," Macao News, 7 November 2017; Nelson Moura, "Global Media Launched Today Its New Portuguese, English, and Chinese News Platforms," Macau News Agency, 2 July 2018.

8. CGTN, "Rioters, Get Your Hands Off Children," Facebook Watch, 23 September 2019, *www.facebook.com/watch/?v=2495151990809474*.

9. Samantha Bradshaw and Philip N. Howard, "The Global Disinformation Order: 2019 Global Inventory of Organised Social Media Manipulation," Working Paper 2019, Oxford Internet Institute, i.

10. "Tom Uren, Elise Thomas, and Jacob Wallis, "Tweeting Through the Great Firewall: Preliminary Analysis of PRC-Linked Information Operations

Against the Hong Kong Protests," Australian Strategic Policy Institute, 3 September 2019; Edward Wong, Matthew Rosenberg, and Julian E. Barnes, "Chinese Agents Helped Spread Messages that Sowed Virus Panic in U.S., Officials Say," *New York Times*, 22 April 2020; "China Media Bulletin: Student Indoctrination, Surveillance Innovation, GitHub Mobilization," Freedom House, *China Media Bulletin* 135 (April 2019); and Sarah Cook, "Welcome to the New Era of Chinese Government Disinformation," *Diplomat*, 11 May 2020.

11. Sarah Cook, "China's Content Manipulation Reaches New Frontiers," *Diplomat*, 16 November 2021.

12. "News Outlets in Argentina Offered Cash to Publish Articles Defaming Falun Gong," Falun Dafa Information Center, 27 April 2020, *https://faluninfo.net/ news-outlets-in-argentina-offered-cash-to-publish-articles-defaming-falun-gong*.

13. Björn Jerdén and Viking Bohman, "China's Propaganda Campaign in Sweden, 2018–2019," Swedish Institute of International Affairs, *UI Brief* 4, June 2019; "Russian Newspaper Criticized China's Threat to Blacklist Journalist," Chinascope, 6 March 2019.

14. Azad Essa, "China Is Buying African Media's Silence," *Foreign Policy*, 14 September 2018.

15. "Nepal Probes Journalists for Dalai Lama News Amid Fears of Growing Chinese Influence," *Hong Kong Free Press*, 14 May 2019.

16. In 2008, the French satellite firm Eutelsat cut its transmission of NTDTV to China, apparently in exchange for the opportunity to broadcast Xinhua's English-language news channel in Europe; Cook, *The Long Shadow of Chinese Censorship*, 42–43. Nathan Vanderklippe, "In Cambodia, Independent Media Close as Chinese Content Moves In," *Globe and Mail*, 29 December 2017; Benjamin Haas, "Radio Silence: 24-Hour Broadcast of BBC World Service Dropped in Hong Kong," *Guardian*, 12 August 2017; Natalie Whiting, "China Boots Media from Pacific Island Leaders Meeting with Chinese President Xi Jinping," ABC.net (Australian Broadcasting Corporation), 16 November 2018.

17. Quoted in Sean Mantesso and Christina Zhou, "China's Multibillion Dollar Media Campaign 'A Major Threat for Democracies' Around the World," ABC.net, 7 February 2019.

18. See Lim and Bergin, "The China Story: Reshaping the World's Media"; Gregory Winger, "China's Disinformation Campaign in the Philippines," *Diplomat*, 6 October 2020; Ed Johnson, "WeChat Deletes Australian PM's Appeal to Chinese Community," Bloomberg, 2 December 2020.

19. Eileen Gud, "How WeChat Spreads Rumors, Reaffirms Bias, and Helped Elect Trump," *Wired,* 20 April 2017.

20. Fanny Potkin, "Exclusive: ByteDance Censored Anti-China Content in Indonesia until mid-2020, Sources Say," Reuters, 13 August 2020.

21. These examples are based on a comparison of results from Pew surveys in 2007 and 2013/2015 depending on data availability for particular states. See Andrew Kohut, "How the World Sees China," Pew Research Center Report, 11 December 2007; Andrew Kohut, "America's Global Image Remains More Positive than China's: But Many See China Becoming World's Leading Power," Pew Research Center Report, 18 July 2013, *pewglobal.org*; Richard Wike, Bruce Stokes, and Jacob Poushter, "Views of China and the Global Balance of Power," ch. 2 in "Global Publics Back U.S. on Fighting ISIS, but Are Critical of Post-9/11 Torture," Pew Research Center Report, 23 June 2015.

22. This is based on a comparison of results from Pew surveys in 2015 and 2019. Wike, Stokes, and Poushter, "Views of China and the Global Balance of Power"; Laura Silver, Kat Devlin, and Christine Huang, "People Around the Globe Are Divided in Their Opinions of China," Pew Research Center, 5 December 2019.

23. Laura Silver, Kat Devlin, and Christine Huang, "Unfavorable Views of China Reach Historic Highs in Many Countries," Pew Research Center, 6 October 2020.

24. Patrick Wintour and Tobi Thomas, "China Loses Trust Internationally over Coronavirus Handling," *Guardian,* 27 October 2020.

25. Wasserman and Madrid-Morales, "How Influential Are Chinese Media in Africa?"; Heidi Holz and Ryan Loomis, "China's Efforts to Shape the Information Environment in the Mekong Region," Center for a New American Security, September 2020.

26. Dean Sterling Jones, "A British Newspaper Has Given Chinese Coronavirus Propaganda a Direct Line to the UK," *BuzzFeed News,* 8 April 2020; Chuck Ross, "Chinese Propaganda Outlet Has Paid U.S. Newspapers $19 Million for Advertising, Printing," *Daily Caller,* 8 June 2020; Marc Tracy, Edward Wong, and Lara Jakes, "China Announces That It Will Expel American Journalists," *New York Times,* 17 March 2020.

27. Di Francesco Bechis and Gabriele Carrer, "How China Unleashed Twitter Bots to Spread COVID-19 Propaganda in Italy," *Formiche,* 31 March 2020; Alex Hern, "UK-Based Chinese News Network CGTN Faces Possible Ban," *Guardian,* 6 July 2020; Aaron Huang, "Combatting and Defeating Chinese Propaganda and Disinformation: A Case Study of Taiwan's 2020 Elections," Belfer Center for Science and International Affairs, July 2020.

CHAPTER ELEVEN

Conclusion: Sharp Power and the Threat to Democracy

CHRISTOPHER WALKER

W E ARE WELL INTO THE SECOND DECADE of an authoritarian resurgence that has reshaped the global landscape. Autocratic powers, led by China and Russia, have become more assertive and ambitious. The authorities in these repressive settings work relentlessly to deny their own people the right to participate in the governments of their countries. They seek to dominate media, education, and the courts to marginalize alternative points of view. Pervasive technologies that were widely thought to offer advantages for greater freedom instead are affording ambitious leaders in Beijing, Moscow, and elsewhere potent new tools of manipulation and control. A global financial system vulnerable to kleptocracy and its networks also favors the autocrats. In crucial and unanticipated ways, the world has become flatter for the authoritarians.

Over a protracted period, the autocrats have tightened the screws at home. Along with other unremittingly repressive regimes—such as Cuba, Iran, and Saudi Arabia—China and Russia also are actively exerting influence beyond their borders and view democratic publics abroad in a manner similar to how they view their own populations: as hostile forces needing to be neutralized or controlled. In today's interconnected world they have the tools to do so. In an era of globalization, the autocrats' domestic standards and behaviors do not remain neatly contained within their borders. The fall of the Soviet Union and China's embrace of market reforms have produced thick linkages between autocracies and democracies. As hopes that these ties would encourage political reform in autocracies faded, authoritarians took the offensive. Autocrats have developed more interactive, multidimensional, and often nuanced ways to project influence. As part of the ambitious global engagement of the Chinese Communist Party

(CCP), for instance, Chinese authorities are training officials from developing countries in censoring the internet, controlling civil society, and building a single-party regime.[1] The Russian authorities have developed their own forms of global engagement that invariably affect democratic standards and values in damaging ways.[2]

As nonmilitary activities falling outside the scope of "hard power," these influence efforts have been commonly understood as "soft power." However, this framing is inadequate and has led to a dangerous complacency among democracies. Unlike soft power, which relies on attraction, these corrosive and compromising influence efforts often rely on manipulation and outward-facing forms of censorship. In 2017, Jessica Ludwig and I first described these influence activities as "sharp power" because they pierce and penetrate the information and political environments of targeted countries in order to "monopolize ideas, suppress alternative narratives, and exploit partner institutions."[3]

Given the new circumstances, a crucial question arises: What happens when repressive powers systematically exert influence in systems and institutions that are central to the functioning of democracy? With a growing body of research available, including the essays that appear in this volume, the answer to this question has become clearer. It should be a cause for concern for anyone who would like to see democracy and the ideas that underlie it flourish.

As authoritarian influence has spread, so too have the risks for democracy. Russia's full-blown attack on Ukraine brought these dangers into sharper relief. Yet democracies have not developed adequate strategies to hold repressive regimes accountable or to address the autocrats' sophisticated and compromising forms of international influence. The authoritarian mobilization that has taken shape over an extended period of time is a powerful reminder of the global stakes for democracy that ineluctably have come into view.

Authoritarian regimes, unlike liberal democracies, rely on a combination of repression, ideological dogma, and political censorship to survive. Autocrats monopolize the generation and dissemination of ideas. Years of repression and increasingly stifling censorship under Vladimir Putin have turned Russia into a police state. Since Russia's invasion of Ukraine in February 2022, the Kremlin has gone so far as to ban calling it a "war" or "invasion"; it prefers the term "special operation." Violators of this ban can land up to fifteen years in prison.

The People's Republic of China (PRC), for its part, has built a state-of-the-art censorship apparatus, increasingly through the use of cutting-edge technology. The so-called Great Firewall aims to seal off internet users in China from the rest of the worldwide web, blocking access to Western sites such as Google and Twitter. Alternative Chinese platforms such as WeChat offer users online conveniences that in practice enable greater censorship and monitoring. These are but one part of a wide-ranging, comprehensive censorship and control apparatus that increasingly relies on automation and big-data capabilities—along with a massive effort to collect DNA from millions of people—to entrap the Chinese population in an integrated, omnipresent web of surveillance. The authorities in Beijing doubtless have built out this encompassing techno-surveillance and censorship capacity in order to cement political control for the long haul. As economic conditions in China weaken and the government's performance legitimacy frays, Beijing will progressively rely upon techno-control for regime security purposes.

"Document Number 9," a 2013 internal CCP memo, underscores the regime's motivation to pursue censorship and is reflective of its ethos. The document warns that democratic values—including constitutionalism, independent civil society, and free expression—pose a grave threat to CCP ideology and one-party rule. As part of Xi Jinping's recentralization of political power within the CCP, there has been a massive scaling up of international outreach, especially in the CCP's relations with other authoritarian ruling parties.[4]

Over the past five years, awareness of the sharp-power threat has grown considerably, but the autocrats are adapting. While journalists and civil society are shining light on the problem, transparency alone is insufficient. Most democracies are at best in the early stages of tackling the threats posed by the elite capture, divide-and-conquer tactics, and technological encroachment that are integral to authoritarians' outward-facing engagement. Free societies must therefore come to grips with the new reality and develop more purposeful means of reversing the authoritarian momentum.

Democratic Complacency

Authoritarian regimes have been waging an active assault on democracy for quite some time. The effects of this battering are now clearly visible.

Authorities in countries from Afghanistan to Zimbabwe have launched massive crackdowns, often with impunity. Cooperation and learning among these repressive regimes has been normalized. Anne Applebaum observes that rather than simply dealing with the government in their home capitals, in this new environment democratic activists and reformers today in fact must fight multiple autocrats, in multiple countries, part of a phenomenon that she calls "Autocracy, Inc."[5]

Free societies' misguided assumptions about the inevitable triumph of liberal democracy have only worsened the authoritarian challenge. In the wake of the Cold War, Western democracies were convinced that deep engagement with Russia and China—particularly economic integration—would yield clear mutual benefits and encourage meaningful political reform. During this period, the West welcomed the PRC into the international system, believing that doing so would lead it to develop into a "responsible stakeholder."

But in retrospect, democracies made a crucial error in their interactions with autocracies. Free societies largely put aside their own inherent competitive advantage—the principles of democratic accountability and transparency. By turning a blind eye to the authoritarians' corrupt practices, succumbing to self-censorship, or otherwise letting the authoritarians set the terms of engagement, democracies and their key institutions ceded much ground. Universities in open societies, for instance, were far too permissive in allowing PRC-affiliated cultural and language centers (known as Confucius Institutes), along with a wide range of other authoritarian-sourced initiatives that might compromise academic integrity, on their campuses. Over time, authoritarian regimes buckled down and asserted their own preferences.

With a first-mover advantage and a keen ability to adapt, the authoritarians have taken the initiative. Their momentum has spread and intensified tyranny around the world. This is apparent, for example, in what is known as "transnational repression,"[6] in which governments reach across borders to silence dissent among diasporas and exiled democrats—shattering international state-sovereignty norms. The gruesome murder of Jamal Khashoggi at the hands of Saudi authorities is arguably the most widely known example of this growing phenomenon. The technological revolution of the past few decades has brought digital forms of transnational repression that make it even easier for dictators to hound and intimidate activists, journalists, and critics, no matter where they are.⁷

Think Different

The global authoritarian offensive is hardly limited to the repression of individual activists or advocacy groups, however. It is far more ambitious. Leading authoritarian powers are targeting the minds of foreign publics by manipulating key institutions in democracies, including universities, publishers, think tanks, policy institutes, media outlets, and entertainment companies.

Knowledge-sector institutions now confront vexing asymmetries in their relationships with authoritarian powers that leave them open to sharp-power efforts to compromise their integrity. For example, foreign scholars of the PRC, Iran, and the United Arab Emirates have encountered a range of repressive tactics; although they are often subtle, they can also be quite crude. As an early indicator of the Chinese party-state's determination to manipulate discourse, at the annual meeting of the European Association of Chinese Studies in 2014 personnel from Confucius Institute Headquarters seized printed conference programs and returned them with several pages missing, including ones touting a sponsorship from a Taiwanese foundation.⁸

China and Russia, in particular, have built out formidable global-media infrastructures, which increasingly collaborate with media enterprises in democracies and autocracies alike in order to disseminate friendly messages about their regimes and block critical coverage. For instance, the Russian authorities have made content from the Russian state-owned news agency Sputnik free to use, whereas Reuters and other international news agencies charge client outlets for their services. Another part of the Kremlin's media strategy includes hidden or indirect pressure through, for example, opaque foreign-media financing or disguised mergers and acquisitions. The Kremlin may even involve foreign news outlets that have no overt connection to Russia.⁹ These methods have enabled Russian authorities to pollute foreign media ecosystems and manipulate their audiences: While the Kremlin's messaging around its invasion of Ukraine has largely fallen on deaf ears in the West, it has gained traction in much of the global South.

The CCP's global information strategy relies on a combination of censorship and propaganda. It now includes, in addition to positive messaging about China and its regime, more bellicose and corrosive narratives targeting perceived enemies. For example, during the 2019 protests in Hong Kong, Chinese state media posted videos to Facebook and Twitter that compared "protesters to the Islamic State militant group and the presence of student activists to the use of child soldiers."[10]

The scope and scale of China's engagement are also apparent in the entertainment industry. Aynne Kokas explains how the CCP increasingly "relies less on the attractive power of Chinese media corporations as partners than on threats to cut off access to the Chinese market," as part of the weaponization of "corporations' dependence on political authorities for market access to control content." Through this controlling approach, the Chinese authorities have effectively conditioned powerful institutions in free societies to "limit what they say about topics that Beijing deems sensitive." Kokas observes that among the things that set soft power apart from sharp power are "the time and location at which the power is exercised." Sharp power is more likely to be exerted as the media content is being produced or distributed, seeking to control content at its source, whereas "soft power would be exerted as the audience reads, hears, or watches the media product."[11] This key observation is also highly relevant to the technological sphere in which control or manipulation of information at its source increasingly is an ambition of the authoritarians.[12]

Sharp-power efforts have reached every corner of the world. Russian authorities propound ideas and concepts (including absolutist approaches to state sovereignty and nationalist or populist visions of democracy) that now course through Latin American academia and the media.[13] China is building a media bridgehead in sub-Saharan Africa; the effects on the local media ecosystem remain poorly understood.[14] Russia has also built out its engagement in Africa, all too often to the detriment of the continent's stability and its democracies.[15] The effects of this global authoritarian media onslaught have become clearer. In the context of Russia's horrific, full-blown war in Ukraine, far too many audiences outside the trans-Atlantic democracies have bought into the Kremlin's distortions, which Chinese state media have readily amplified around the world.[16]

The application of sharp-power tactics globally has accelerated a worldwide shift toward authoritarianism and away from democracy. But as Edward Lucas observes, free societies are "losing the battle of ideas with authoritarian regimes, not because [democratic] ideas are weak, but because the battlefield is skewed against them."[17] To gain the upper hand, democracies need new ways to level the field and respond to the challenge.

The Cutting Edge of the Sharp-Power Struggle

Most democracies have remained complacent in the face of the sharp-power threat. But when put to the test, a few countries have responded adeptly. Australia was arguably the first country to mobilize in earnest against the China challenge. Over the past two decades, the Chinese party-state increased its intrusive activities in Australia across a diverse range of sectors. John Fitzgerald describes how Beijing's "integrated networks" of influence had four key goals: to 1) directly control Chinese-language media in Australia; 2) cow community groups and universities into suppressing criticism of the PRC; 3) shape the foreign-policy preferences of political parties; and 4) build a formal presence for the CCP's insidious international arm, the United Front Work Department. For instance, Australian stations owned by Beijing's China Radio International ran "programs supporting Beijing's claims while ignoring other views."[18]

By the time Australian society started to mobilize against this authoritarian encroachment, the party-state and its surrogates had already infiltrated core democratic and civic institutions. Local elites and organizations were in effect repurposed to advance the strategic goals of the world's most formidable authoritarian regime. Among the most visible and critical examples is that of former Australian senator Sam Dastyari. He offered Chinese billionaire Huang Xiangmo "countersurveillance" advice and promised to respect Beijing's claims in the South China Sea at a public campaign event that he held with Huang in 2016. Huang had paid Dastyari's legal fees in 2014 and promised to donate to his party. Revelations of these dealings by Australian media compelled Dastyari to resign in 2018. This elite capture is not a garden-variety form of corruption, but a method for short-circuiting democratic accountability.

This pattern is even playing out at the international level. Although China contributes less than 1 percent of the total budget of the World Health Organization (WHO), Beijing has wielded its influence to become "deeply integrated into the WHO politically" and to gain the WHO leadership's "unreserved support."[19] These efforts have made the world's leading public-health body vulnerable to manipulation: The WHO's hobbled response at the outset of the covid pandemic was doubtless related to the PRC's furtive approach to the breakout of the virus. The CCP's manipulation of the WHO is a small part of its efforts to inject its ideological concepts and preferences into the United Nations, often in ways that run counter to the organization's stated tenets.[20]

Critically, in the Australian case, it was the nongovernmental sector that took the lead in mobilizing against China's authoritarian influence. Given the party-state's targets—such as Australia's media, political, and educational institutions—Fitzgerald notes that civil society was effective because it "took its charge not from the angle of geopolitics and international rivalries, but rather with a concern with freedom, rights, and equal treatment for all Australian citizens."[21] Nongovernmental and governmental action became mutually reinforcing, leading Australian society to recalibrate its relationship with Beijing.

The Czech Republic is another recent target of China's full-spectrum engagement. As in Australia, the nongovernmental sector has played a pivotal role in communicating to the public the dangers of the Chinese party-state and in identifying ways to rebuff sharp-power activities. Among the most striking examples of influence in the Czech case concerned Chinese energy and finance conglomerate CEFC, which appeared "seemingly out of nowhere with loads of cash available for high-profile overseas acquisitions." In 2015, CEFC went on a "weeklong shock-and-awe shopping spree in Prague, buying some prime real-estate, a football club, a brewery, and a media conglomerate." Stunningly, as part of China's sweeping engagement in the Czech Republic that year, it was announced that CEFC chairman Ye Jianming had been named as an advisor to Czech president Miloš Zeman.[22]

At the outset, distinct challenges in the Czech case arose from a lack of understanding of the threat. Martin Hála describes the CCP's approach to "making friends" in high places as a way of coopting foreign elites not only to advance Chinese interests but also to manipulate and control foreign institutions. "The unwitting foreigners are not entering a spontaneous relationship with the Chinese counterparts whom they meet in person," writes Hála, "but with a hidden yet formidable top-down bureaucracy that is beyond the ability of most people in open societies to understand because they have encountered nothing remotely comparable to serve as a reference."[23] In other words, people and organizations engaged with the CCP and its proxies are too often running blind.

As in Australia, the Chinese party-state's engagement in the Czech Republic was extensive: Xi Jinping visited Prague in 2016, and the CCP and its surrogates, including CEFC, deepened their ties across Czech society. But Beijing's manipulative approach helped to alert Czechs to the threat, galvanizing resistance. The Czech government and civil society progressively marshaled a strong response to Chinese attempts to compromise the integrity of democratic institutions.

Similar to the Czech Republic, Lithuania has stuck to its democratic principles in the face of Chinese sharp power. When Lithuanian authorities discovered that some Chinese-made smartphones had a built-in censorship tool capable of blocking certain web search terms, they removed the devices from government use and told citizens to throw them away. Lithuania has been on the receiving end of a full-bore intimidation campaign that includes diplomatic isolation, economic coercion, and the CCP's formidable global-propaganda machine. Part of the motivation for the PRC's aggressive behavior is Lithuania's cordial relations with Taiwan, a vibrant, independent democracy which the CCP regards as a part of China. In 2021, Lithuania allowed the Taiwanese government to open a representative office under the name "Taiwan"—a first in Europe.

Taiwan, a frontline state in the struggle against the CCP, has often been Beijing's test case for its influence activities. The CCP's sharp-power efforts in Taiwan are designed to degrade and manipulate its democratic institutions, to demoralize and divide the Taiwanese, to recruit influencers and thought leaders, and to intimidate CCP critics into silence.[24] These efforts aim to push Taiwan toward "reunification" with China and to extinguish Taiwan's democracy as proof of concept that "gives the lie to the CCP's narrative that liberal democracy is a purely Western product that cannot work in a Chinese or Asian culture."[25]

Nevertheless, Taiwan has emerged as an "island of resilience," whose society and government are developing innovative ways to combat the growing threat. In 2022, the government established a digital-affairs ministry to promote technological resilience. Doublethink Lab, a civil society organization, is among the initiatives dedicated to dissecting Chinese influence activities and their impact using digital tools and methodologies. It also builds networks among democracy watchdogs, technology experts, and China watchers to strengthen democratic resilience by adapting to the CCP's ever-changing influence efforts.

Technology for Autocracy?

As part of their overall mobilization to exert influence, authoritarians have used first-mover advantage in the digital sphere to wide effect. The digital revolution has helped to flatten the global operating environment for authoritarian powers, affording them opportunities to exert influence at scale. New tools make it easier for authoritarian regimes to manipulate and surveil their populations—and to help antidemocratic forces in other countries do the same.

In key respects, autocracies have already aligned modern technology with their values. In essence, the powerful technological surveillance model that has come to predominate globally lends itself to the application of sharp power. Democracies, meanwhile, have struggled to make now ubiquitous technologies compatible with basic democratic principles of transparency and accountability. Modern social media, built around personal-data surveillance and programmed to play on human emotions for targeting advertisements, are at odds with a political culture of consensus, accountability, and restraint. The algorithms underlying social media enable large-scale manipulation and stoke polarization.[26] Peter Pomerantsev observes that "Russia distorts the truth about its crimes in Ukraine simply by using Western social media, which is built in a way that a citizen has little right to know who is manipulating them and how, why algorithms show you one piece of content and not another."[27]

China's global tech ambitions have grown since Xi Jinping assumed power. Even if China and other authoritarian powers do not explicitly seek to remake the world in their image, civil liberties everywhere are in danger as authoritarian styles of social management are being embedded in the global technological infrastructure. For instance, governments in more than eighty countries have acquired Chinese-made surveillance systems that can strengthen state control. In Zimbabwe, China is helping to put the pieces in place for a surveillance state, enabling the authorities in Harare to better amass data and process it.[28] In Uganda, as in Zimbabwe, the Chinese state-aligned company Huawei has played a key role in the establishment of technological capabilities. Uganda's president, Yoweri Museveni, has been in power since 1986. Journalists Josh Chin and Liza Lin recount how the authorities in Kampala enlisted Huawei through a classified bidding process to work with "Ugandan security officials to design a full-sized Safe Cities system to suit the government's needs." While the authorities pushed this system as a tool for enhancing law enforcement, in practice Museveni's regime "followed the Chinese model and used it to track political threats."[29] Internet services using Russia's SORM system send copies of all internet traffic to authorities. So-called smart-city systems that purportedly improve public security and municipal service delivery in practice can enable regimes to track political opponents.[30]

Firms linked to authoritarian governments may provide foreign countries technology (such as facial-recognition software, translation services, and data-visualization programs) with prices and sometimes capabilities that cannot be matched by companies in democratic states. But a critical risk is that these authoritarian governments may gain or retain access to the data that these systems process. Autocratic regimes can leverage relationships with private firms to police, alter, and constrict expression outside their borders, in invisible yet significant ways. The Chinese government is piloting surveillance systems that can recognize emotions and discern ethnicity. Beijing is using advanced data-analysis software to gather information from social media and the internet. As the authorities in Beijing "cast an ever-wider net for collecting user data, [they benefit] from Chinese-owned apps that are transnational in scope and scale, such as ByteDance's TikTok, Tencent's WeChat, and Alibaba's AliPay."[31]

If left unaddressed, the authoritarian transformation of the technological domain will leave free societies open to even greater sharp-power exploitation by authoritarian governments. The rapid advance and application of artificial-intelligence–driven technologies—especially for surveillance—raise the stakes even further. Addressing this challenge will require a level of conceptual clarity that is still missing from most authoritarian-influence discussions.

The "Soft Power" Fallacy

In a March 2017 article entitled "China Is Spending Billions to Make the World Love It," the *Economist* detailed Chinese authorities' extraordinary efforts to "sell [the PRC] as a brand" and "attract people from other countries." The party-state's outreach spanned multiple fronts: educational initiatives including Confucius Institutes and people-to-people exchanges; global media; and international commerce and development programs, namely, the Belt and Road Initiative. But the results have disappointed China: "Money has not brought China anything like the love it would like."[32] More recently, analyst Joshua Kurlantzick observed that despite having launched "a massive soft power campaign" across multiple regions of the developing world, China has seen its global image deteriorate "extensively" in the past four years. China's reputation has declined not only among Western democracies but also among those in Africa and Asia.[33]

These examples are emblematic of the scholarly and journalistic ink that continues to be spilled explaining why repressive regimes, despite investing enormously in efforts often associated with soft power, so often are *not* successful at generating it. There are four key reasons for this conundrum. First, the metrics that are often used to demonstrate the failure of authoritarian influence efforts are poorly suited to the task. Public-opinion surveys, which serve as the go-to measurement of soft power, do reveal a country's favorability among certain audiences. Surveys are not, however, an appropriate measurement for how much a foreign power is coopting local elites, inducing forms of political censorship, or compromising the integrity of local institutions.[34]

A second reason results from confusing the means of influence with their effects. The tools autocrats employ—such as the PRC's Confucius Institutes and media outlets such as Russia's RT and Sputnik—are themselves not "soft" or "sharp" power. Rather, it is the effects and outcomes of these tools that determine whether their influence is soft or sharp. Since authoritarians increasingly use these tools for manipulation and outward-facing censorship, we can usually identify them as sharp power.

A third and related factor contributing to muddied understandings of authoritarian influence is the indiscriminate use of the term "soft power." Over time, the soft-power concept has become a sort of Maslow's hammer. Take as an example a 2022 report from the Tony Blair Institute entitled *Security, Soft Power and Regime Support: Spheres of Russian Influence in Africa.* The report applies a soft-power framing to Russia's influence activities in Africa, which include "indoctrination" campaigns and the deployment of professional political and social-media manipulators. Investment in Africa by the Kremlin and its surrogates often aims to manipulate or monopolize local partners in a manner that is more consistent with sharp power than soft power.[35] In these instances and many others, sharp and soft power are being confused for one another, muddying the analytical waters.

Fourth, "it is not the case that countries can exert either 'sharp' or 'soft' power, but not both."[36] China's investment and infrastructure-building around the globe doubtless have soft-power appeal. Yet when influence efforts result in self-censorship or corrode the integrity of independent institutions, states move from the generation of soft power to the exertion of sharp power.[37]

A lack of conceptual clarity regarding the types and effects of authoritarian influence has produced analytical confusion, with troubling policy implications. If we have difficulty distinguishing soft from sharp power, we will do no better combating authoritarian manipulation as it evolves.

The Democratic Countermobilization

Most free societies are still not adequately prepared to meet the multidimensional sharp-power strategies employed by China, Russia, and likeminded states. Authoritarians' international engagement tends to mimic their domestic governance, often including outward-facing censorship, elite capture, and corrupting practices.

Australia, the Czech Republic, Lithuania, and Taiwan have confronted threats to the integrity of their democratic institutions and offer valuable lessons. In each country, the nongovernmental sector played a critical role in alerting policymakers and the public at large to authoritarian encroachments by producing reliable yet easy-to-understand information and analysis, fostering needed debate, and stimulating resilience through openness and transparency. These efforts spurred governmental responses and shifted the public mindset from complacency to action.

These four countries were unusual in that, unlike most states, they possessed critical features essential for rebuffing sharp power. Their responses drew upon dogged civil societies and news media to present crucial issues without fear or favor. Australia, the Czech Republic, and Taiwan in particular had independent experts on China who were ready to inform the public about authoritarian influence in a clear-eyed manner. But only a small number of countries, including those mentioned in this essay, are equipped to address Chinese or Russian sharp power—particularly in Latin America and sub-Saharan Africa.

Authoritarian powers' full-spectrum set of influence tactics can be overwhelming for many countries. Countries lacking a robust civil society, capable news media, and independent China (and Russia) expertise are much more vulnerable. To address the growing sharp-power challenge, democratic societies should:

ROLL BACK SECRECY AND OPACITY. Open societies need to more directly and creatively confront the authoritarians' opacity and secrecy. When engaging with foreign partners, autocrats prefer to work directly (and often exclusively) with executive-branch elites. This state-oriented approach enables a culture of secrecy and corruption. Operating abroad as they do at home, the leaderships of China, Russia, and other authoritarian powers do not welcome nongovernmental voices in decisionmaking processes, whether in bilateral relations or international organizations. Democracies should not cede this ground. Open societies need to recommit and intensify their efforts to incorporate nongovernmental voices into key forums, discussions, and decisionmaking processes.

The nongovernmental sector has a vital role in the sharp-power struggle. In targeted countries, nongovernmental resources must be tailored to fit the local context and the complexity of sharp-power tactics in order to respond to authoritarian influence. These resources are especially needed in cases when authoritarian powers have successfully captured official elites, because it then falls to civil society to tackle the sharp-power challenge.

REBUFF ELITE CAPTURE. The more elite capture in a country, the more treacherous the path to safeguarding institutional integrity becomes. But authoritarian cooptation of local elites does not lend itself to garden-variety transparency and accountability initiatives. Going forward, new initiatives must address elite capture where it has already metastasized and prevent its spread to new places.

Targeted forms of investment and partnership with authoritarian powers can be particularly risky, as they provide prime opportunities for foreign autocrats to coopt local elites and gain indirect leverage in key sectors. Open societies can and should reduce their vulnerability to elite capture through a combination of tighter investment rules and, where needed, economic deterrence. Developed democracies could create standardized procedures for screening foreign investments and tracking the resulting ties that form with local elites. These efforts should include developing countries where possible.

DEFEND THE FREEDOM OF EXPRESSION. Rewriting the rules of free expression is a central aim of authoritarian powers. Institutions in open societies—including universities, publishers, think tanks, technology firms, media, and entertainment companies—must develop new ways to resist the efforts of authoritarian powers and their surrogates to limit freedoms of expression or association. Given the extent to which authoritarian powers have already cowed even powerful institutions into self-censorship, the need to rebuild eroded free-expression norms is even greater.

ADDRESS KNOWLEDGE ASYMMETRIES. The targets of sharp power often lack the necessary knowledge to resist. Scholars, journalists, and publics alike need deeper understandings of how sharp-power tactics and Chinese and Russian influence manifest in local contexts as well as how to bolster transparency and accountable governance. New, interdisciplinary networks should be developed in individual countries to act as "knowledge hubs" for accelerating learning and adaptation.[38] By cooperating with civil society, media, and watchdog organizations, these hubs should bridge cognitive gaps among the general public, sharing knowledge beyond narrow communities of analysts. These local efforts must be supplemented by international cooperation among knowledge hubs and independent analysts.

COMPETE IN THE GLOBAL MEDIA SPHERE. Related to persistent knowledge asymmetries is the lopsided competition that has taken shape in the global media context. China and Russia, in particular, have developed massive outward-facing media capabilities that are able to curate content to suit the preferences of the CCP and the Kremlin. Narratives projected by these media initiatives increasingly are aligned with each other. Through their lavishly resourced media outlets, autocrats rarely shy away from criticizing democracies. In terms of narrative competition, autocracies' relentless assailing of democracy and the ideas that underlie it has undoubtedly had an impact. Democracies will need to invest far more effort and resources into media-related initiatives that can meaningfully compete with the already well-developed authoritarian media infrastructure.

CREATE NEW METRICS. The reflexive use of the term "soft power" to describe virtually all forms of nonmilitary international engagement has led to an analytical dead end for journalists, scholars, and policymakers. Many forms of authoritarian influence—especially those that induce political censorship or involve elite cooptation—cannot be measured by opinion polls, the conventional soft-power measurement. We need new metrics suited to understanding all aspects of sharp power, which will require deeper forms of investigative journalism and specialized nongovernmental efforts to expose the opaque activities of the CCP, the Kremlin, and their proxies.

INCENTIVIZE TRANSPARENT AND ACCOUNTABLE TECHNOLOGY. Authoritarian powers are working to reshape the global technological environment to fit their chief priorities: control and surveillance, both inside and outside their borders. For this reason, democracies must accelerate and deepen their efforts to adopt common technological standards that embrace transparency and accountability.

The stakes for implementing a proactive democratic response to sharp power are rising as emerging technology offers autocrats the promise of even greater influence at once-unimaginable scales. The internet's openness has provided considerable opportunities for intrusion and manipulation by authoritarian powers. And China, Russia, and other autocracies are only scratching the surface of their technological opportunities.

Finally, we should not lose sight of the fact that these ruthless and unaccountable regimes do not hold the moral high ground. In addition to systematically repressing their own people, the regimes in Beijing and Moscow are prosecuting their own forms of modern genocide in the Xinjiang Autonomous Region and Ukraine, respectively. The leaderships in Tehran and Riyadh commit unspeakable brutality against women, who are courageous and fearless in striving for greater freedoms in the face of their governments' unrelenting repression. Venezuela has become an impoverished, cruel, hollowed-out state under the leadership of Hugo

Chávez and Nicolás Maduro. In unfree systems, the regimes instrumentalize and degrade their own people, whom the countries' leaderships invariably fear. Democratic societies can become inured to autocrats' extraordinary depredations, in part due to the neutralizing and conditioning effects of present-day disinformation and propaganda. But deep into the second decade of the global authoritarian resurgence in which unfree regimes are projecting their standards and values into the wider world, policymakers and citizens in free societies must be clear-eyed about what is at stake. Unless democratic societies rise to the challenge by leveraging their inherent competitive advantages—innovation, free expression, openness, and accountability—the sharp-power challenge will continue to mount.

Notes

The author thanks Ariane Gottlieb for research assistance.

1. Elizabeth C. Economy, *The World According to China* (Cambridge: Polity, 2022).

2. Kathryn E. Stoner, *Russia Resurrected: Its Power and Purpose in a New Global Order* (Oxford: Oxford University Press, 2021).

3. Christopher Walker and Jessica Ludwig, "From 'Soft Power' to 'Sharp Power'" in *Sharp Power: Rising Authoritarian Influence* (Washington, D.C.: National Endowment for Democracy, 2017), 13.

4. Christine Hackenesch and Julia Bader, "The Struggle for Minds and Influence: The Chinese Communist Party's Global Outreach," *International Studies Quarterly* 64 (September 2020): 723–33.

5. Anne Applebaum, "Autocracy, Inc: How the World's Authoritarians Work Together," Nineteenth Annual Seymour Martin Lipset Lecture on Democracy in the World, 1 December 2022, *www.ned.org/events/nineteenth-lipset-lecture-anne-applebaum-autocracy-inc*.

6. "Defending Democracy in Exile," Freedom House, 2021–2022.

7. Ronald J. Deibert, "Subversion Inc: The Age of Private Espionage," *Journal of Democracy* 33 (April 2022): 28–44.

8. Glenn Tiffert, "The Authoritarian Assault on Knowledge," *Journal of Democracy* 31 (October 2020): 29.

9. Edward Lucas, "How Autocrats Undermine Media Freedom," *Journal of Democracy* 33 (January 2022): 131–46.

10. Sarah Cook, "Countering Beijing's Media Manipulation," *Journal of Democracy* 33 (January 2022): 120.

11. Aynne Kokas, "How Beijing Runs the Show in Hollywood," *Journal of Democracy* 33 (April 2022): 90–102.

12. Christopher Walker, Shanthi Kalathil, and Jessica Ludwig, "The Cutting Edge of Sharp Power," *Journal of Democracy* 31 (January 2020): 124–37.

13. Claudia González Marrero and Armando Chaguaceda, *Russia's Sharp Power in Latin America* (Montevideo, Uruguay: Konrad-Adenauer-Stiftung, 2022).

14. Chrispin Mwakideu, "Experts Warn of China's Growing Media Influence in Africa," *Deutsche Welle*, 29 January 2021, *www.dw.com/en/experts-warn-of-chinas-growing-mediainfluence-in-africa/a-56385420*.

15. Joseph Siegle, "Russia's Asymmetric Strategy for Expanding Influence in Africa," London School of Economics, 17 September 2021

16. See, for example, David Bandurski, "China and Russia are joining forces to spread disinformation," Washington, DC: Brookings Institution, *TechStream*, March 2022; and Elizabeth Dworkin, "China Is Russia's Most Powerful Weapon for Information Warfare," *Washington Post*, 8 April 2022.

17. Lucas, "How Autocrats Undermine Media Freedom," 144.

18. John Fitzgerald, "Combating Beijing's Sharp Power: How Australia's Civil Society Led the Way," *Journal of Democracy* 33 (July 2022):138.

19. Economy, *The World According to China*.

20. Kristine Lee and Alexander Sullivan, *People's Republic of the United Nations: China's Emerging Revisionism in International Organizations* (Washington, D.C.: Center for a New American Security, 2019).

21. Fitzgerald, "How Australia's Civil Society Led the Way," 131.

22. *China Digital Times*, "Martin Hála on Chinese energy and finance conglomerate CEFC and CCP Influence in Eastern Europe," 8 February 2018.

23. Martin Hála, "Combating Beijing's Sharp Power: Transparency Wins in Europe," *Journal of Democracy* 33 (July 2022): 161–62.

24. Ketty W. Chen, "Combating Beijing's Sharp Power: Taiwan's Democracy Under Fire," *Journal of Democracy* 33 (July 2022): 149.

25. Chen, "Taiwan's Democracy Under Fire," 149.

26. See Ronald J. Deibert, "The Road to Digital Unfreedom: Three Painful Truths About Social Media," *Journal of Democracy* 30 (January 2019): 25–39.

27. Peter Pomerantsev, "Autocrats Are Weaponizing Globalization: Ukraine Is Where They Must Be Stopped," *Time*, 21 December 2022.

28. "Big Brother Will See You Now: China Is Helping Zimbabwe Build a Surveillance State," *Economist*, 17 December 2022.

29. Josh Chin and Liza Lin, *Surveillance State: Inside China's Quest to Launch a New Era of Social Control* (New York: St. Martin's Press, 2022), 133–34.

30. Walker et al., "The Cutting Edge of Sharp Power."

31. Aynne Kokas, "Why TikTok Is a Threat to Democracy," *Journal of Democracy*, October 2022.

32. "China Is Spending Billions to Make the World Love It," *Economist*, 23 March 2017.

33. Joshua Kurlantzick, "China's Collapsing Global Image," Council on Foreign Relations, Asia Unbound blog, 20 July 2022, *www.cfr.org/blog/chinas-collapsing-global-image*.

34. Christopher Walker, Shanthi Kalathil, and Jessica Ludwig, "Forget Hearts and Minds," *Foreign Policy*, 14 September 2018.

35. Emman El-Badawy et al., *Security, Soft Power and Regime Support: Spheres of Russian Influence in Africa* (London: Tony Blair Institute for Global Change, 2022), 18.

36. Christopher Walker, "What Is 'Sharp Power'?" *Journal of Democracy* 29 (July 2018): 18.

37. Joseph S. Nye, "China's Soft and Sharp Power," Project Syndicate, 4 January 2018, *https://tinyurl.com/bddh7v6z*.

38. Martin Hála, *A New Invisible Hand: Authoritarian Corrosive Capital and the Repurposing of Democracy* (Washington, D.C.: National Endowment for Democracy, 2020), 10.

ABOUT THE AUTHORS

KETTY W. CHEN is a political scientist. She is currently the vice-president of the Taiwan Foundation for Democracy and a member of the board of the Prospect Foundation. She also serves on the advisory board of the National Bureau of Asian Research, and was acting director and deputy director of international affairs for the Democratic Progressive Party of Taiwan from May 2014 to May 2016. "Combating Sharp Power: Taiwan's Democracy Under Fire" originally appeared in the July 2022 issue of the *Journal of Democracy*.

SARAH COOK is research director for China, Hong Kong, and Taiwan at Freedom House. She oversees the monthly digest *China Media Bulletin* and is the coauthor, most recently, of the special report *Beijing's Global Media Influence: Authoritarian Expansion and the Power of Democratic Resilience* (2022). "Countering Beijing's Media Manipulation" originally appeared in the January 2022 issue of the *Journal of Democracy*.

WILLIAM J. DOBSON is coeditor of the *Journal of Democracy* and the author of *The Dictator's Learning Curve: Inside the Global Battle for Democracy*. He previously served as the Chief International Editor at NPR, the Washington Bureau Chief of *Slate* magazine, and Managing Editor of *Foreign Policy*.

JOHN FITZGERALD is emeritus professor at Swinburne University of Technology in Melbourne and a fellow of the Australian Strategic Policy Institute in Canberra. From 2008 to 2013, he lived in Beijing and oversaw the Ford Foundation's operations in China. His latest book is *Cadre Country: How China Became the Chinese Communist Party* (2022). "Combating Sharp Power: How Australian Civil Society Led the Way" originally appeared in the July 2022 issue of the *Journal of Democracy*.

MARTIN HÁLA is founder and director of Project Sinopsis, which tracks topics related to China in the Czech Republic and beyond. He is coeditor of *Investigative Journalism in China: Eight Cases in Chinese Watchdog Journalism* (2010). "Combating Sharp Power: Transparency Wins in Europe" originally appeared in the July 2022 issue of the *Journal of Democracy.*

SAMANTHA HOFFMAN is a senior analyst at the Australian Strategic Policy Institute's International Cyber Policy Centre, where she focuses on the domestic and global implications of the Chinese Communist Party's approach to state security. She is the author of the report "Engineering Global Consent: The Chinese Communist Party's Data-Driven Power Expansion" (2019). "China's Tech-Enhanced Authoritarianism" originally appeared in the April 2022 issue of the *Journal of Democracy.*

AYNNE KOKAS is director of the East Asia Center and associate professor of media studies at the University of Virginia and the C.K. Yen Chair at the Miller Center for Public Affairs. Her books include *Hollywood Made in China* (2017) and *Trafficking Data: How China Is Winning the Battle for Digital Sovereignty* (2022). "How Beijing Runs the Show in Hollywood" originally appeared in the April 2022 issue of the *Journal of Democracy.*

EDWARD LUCAS is senior nonresident fellow at the Center for European Policy Analysis and an aspiring Liberal Democrat member of the U.K. Parliament. His books include *The New Cold War: Putin's Russia and the Threat to the West* (2008), *Deception: The Untold Story of East-West Espionage Today* (2012), and *Cyberphobia: Identity, Trust, Security, and the Internet* (2015). "How Autocrats Undermine Media Freedom" originally appeared in the January 2022 issue of the *Journal of Democracy.*

TAREK MASOUD is the Ford Foundation Professor of Democracy and Governance at Harvard University's John F. Kennedy School of Government and coeditor of the *Journal of Democracy.*

NADÈGE ROLLAND is senior fellow in political and security affairs at the National Bureau of Asian Research in Washington, D.C. Her books include *China's Eurasian Century? Political and Strategic Implications of the Belt and Road Initiative* (2017). This essay originally appeared in the July 2020 issue of the *Journal of Democracy*.

RUSLAN STEFANOV is the program director at the Center for the Study of Democracy. "The Kremlin Playbook for Latin America" draws on the 2020 report *Deals in the Dark: Russian Corrosive Capital in Latin America,* published by the National Endowment for Democracy's International Forum for Democratic Studies.

GLENN TIFFERT is a historian of modern China and a research fellow at the Hoover Institution, where he cochairs its project on China's Global Sharp Power. "The Authoritarian Assault on Knowledge," which originally appeared in the October 2020 issue of the *Journal of Democracy,* draws on his 2020 report *Compromising the Knowledge Economy: Authoritarian Challenges to Independent Intellectual Inquiry,* published by the National Endowment for Democracy's International Forum for Democratic Studies.

MARTIN VLADIMIROV is the director of the energy and climate program at the Center for the Study of Democracy. "The Kremlin Playbook for Latin America" draws on the 2020 report *Deals in the Dark: Russian Corrosive Capital in Latin America,* published by the National Endowment for Democracy's International Forum for Democratic Studies.

CHRISTOPHER WALKER is vice-president for Studies and Analysis at the National Endowment for Democracy. His work on modern authoritarian influence includes the coedited volume (with Larry Diamond and Marc F. Plattner) *Authoritarianism Goes Global: The Challenge to Democracy,* as well as the coedited reports (with Jessica Ludwig) *Sharp Power: Rising Authoritarian Influence,* and *Sharp Power and Democratic Resilience.* "Sharp Power and the Threat to Democracy" originally appeared in the October 2022 issue of the *Journal of Democracy* as "Rising to the Sharp Power Challenge."

China, People's Republic of *(cont.)*
98–111; danger to foreign scholars
in, 15–16; data-gathering practices,
92; Data Security Law, 53, 91; diaspora communities, 151, 177; disinformation operations, 89, 141, 142,
143; economic power of, 99, 118–23,
125–27, 177; elite capture practices,
123–26; espionage, 25; ethnonationalist curriculum in, 20–21; European policy, 117–31; global information strategy, 8, 42, 167–81, 189–90;
health initiatives, 107–8; human
rights record, 17, 21, 55, 57, 60;
international influence of, 4, 5, 15,
17–20, 35–36, 106–9, 168, 185–86;
maritime disputes, 156, 158, 159,
175, 176, 191; "one country, two
systems" framework, 148n6; Personal Information Protection Law,
91; positive publicity of, 101–2, 195–
96; SARS crisis, 109; sharp-power
methods, 139–40, 165n6; smart cities in, 83–84; social media platforms, 42, 53, 58, 59; soft-power of,
7; state-controlled media, 41–42, 53,
141–42, 175–76, 189; state-owned
enterprises (SOEs), 122, 123;
state-security strategy, 23, 35, 87,
91–92, 123; surveillance capabilities,
6, 13, 15, 91; Taiwan policy, 8, 13,
110, 134–47; tech-enhanced authoritarianism of, 6, 81–82, 90, 92–94,
194–95; "Thousand Talents" recruitment program, 18; Turkey's relations
with, 86; US relations with, 137;
Western policy of engagement with,
188; wolf-warrior diplomacy of, 117;
World Health Organization and,
103, 108, 109–10, 113n22
China, Republic of (ROC). See Taiwan
China Central Television, 171, 174
China Daily, 41, 126, 160
China Defence Universities Tracker,
162
China Development Bank, 124
China Global Television Network
(CGTN), 41, 104, 126, 170, 171,
179

China Quarterly, 23
China Radio International (CRI), 126–
27, 159, 160, 169, 191
China Review News, 141
China Scholarship Council, 19–20
China Standards 2035 plan, 90
China Times, 143
Chinese-Australian communities, 150,
151, 152, 155, 157–58, 161–62
Chinese-Australian relations, 8, 150,
151–54, 155–56
Chinese Communist Party (CCP): censorship policy of, 23, 25, 173; Central Propaganda Department of, 53,
88, 89; concept of "community of
shared future," 99; concept of
"social management," 83; concept
of "state security," 87–88; democratic systems and, 129–30; discourse power of, 99, 100, 126;
"Document Number 9" internal
memo, 187; domestic authority of,
98–99, 100–101; economic diplomacy of, 117; ideological discipline
in, 13; International Liaison
Department of, 124; manipulation
of international audiences, 88, 120;
media influence, 4, 25, 53, 167–68,
174, 177–78, 180–81, 183n16;
national and ethnic unity policy of,
21; tech initiatives of, 87–89;
United Front Work Department of,
191; weaknesses of, 178
Chinese entertainment industry: censorship of foreign movies, 54–55, 56;
Hollywood and, 51, 54, 55–56; legislation on, 53; movie market, 50–51,
53; social media platforms, 51; state
control of, 5–6, 52–55; Western
companies and, 5–6, 52, 56–57
"Chinese Infodemic in Taiwan, The,"
145
Chinese-language media, 22, 179
Chinese Overseas Engineering Group
(COVEC), 121
Chinese propaganda: active-interference campaigns, 105; "borrow a
boat" approach, 126–27; "community of shared future for mankind"

concept, 106–7; control of "forbidden subjects," 22, 52, 58, 173; during covid-19 pandemic, 98–99, 101–5; dissemination of conspiracy theories through, 105; effectiveness of, 43, 57, 175–77; foreign audience of, 87–88, 126–27, 171; "guiding light" narrative, 103–4; "helping a world in need" narrative, 102–3; media as tools of, 168–71; offensive turn, 104–6; persuasion campaigns, 105; recruitment of foreign journalists and, 169–70; "selfless hero" narrative, 102; on social-media platforms, 4, 42, 169; soft power tools of, 196

Chinese students abroad: behavior of, 21–22; Chinese-language media and, 22; information collection by, 16; surveillance of, 13, 22; tuition revenue generated by, 19–20

Chinese Students and Scholars Associations (CSSAs), 16, 22

"city brain" system, 85

civil society actors: response to media manipulation, 178–79

Clinton, Hillary, 41

CloudWalk (Chinese firm), 86

CoFacts, 146, 147

Comcast (media conglomerate), 52

Confucius Institute Headquarters (a.k.a. Hanban), 15, 17–18, 188, 189, 196

Cook, Sarah, 8

corrosive capital investments, 67–68, 69, 70, 71, 72–73, 76–77

Council on Government Relations, 26

covert taping, 38–39

covid-19 pandemic: China's response to, 7, 98–99, 101–6, 107–8, 110–11; conspiracy theories about, 89, 105; disinformation about, 105, 176; financial impact of, 19, 25–26; international cooperation during, 107–8; online gaming during, 58; origin of, 105, 176; vaccine development, 111

Cruise, Tom, 54

CtiTV, 143

Cuba: political development of, 69; Russia's influence in, 65, 68

cyberattacks, 5

Czech Republic: China's influence in, 7, 124–25, 127–28, 130, 192–93; democracy in, 9; media outlets, 127; mobilization against sharp power in, 197; relations with Taiwan, 130; Russia's influence in, 71; Xi Jinping visit to, 125, 193

Dahua, 90, 93

Dalai Lama, 19, 20, 22

Dastyari, Sam, 159, 191

Dawisha, Karen, 24

DCLeaks (website), 41

deep fakes, 89

democracy: authoritarian assault on, 3, 187–89; foundations of, 14–15; global media sphere and, 199–200; manipulation of institutions of, 189; openness of, 7, 129; resilience of, 8, 9–10, 129–30; response to sharp power, 200–201; vulnerabilities of, 3–4, 6, 8–9, 128–29

democratic countermobilization, 9, 197

Democratic Party emails leak, 39, 41

Democratic Progressive Party (DPP) (Taiwan), 135, 136, 137–38, 140, 144, 145

Deng, Xiaoping, 98, 154

discourse power, 99, 100

Discovery (media conglomerate), 52

disinformation: authoritarian regimes and, 6; new technology and, 33; politics and, 135–36; on social media, 4, 89, 136, 142, 143, 148n11, 172, 176–79, 190

Disney, 56, 57

Doublethink Lab (DTL), 144–45, 193

DreamWorks Animation, 56, 57–58

Dynamic Portrait System, 93

East China Sea Air Defense Identification Zone (ADIZ), 155–56

economic coercion, 117, 129, 131

Economist Intelligence Unit (EIU), 69, 134

elite capture, 123–24, 198–99

Enarsa (Argentine state oil and gas company), 72

Putin, Vladimir, 24, 65, 67, 186
Putnam, Robert, 61

Qadhafi, Muammar al-, 17
Qatar: funding of research programs, 18; media systems in, 37
Qingdao Publishing Group, 160
Quintana, Juan Ramón, 74

Radio Television Hong Kong, 110
Realpolitik, 111
relationship mapping, 82
Rhasa (Argentine oil-storage firm), 72
Rolland, Nadège, 7
Rosatom, 65, 70, 71, 75
Rosner, Ignacio, 73
Rossiyskaya Gazeta, 40
Rostec, 75
RT (television broadcaster), 4, 40, 43, 196
Rudd, Kevin, 164
Russia: disinformation operations, 6, 87, 171; funding of research programs, 18; interference in U.S. elections, 4, 39, 41; international influence, 36, 66, 185, 190; invasion of Georgia, 69; media strategies, 36, 39, 40–41, 189; online "troll factories," 4, 45; as police state, 186; propaganda machine, 4, 6, 36, 40–41, 66; surveillance tactics, 195; war on freedom, 4, 10; war on Ukraine, 3, 65, 78, 78n3, 186; weapon trade, 75; Western policy of engagement with, 188
Russia's international-influence strategy: in Argentina, 70–73; in Bolivia, 73–75; methods of, 67–68, 69, 72–73, 74, 75, 76; responses to, 76
Rzeczkowski, Grzegorz, 39

Safe Cities system, 195
Sambucetti, Horacio, 72
Sandler, Adam, 54
San Lorenzo refinery, 73
SARS-CoV-2 virus, 105
Saudi Arabia: diplomacy of, 20; social media in, 4; violence against women, 200
Saudi Research and Marketing Group, 36

Senkaku (Diaoyu) Islands, 155
sensationalist news, 37
Shanghai Disney Resort, 51, 56
Shanxi Provincial Public Security Department, 90
Sharp Eyes, 84, 91
sharp power: conception of, 4, 5, 52, 186; in entertainment industry, 55; global reach of, 190–91; mobilization against, 7, 9, 187, 191–94, 198–201; nongovernmental sector and, 198; technology and, 82–83
Shen, Puma, 144
Sikorski, Radosław, 38
Silent Invasion (Hamilton), 24, 158
Sina Weibo, 142, 164
Singapore: pressure on independent media, 24, 35
Sinohydro, 122
16+1 initiative, 118–19, 120, 121, 123, 131n3
Sklenář, Miroslav, 125
Skynet, 84, 91
Sky News, 36, 160
smart-city projects: in Africa, 85; benefits of, 83, 84, 85; hazards of, 6, 83–86; interoperability of, 90–91; public security and, 84, 85; social management and, 84; surveillance capabilities, 91, 195
social management, 83, 84
social media: authoritarian control of, 4, 187; censorship of, 58; content dissemination through, 42, 174–75; disinformation on, 4, 89, 136, 142–43, 148n11, 171–72, 176–79, 190; manipulation of, 77, 194
soft power, 186, 196–97, 200
SORM system, 195
South China Sea: territorial disputes in, 156, 158–59, 175, 176, 191
South Ossetia: international recognition of, 69
sports: politics and, 57, 59–61
Sputnik (radio broadcaster), 40–41, 196
StarTimes, 174
state-capture practices, 67, 76
Stefanov, Ruslan, 6
Stiglitz, Joseph, 32, 33

Milton Keynes UK
Ingram Content Group UK Ltd.
UKHW012156270923
429502UK00001B/2